trust
but
verify

# trust
# but
# ····················➤ verify

## Imagery Analysis in the Cold War

David T. Lindgren

Naval Institute Press
*Annapolis, Maryland*

Naval Institute Press
291 Wood Road
Annapolis, MD 21402

Library of Congress Cataloging-in-Publication Data
Lindgren, David T.
    Trust but verify: imagery analysis in the Cold War / David
T. Lindgren.
        p.    cm.
    Includes bibliographical references and index.
    ISBN 1-55750-518-7 (alk. paper)
    1. Aerial reconnaissance, American—Soviet Union. 2.
Space surveillance—United States. 3. Space surveillance—
Soviet Union. 4. Cold War. I. Title.
UG763 .L56 2000
355.3'432—dc21                                    00-22464

Printed in the United States of America on acid-free paper ∞
07 06 05 04 03 02 01 00   9 8 7 6 5 4 3 2
First printing

*To those who served in silence*

NSA's memorial to those who died on aerial
reconnaissance missions during the cold war.

# Contents

# Preface

In the years since the cold war's end, a vast amount of formerly classified material on the cold war has been made available to the American public. The Center for the Study of Intelligence (CSI) is systematically examining the intelligence collections of all CIA directorates to determine which should be declassified. The CSI has given highest priority to materials focusing on the former Soviet Union. Among the documents being declassified are the national intelligence estimates. Several hundred NIEs have already been processed and delivered to the National Archives. The CSI has also declassified over a thousand articles and book reviews that have appeared over the years in its journal, *Studies in Intelligence.* To these materials must be added the satellite imagery taken between 1960 and 1972 and authorized for release by President Clinton in 1995. These various materials were of immeasurable value to this study. As additional documents and imagery are declassified, they will allow more in-depth analysis of many of the issues touched upon here only briefly.

In any project of this type, there are individuals whose assistance proves to be invaluable. In this instance I am indebted to a number of imagery analysts, several now retired, who graciously agreed to read and make suggestions on various drafts of this manuscript. Since in most cases these individuals continue to maintain an affiliation with the intelligence community, they will remain anonymous. Nevertheless, they were all supportive of this project; they were also proud of any contribution, however small, they may have made to the successful resolution of the cold war.

As a former imagery analyst myself, I was obliged to submit this manuscript to the Central Intelligence Agency's Publication Review Board. The board's review of the manuscript was meticulous but expeditious, and although a number of statements concerning classified systems were deleted, board members made no attempt to correct errors, dilute harsh judgments, or in any way to recast the author's conclusions. Any shortcomings in the manuscript, therefore, are entirely of my own making.

# Abbreviations

| | |
|---|---|
| ABM | Antiballistic Missile |
| ACDA | Arms Control and Disarmament Agency |
| BMD | Ballistic Missile Defense |
| CIA | Central Intelligence Agency |
| CIO | Central Imagery Office |
| CIS | Commonwealth of Independent States |
| COMINT | Communications Intelligence |
| COMIREX | Committee on Imagery Requirements and Exploitation |
| COPUOS | Committee on Peaceful Uses of Outer Space |
| DCI | Director of Central Intelligence Agency |
| DI | Directorate of Intelligence |
| DIA | Defense Intelligence Agency |
| DMA | Defense Mapping Agency |
| DOD | Department of Defense |
| ELINT | Electronics Intelligence |
| EXCOM | Executive Committee of National Security Council |
| FROG | Free Rocket over Ground |
| FY | Fiscal Year |
| GRD | Ground-Resolving Distance |
| I&W | Indication and Warning |
| ICBM | Intercontinental Ballistic Missile |

| IFOV | Instantaneous Field-of-View |
| IMINT | Imagery Intelligence |
| INF | Intermediate-Range Nuclear Forces |
| ISMA | International Satellite Monitoring Agency |
| IRBM | Intermediate-Range Ballistic Missile |
| KH | Keyhole |
| LPAR | Large Phased-Array Radar |
| LTBT | Limited Test Ban Treaty |
| MAD | Mutually Assured Destruction |
| MIRV | Multiple Independently Targetable Reentry Vehicle |
| MOL | Manned Orbiting Laboratory |
| MRBM | Medium-Range Ballistic Missile |
| MRV | Multiple Reentry Vehicle |
| NASA | National Aeronautics and Space Administration |
| NATO | North Atlantic Treaty Organization |
| NFIB | National Foreign Intelligence Board |
| NID | National Intelligence Daily |
| NIE | National Intelligence Estimate |
| NIMA | National Imagery and Mapping Agency |
| NIO | National Intelligence Officer |
| NPIC | National Photographic Interpretation Center |
| NREC | National Reconnaissance Executive Committee |
| NRO | National Reconnaissance Office |
| NSC | National Security Council |
| NTM | National Technical Means |
| OIA | Office of Imagery Analysis |
| ONE | Office of National Estimates |
| OSIA | On-Site Inspection Agency |
| PDB | President's Daily Brief |
| PFIAB | President's Foreign Intelligence Advisory Board |
| PIC | Photographic Interpretation Center |
| PID | Photo Intelligence Division |
| PIR | Photographic Intelligence Report |
| RSMA | Regional Satellite Monitoring Agency |
| SAC | Strategic Air Command |
| SALT | Strategic Arms Limitation Talks |

| | |
|---|---|
| SAM | Surface-to-Air Missile |
| SCC | Standing Consultative Commission |
| SDI | Strategic Defense Initiative |
| SIGINT | Signals Intelligence |
| SIPRI | Stockholm International Peace Research Institute |
| SLBM | Submarine-Launched Ballistic Missile |
| SPOT | Système Pour l'Observation de la Terre |
| START | Strategic Arms Reduction Talks |
| TELINT | Telemetric Intelligence |
| TKH | Talent-Keyhole |
| TM | Thematic Mapper |
| USAAF | U.S. Army Air Force |
| USAF | U.S. Air Force |
| USIB | U.S. Intelligence Board |

In December 1991, with the collapse of the Soviet Union, the cold war came to an abrupt conclusion. By almost any definition it ended in total victory for the West: the nations of Eastern Europe regained their freedom, Germany was reunited within the North Atlantic Treaty Organization (NATO), the Soviet Union disintegrated, and the threat of global communism all but disappeared. Just as important, the cold war was resolved without recourse to the use of nuclear weapons. This was no small achievement. By the late 1980s the combined arsenals of the United States and the Soviet Union contained over twenty-three thousand nuclear warheads on long-range launchers. That neither side, either intentionally or accidentally, ever launched even one of its missiles in the direction of the other can only be considered one of mankind's great fortunes, although this threat has yet to be entirely eliminated.

The contribution of the United States to the successful outcome of the cold war was decisive, although it paid a heavy price, politically and economically. As in previous wars, it would be America's superior financial resources, technological know-how, and aggressive leadership that would make the difference. To many, the real surprise over the collapse of the Soviet Union was neither its suddenness nor its completeness but rather that it took so long. Some have blamed this prolonged existence on the Reagan-Bush decision to expand the cold war during the 1980s, which, they claim, only provided the Kremlin leadership with an excuse to postpone badly needed reforms (Goodman 1997, 128). Whatever the explanation, once Gorbachev assumed party leadership and initiated his program of perestroika, the Soviet economy began a decline from which it is only now beginning to recover. In the span of just five years Gorbachev would oversee not only the cold war's end but also the demise of the Soviet Union.

In assessing the various factors that contributed to the West's overwhelming victory, it is fashionable to downplay the role of intelligence. The many failures attributed to the intelligence community, including its most glaring failure—to provide any meaningful warning that the Soviet Union was about to disintegrate—have served to deflect attention from those things done well. In this regard there is probably some truth to the intelligence community's oft repeated claim that its failures are trumpeted while its successes go unrecognized. As just one case in point, the surprise Japanese attack on the naval facilities at Pearl Harbor on 7 December 1941 remains America's greatest intelligence failure, yet the role of the intelligence community in deterring a surprise attack by the Soviet Union on the United States or on its forces in Europe is at best taken for granted. While admittedly neither side was anxious to dip into its nuclear arsenal, the fact remains "the Cold War provided any number of occasions that would earlier have justified resort to the most sophisticated armaments available" (Gaddis 1997, 86).

The prevention of "another Pearl Harbor" was due in no small part to the community's development of a technical intelligence collection system that by the late 1970s was capable of monitoring a wide range of activities in the most remote corners of the Communist world. The system, comprising specialized reconnaissance aircraft as well as a vast array of early warning, communications, signals, and imaging satellites, came to provide U.S. policymakers with timely information on the order-of-battle and combat readiness of Soviet and Warsaw Pact troops; it also played a critical role in exposing such myths as the "bomber gap" and "missile gap." The system's monitoring capabilities made possible the signing of the first significant arms control agreements, SALT I and ABM. The trust and confidence generated by these treaties would lead directly to INF and START, which required the destruction of entire generations of nuclear weapons by both sides. It was the elimination of the nuclear threat that played such a great role in helping to destabilize the Soviet system; perestroika would simply speed up the pace of a disintegration already well under way.

The United States entered the cold war with neither an intelligence service nor any significant overhead reconnaissance capability. America's defense rested primarily upon the Strategic Air Command's (SAC) fleet of World War II vintage bombers, whose commanders possessed only the most rudimentary information on Soviet targets and air defenses. Much of the information available to SAC's planners was derived from captured German and Japanese maps and aerial photos. Attempts by the U.S. Air Force to improve upon this information by converting World War II bombers into reconnaissance aircraft for purposes of overflying Soviet territory proved risky, largely ineffective, and often provocative. Yet in the absence of other, more effective means of obtaining information from behind the Iron Curtain, these overflights were considered essential.

The expansion of Communist influence across Eastern Europe and much of Asia frightened many in Washington; global domination by the Communists under Moscow's leadership seemed entirely possible. The need for more and better information on Soviet strategic capabilities led directly to the development of highly specialized reconnaissance aircraft, such as the U-2 and the SR-71. The U-2, developed by the CIA in the mid-1950s, was a spectacular technical achievement. Capable of flying long distances at an altitude of nearly eighty thousand feet, this aircraft would help fill America's growing intelligence gap until surveillance satellites became available in the early 1960s. The success of the U-2 program, in terms of both its design and the strategic information it acquired, would also enhance the CIA's standing within the intelligence community and make it the dominant player in the overhead reconnaissance program.

U-2 overflights of the Soviet Union went on for nearly four years before Francis Gary Powers was shot down in May 1960. The program had, by its designers' estimates, exceeded the maximum length of time it could last, and it was enough. By the time Powers went to trial in August of that year, the first imaging satellite had been successfully placed in orbit. Over the next three decades larger and more sophisticated satellites would obtain increasingly more detailed information on Soviet and Warsaw Pact military forces. Similarly, the Soviet Union would develop its own reconnaissance satellite program. In combination the two programs would assure that each side in the cold war had a realistic assessment of the other side's strategic capabilities.

From SAC's earliest efforts during the immediate postwar years to acquire data on Soviet targets and air defenses, the overhead reconnaissance program has grown today into a multi-billion-dollar operation involving literally all agencies within the intelligence community, thousands of military and nonmilitary analysts, and scores of civilian consultants and defense contractors. As much as two-thirds of the intelligence community's $28 billion budget may be spent in this way. The organization that has evolved over the years to manage this program is complex, reflecting in part the heavily classified nature of the program's activities but also the need to eliminate interagency disputes over the utilization of reconnaissance assets.

During the course of the cold war several organizations were created to manage the overhead reconnaissance program. At the top was the United States Intelligence Board (USIB), composed of representatives from the entire intelligence community and chaired by the director of the Central Intelligence Agency (DCI). The board met weekly to discuss the most pressing intelligence problems and determine requirements for intelligence gathering. One of the most contentious issues with which the board has had to deal concerns the conflicting demands generated by the air force and CIA over target coverage. In general, the air force has been most interested in tactical intelligence, that is, in locating the specific targets that will have to be destroyed in any conflict. This requires frequent coverage in a high-resolution mode. CIA analysts, on the other hand, have tended to demand less frequent coverage of a wider range of targets, reflecting their concern with longer-term assessments of Soviet capabilities and intentions (Leary 1984, 87).

It was to help resolve these conflicts that the National Reconnaissance Office (NRO) was established in September 1961. The NRO was given responsibility for the overall management of the nation's satellite reconnaissance systems. When first formed, it was hidden under cover of the Office of Missile and Satellite Systems within the Office of the Secretary of the Air Force, and so great was the secrecy surrounding it, the media did not learn of the NRO's existence until 1973. The intent in establishing the NRO was to balance the competing interests between the CIA and the air force. Unfortunately, the competition between the two organizations did not end but, in fact, intensified after the NRO was created because, although the air force was given responsibility for the missiles, bases, and the recovery of satellites, the CIA was given control over the collection and analysis of all imagery intelligence (IMINT). The NRO would have to be restructured twice more before a compromise acceptable to both the air force and the CIA was finally reached in 1965. Thereafter, the system worked reasonably well, though the basic conflict in missions between the two organizations remained a source of tension.

From 1967 to 1992 the day-to-day operation of imagery reconnaissance systems was in the hands of the Committee on Imagery Requirements and Exploitation (COMIREX), the successor to the Committee on Overhead Reconnaissance (COMOR) established by President Eisenhower in August 1960. Chaired by a representative from the CIA, COMIREX was responsible for gathering requests for target coverage from throughout the intelligence community and determining collection priorities. A subcommittee worked out the details on orbital paths and determined when to turn cameras or imaging systems on and off, then forwarded this information to the Satellite Control Facility in Sunnyvale, California, which programmed the daily collection schedules for all imaging satellites (Lardner 1990, A29). The task of assigning target priorities was normally a fairly routine procedure, but in times of crisis, such as the Gulf War, COMIREX had to find a way to balance the military's demands for tactical information against the intelligence community's continued need for strategic information.

From its inception the success of the overhead reconnaissance program has depended upon two things—the ability to acquire data from so-called denied areas and the ability to turn these data into useful information or intelligence. The overhead reconnaissance systems developed for the intelligence community represent outstanding examples of American technological prowess. With a facility almost undreamed of at the beginning of the cold war, Americans could by cold war's end routinely conduct a variety of operations from space—from acquiring high-resolution images of the Soviet missile sites to recording long-distance telephone calls between officials in Moscow and their counterparts in the provinces.

To produce useful information from these data is the job of intelligence analysts; they are the heart of the intelligence production process. The art of acquiring intelligence from aerial platforms is not new and has been used by the military services for years. Aerial reconnaissance for military purposes was used as early as the American Civil War. John Wise, a balloonist from Pennsylvania, may have been the first to acquire information of military significance when in July 1861, as General McDowell was preparing to engage Confederate forces approaching Manassas, he "ascended high enough in his balloon to spot numerous Confederate detachments scouting Union lines and reported enemy artillery pieces being positioned about three miles distant" (Infield 1970, 21).

During World War I aircraft quickly replaced the more vulnerable balloons for acquiring photographs of enemy positions, and by World War II aerial photointerpretation had become indispensable to the Allied effort against Nazi Germany. The work of photointerpreters enabled the British to disrupt Nazi preparations for the invasion of England, led to the discovery of German V-1 rocket sites near Peenemünde, and aided in the preparation of maps and three-dimensional models crucial for the Allied invasion at Normandy. Many of these photointerpreters would be among the first to join cold war organizations established for similar purposes.

By cold war's end literally all agencies within the intelligence community were employing imagery analysts in some fashion, though the bulk of them could be found in the National Photographic Interpretation Center (NPIC), the CIA's Directorate of Intelligence (DI), and especially its Office of Imagery Analysis (OIA), the Defense Intelligence Agency (DIA), the Defense Mapping Agency (DMA), and a number of other Department of Defense components, including the intelligence services of the army, navy, and air force. In conducting their interpretation, most analysts have continued to depend on manual techniques developed during World War II, such as the use of stereoscopes to magnify objects, although today these devices have become far more sophisticated and can magnify objects on photos as much as five hundred times. They may also make use of soft-copy analysis, using computers to analyze the digital data from which hard-copy images are made. What is most surprising, however, is that while the quality of the imagery (in terms of spatial resolution and frequency of acquisition) and the analytical equipment (computers, stereomicroscopes, stereocomparators) has improved dramatically since the program's inception, the task of the imagery analyst has not become any easier; better imagery has only led policymakers to ask tougher questions.

Early in the program photointerpreters/imagery analysts were largely in the business of building the air force's Strategic Library Bombing Encyclopedia (BE) for use in generating target maps for SAC bombers and, later, target coordinates for intercontinental ballistic missiles (ICBMs). Included within the index were Soviet missile sites, command centers, air defense systems, airfields, naval bases, petroleum storage facilities, factories, power stations, railroad yards, bridges, and so on. As the quality and frequency of imagery improved, analysts moved away from an emphasis on targeting to developing and applying methodologies for estimating the annual production of everything from aircraft plants and missile factories to oil fields and agricultural crops. Without the development of high-resolution, near-real-time reconnaissance systems information of this kind simply could not have been produced for Iron Curtain countries.

The quality of imagery analysis over the years has been remarkable, and far better than generally understood. However, there is a significant political dimension to the intelligence process that has resulted in numerous disputes within the intelligence community over weapons capabilities. Most disputes have pitted DIA analysts against CIA analysts. The DIA, along with other military service intelligence organizations, has been criticized for resorting "to worst-case assessments to justify higher defense spending" (Goodman 1997, 134). Critics of the CIA, on the other hand, have contended that the agency is equally guilty of putting its own spin on Soviet actions. By their reckoning the CIA has presented a more benign interpretation of Soviet actions so as to encourage arms control negotiations in which it is a major player.

But arms control, too, is a very politicized process, and imagery analysts have often found themselves caught in the middle of disputes here as well. Analysts have the responsibility of monitoring certain activities to ascertain whether violations have occurred; the responsibility is to "monitor," not "verify." Verification is a political decision made by the National Security Council (NSC). Thus, if a possible violation of an arms control agreement is detected by an imagery analyst, that information is forwarded to the NSC, where the decision is made whether the activity constitutes a conscious violation; whether it appears to be part of a pattern to deceive; and whether the existence of the violation should be publicly protested, mentioned privately to the offending party, or ignored. In either of the latter two instances, if the violation later becomes public knowledge, the intelligence community, and imagery analysts in particular, may stand accused of having missed it.

It is also the case that an analyst may monitor for months an activity for which there appears little interest outside the intelligence community. Suddenly that activity becomes a major political issue in the hands of a journalist or political candidate and assumes an importance far beyond any conceivable national security consideration. The "discovery" by a U.S. senator, casting about for a reelection issue, of a Soviet brigade in Cuba played a significant role in preventing ratification of the SALT II agreement. The CIA was aware that some Soviet troops had been permitted to remain in Cuba after the missile crisis, but over the years this fact was forgotten. When the issue of their presence was suddenly raised in the fall of 1979, the CIA was caught by surprise, forcing President Carter to delay action on the treaty. The delay would prove costly. By the time the issue was resolved the Soviet Union had invaded Afghanistan and the SALT II Treaty would never be formally ratified, though in fact both sides informally agreed to abide by its conditions.

In somewhat similar fashion, a retired air force general would stir up a political firestorm over the Soviet Union's construction of a vast network of civil defense shelters in the late 1970s. Why hadn't the intelligence community discovered this activity? According to the general this construction indicated the Soviets were anticipating a first strike against the United States. In fact, the activity was being monitored, but no one in Washington was interested until the general succeeded in making it a political issue. Although the issue would die away in time, it would not do so before thousands of hours of imagery analysts' time were spent documenting the extent of this construction activity. Ironically, the Russians are engaged in similar activity today. In light of the fact the cold war ended several years ago, one might think this activity would become more of a political issue than it has.

In spite of the advances in imagery exploitation, however, there remain limitations to the kinds of intelligence overhead reconnaissance systems can provide. For example, while it is possible to assess a nation's military capabilities on the basis of information derived from satellite imagery, it is impossible to determine the intentions of that nation's political and military leaders. Similarly, estimates of the timing of events are difficult to calculate with any precision, although on occasion photos may provide certain indicators that may narrow the time period within which an event may take place. For all its limitations, however, imagery analysis remained a significant source of information on the Soviet Union, even as that society became more open to Westerners during the latter stages of the cold war.

It is an unfortunate truth that even when the intelligence provided is accurate, it cannot by itself guarantee that good policy will result; the corollary, however, is a certainty: "Poor intelligence inevitably leads to poor policy." The greatest problem faced by analysts is just getting through to policymakers, a complaint made more often by imagery analysts than any other group. The intelligence produced by imagery analysts is normally incorporated into "all source" analytical reports which are circulated to policymakers and other members of the intelligence community in a number of ways, but primarily through written reports. These include intelligence memoranda, photographic intelligence reports (PIRs), and a variety of monthly, weekly, and daily reports, including the president's daily brief (PDB) and the national intelligence daily (NID). Many of the complaints stem from the review process. Written documents are subjected to so many rewrites as they pass through the administrative hierarchy that by the time they reach the level of the policymaker, their impact is often lost. Only the most experienced analysts are normally capable of negotiating this bureaucratic maze (Ranelagh 1986, 685).

Historically, the most important documents produced by the intelligence community have been the national intelligence estimates (NIEs). Initially prepared by the CIA's Office of National Estimates (ONE), NIEs became the responsibility of the National Intelligence Officers (NIO) system after 1973. Estimates were drafted by intelligence community analysts on topics authorized by the National Security Council; supervision of the estimates was the responsibility of the USIB. Over time the annual estimate of Soviet strategic force capabilities became the intelligence community's most influential document. Although its projections of Soviet strategic weapons systems were frequently criticized for underestimating the magnitude of the Soviet arms buildup during the 1960s, there was no phase "of the strategic arms control and reduction process [that] would have been possible without the Estimates" (Steury 1996, 502).

With the cold war at an end, the overhead reconnaissance program has lost the primary mission for which it was designed. As one result, Congress has approved a consolidation of most imagery resources into a single new organization, the National Imagery and Mapping Agency (NIMA). In the congressional debates surrounding the reorganization, however, it has become clear that much of what the imagery community accomplished during the cold war has already been lost. Some of this is a direct result of the secrecy that surrounded the imagery community's activities for so long. A major breakthrough in this regard occurred in February 1995, when President Clinton ordered the declassification of intelligence imagery from the earliest satellite systems. The most important of these was the Corona system, which from its first successful mission in August 1960 until its retirement in 1972 provided the intelligence community with extraordinary photographic coverage of the Soviet Union, Communist China, and many other "denied areas." While the photos from many of these systems are now part of the cold war's public record, the analysts who worked with these systems have largely retired from government service. This book is meant as one attempt to document the contribution of the imagery community while it is still fresh in mind.

The book focuses on the efforts of imagery analysts during the cold war to penetrate the Iron Curtain in order to provide American policymakers with a realistic assessment of the Soviet Union's strategic capabilities. It is not meant as a comprehensive analysis of the entire imagery field. There is, for example, no systematic discussion of the critical role imagery analysts played during the Korean and Vietnam Wars in providing the more tactical information required for operation planning, target selection, and damage assessment. One apparent exception is the Cuban missile crisis, though in fact, it is not, since Khrushchev's purpose in placing the missiles on the island was to dramatically alter the strategic missile balance then heavily favoring the United States. More important, the incident serves as an almost textbook example of how a foreign policy crisis was resolved largely on the basis of information derived from aerial photographs.

Following a brief discussion of the cold war's origins, chapter 1 describes the earliest efforts by the United States to acquire information on Soviet military activities by means of aerial overflights. Chapter 2 focuses on the events leading to Eisenhower's decision to approve development of the U-2 reconnaissance aircraft; it also assesses the impact the U-2 had upon national security policy and especially its role in exposing Khrushchev's policy of "strategic deception." In the aftermath of the Powers incident, U-2 overflights of the Soviet Union were ended, though they continued to overfly other "denied areas." One of these "denied areas" was Castro's Cuba, and chapter 3 examines the contribution the U-2, along with other forms of aerial reconnaissance, made to the successful resolution of the Cuban missile crisis. The U-2's role was indispensable both to the early detection of the missiles as well as to the provision of critical information during the crisis that enabled the Kennedy administration to eventually require Khrushchev to dismantle and remove the missiles from the island.

The book's remaining chapters focus almost exclusively on satellite systems. Chapter 4 examines the early years of the satellite program, with particular emphasis on the origins and contributions of Project Corona. Chapters 5 and 6 attempt to describe the satellite systems that succeeded Corona but remain heavily classified even today. These systems, providing high-resolution digital images on a near-real-time basis, were directly responsible for the arms control agreements that slowed the arms race and led to the destruction of entire generations of intercontinental and intermediate-range ballistic missiles. In no small way, therefore, they contributed to the Soviet Union's ultimate collapse. With the Soviet threat gone, however, America's overhead reconnaissance program faces an uncertain future. Chapter 7 examines the role of imagery analysis in a post–cold war world.

I should say a brief word about terminology. Historically, those who worked with aerial photographs were referred to as "photointerpreters" or "aerial photointerpreters," but during the 1970s this term was dropped in favor of the term "imagery analyst." This change reflected in part the fact that new reconnaissance satellites, like NASA's *Landsat* and the CIA's KH-11, no longer employed camera systems but electro-optical scanners; hence, analysts were working with images created from electronic data rather than with photographs produced from film. The new term was also meant to enhance the status of government photointerpreters, who increasingly worked not only with imagery but a wide range of intelligence sources. For purposes of this book I have attempted to employ these terms within their historical contexts, though it should be remembered the terms are meant to be synonymous. A third term, which I have chosen not to use, is "remote sensing." Coined during the 1970s to refer to the broad field of aerial photointerpretation and digital imagery analysis, it is a term commonly used in the private sector, and especially in academia, but it never caught on within the intelligence community and for that reason does not appear here.

One other term that requires some elaboration because of its importance to this discussion is "spatial resolution" (also called "ground resolving distance," or GRD). This term represents a measure of the smallest object on a photo or the smallest interval between two objects that can be precisely determined; hence, the spatial resolution or GRD of a set of photos is typically expressed in such terms as three feet or, perhaps, three inches. Spatial resolution, the term I have tended to employ in this text, is affected by a number of factors including the resolution of the film, the focal length of the camera, the altitude of the camera platform (or scale), and the condition of the atmosphere (e.g., hazy, partly cloudy) at the time the photos were acquired. The spatial resolution of a camera system is usually expressed as the theoretical maximum at nadir, or the spot on the terrain directly beneath the camera's lens. For panoramic cameras whose optical axis sweeps back and forth across the platform's flight path, spatial resolution is highest at nadir and decreases as the optical axis moves away from nadir toward the horizon; strip cameras, on the other hand, typically photograph the terrain below only at nadir.

For nonphotographic or electro-optical systems, like those on *Landsat* or the KH-11, there are several types of resolution. Spatial resolution is "the dimension of the ground projected instantaneous field-of-view (IFOV) of the sensor system collecting the information" (Jensen 1986, 4). The Landsat Thematic Mapper, for example, has an IFOV of thirty meters by thirty meters; it may be said to have a spatial resolution of thirty meters. There are also radiometric and spectral resolutions. Radiometric resolution refers to the sensitivity of the detectors acquiring reflected or emitted radiation from the earth's surface, while spectral resolution defines the number and width of the spectral bands for which the sensor system gathers data. The remarks made about electro-optical systems in this text will focus for the most part on their spatial resolutions.

# 1

## The Cold War Begins

The cold war had its roots in the Bolshevik Revolution of 1917. From the beginning most Americans found the ideological assumptions of bolshevism repugnant, but they expressed little fear of the Soviet Union itself because its government appeared so weak and unstable. If there were any danger to the American way of life it came from the various forms of radicalism being brought here by immigrants from Eastern Europe; during the twenties there was accordingly a greater interest shown in immigration policy than foreign policy. By the mid-1930s the threats to our national security posed by Nazi Germany and Imperialist Japan overshadowed any remaining concerns we may have held about the Soviet Union. In fact, common geopolitical interests would combine to make the United States and the Soviet Union allies in the struggle to halt the spread of fascism. When the war ended, fascism was defeated, but the Red Army occupied much of Central Europe; Soviet communism came quickly to replace fascism as the greatest threat to democratic capitalism. "The Cold War took shape," Melvyn Leffler has observed, "when a sense of ideological rivalry merged with a fear of Soviet power" (Leffler 1994, vii).

Martin Malia has concluded that the cold war was probably "inevitable given the simple existence of the Soviet Union" (Malia 1994, 298). For a brief period in the immediate aftermath of World War II, however, a different set of assumptions and policies on the part of both governments might have allowed for a more positive postwar relationship. Stalin, well aware of his nation's weak position vis-à-vis the United States, displayed a surprisingly cautious approach to international affairs. There is every indication, for example, that he wanted to continue a cooperative relationship with the West for reasons of both security and economics; he needed and hoped to obtain Western aid to rebuild his shattered economy. Additionally, he wanted to exercise some measure of influence over Eastern Europe, especially Germany, and, in fact, there were many in the West, including Churchill himself, who were prepared to make concessions to him on some of these issues in recognition of the critical role the Soviet Union had played in Germany's defeat. Yet it is during this period, mid-1945 to mid-1947, that the relationship between the Soviet Union and the West changed to a more openly adversarial one.

The period began with Roosevelt's death in April 1945. Harry Truman, who succeeded Roosevelt, was totally unprepared for the challenges facing him, due in no small part to Roosevelt's having kept him isolated from any involvement in foreign affairs. As it was Truman barely had time to familiarize himself with the most important military and foreign policy issues before meeting with Stalin in Potsdam the following July. Truman came away from the meeting unimpressed by the Soviet leader but nevertheless ready to work with him. Like many Western leaders, Truman was prepared to give Stalin the benefit of the doubt because of the enormous losses his country had suffered at the hands of the Nazis.

As it turned out, the problems facing Truman in his first few months would be generated less by Stalin's diplomatic initiatives than by the condition of the international system. In Europe the economic and political situation was critical; food and fuel were scarce, and the democratic governments there were hanging on by the thinnest of threads. With Soviet troops occupying Eastern Europe and with Communist parties seemingly about to come to power in France and Italy, the prospect that Western Europe might fall to communism became very real to the Truman administration. The situation was little better in Asia, where Soviet troops occupied North Korea and Communist forces in China were making progress in their civil war with Chiang Kai-shek's Nationalist forces.

Ironically, as the international scene was worsening, Truman was under great pressure to "bring the boys home." Demobilization of the army was proceeding at a rapid rate, and by May 1946 there were just over two million men in uniform, down from a wartime high of just over eight million (Newton 1991, 135). Truman's "ace in the hole," as he called it, was the atom bomb, the use of which he had already authorized at Hiroshima and Nagasaki. To make the bomb an even more credible threat, Truman created the Strategic Air Command in March 1946 under the authority of the U.S. Army Air Force (USAAF) and, later, its successor, the U.S. Air Force (USAF). SAC became America's long-range strike force, prepared to deliver a nuclear payload anywhere on the globe. To further enhance this capability the United States acquired exclusive control over a number of formerly British air bases in the Atlantic and Pacific from which SAC bombers could easily strike Communist countries.

During 1947 the situation in Europe became even more critical. In February the British informed the Truman administration they were going to pull out of Greece and suspend aid to Turkey. The United States, they acknowledged, would have to assume these commitments. Truman's response, which became known as the Truman Doctrine, was to wring from Congress an emergency appropriation of $400 million to help stabilize the Greek and Turkish governments and prevent the Soviets from dominating the eastern Mediterranean, including the strategically important Turkish Straits.

But the Truman Doctrine would signal just the beginning of a wider American involvement in European affairs. Later in 1947 the United States would announce the creation of the Marshall Plan, a massive program of economic aid for the reconstruction of Europe; even the Soviet Union would be eligible to receive assistance. Discussions with representatives of the various European nations would extend well into 1948, by which time Stalin had made his decision to reject participation in the plan; neither the Soviet Union nor Eastern Europe would apply for economic assistance. Although such aid would almost certainly have expedited the reconstruction of the Soviet economy, the control the United States would have exerted was, in Stalin's view, too high a price to pay. By the end of 1947 any remaining hope that the West and the Soviet Union could establish some basis for a postwar collaboration had vanished; the cold war had begun.

East-West tensions over central and Eastern Europe increased dramatically during 1948. In February, under pressure from Stalin, all non-

Communists in the Czech cabinet were forced to resign and a new government, more "friendly" to the Soviet Union, was formed by the Czech Communist Party. This coup came as a great shock to the West, not only because Czechoslovakia was the most democratic of Eastern Europe's governments, but because it conjured up images of the Nazi coup just ten years earlier. Soviet control was also tightening over Poland, the main invasion route to the Soviet Union: "The obliteration of 'the bastard of Versailles' as Molotov contemptuously called Poland, had been the cornerstone of the Nazi-Soviet Pact. . . . Stalin had no intention of handing back eastern Poland, part of his booty from his alliance with Hitler, or restoring Poland's independence" (Newton 1991, 54).

Czechoslovakia and Poland, whatever their historical ties to the West, were under the control of the Red Army. Germany was a different matter entirely; both sides had a stake in Germany's future. The United States saw an industrialized and unified Germany as critical to the economic and political stability of Western Europe. Stalin had in mind a different Germany than the nation that had twice invaded Russia in the span of a mere quarter-century. He envisioned a Germany economically and militarily incapable of ever again attacking his country. To ensure this, he demanded that the Soviet Union have a hand in governing postwar Germany. When it became clear that the United States had no intention of allowing him such control, Stalin decided to keep his military forces in Germany and administer the Soviet zone as a separate political unit. The Allies responded by announcing their plans to consolidate their three occupation zones into the new Federal Republic of Germany (FRD).

In a crude attempt to prevent the Allies from creating a unified West Germany, Stalin announced on 24 June that he was blockading all land, rail, and canal access to Berlin's three western zones. He hoped that by doing so he could pressure the Allies into reversing their decision on West Germany's unification and perhaps even force them out of Berlin. Truman would have none of it. He concluded that to withdraw from Berlin would only encourage Stalin's aggressive tendencies, much as the Munich agreement had done with Hitler. Instead, Truman ordered an airlift to supply the city with needed food and fuel; it was the cold war's first significant confrontation.

The airlift proved a spectacular success in large part because Stalin did not dare to interdict the three air corridors that had been established in

1945 to provide safe air connection between Berlin and West Germany. The Allies quickly began exploiting these corridors to supply Berlin residents. Over the course of the next eleven months British and American aircraft flew nearly three hundred thousand missions delivering over two million tons of supplies to the city's inhabitants. The astonished Stalin "was left with the choice he had hoped to avoid—capitulation or war—and in May, 1949, in one of the most humiliating of all setbacks for Soviet foreign policy, he selected the first alternative by lifting the blockade" (Gaddis 1997, 48).

The Berlin blockade simultaneously accomplished two things. First, it made clear to the Soviet leadership that any attempt to expand its influence westward would run the direct risk of a military confrontation with the United States. In addition, it also accelerated American efforts to put in place the military and political institutions necessary for Western Europe's defense. By April, for example, the creation of the North Atlantic Treaty Organization was completed. This was followed in rapid succession by a $4 billion aid package for the purpose of rearming Europe, the assigning of American troops to NATO, and the naming of General Eisenhower as supreme commander of Allied forces in Europe. The Allies would also complete the establishment of the Federal Republic of Germany. It was their belief that the "Germans would be more inclined to support NATO if they had a country to fight for" (Brands 1993, 51). When the Soviet Union responded by reconstituting its occupation zone as the German Democratic Republic (GDR), the division of Europe into "two hostile camps" became a reality; the only unfinished task was the completion of the barbed-wire fences and mine fields marking the borders between the two camps.

If events in Europe were unsettling for most Americans, Asia presented an even gloomier picture. In China Mao Tse-tung's armies were moving steadily southward, and by spring of 1949 not even the staunchest supporters of Chiang Kai-shek could any longer doubt the outcome of this conflict. Shocked by the prospect of the world's most populous nation becoming Communist, Americans searched desperately for an explanation. Republicans, with the help of the so-called China Lobby, quickly and conveniently found one. It was none other than President Truman and his secretary of state, Dean Acheson, they declared, who along with other "liberals" in the State Department were responsible for China's loss. When barely a year later the armies of North Korea swept southward across the thirty-eighth parallel with the intention of unifying the Korean peninsula under Communist control, Truman had no choice but to make a stand; he feared, however, that this might be the beginning of World War III (McCullough 1992, 749). If there were any consolation it was that "Communism's aggressive intentions" were no longer in doubt, and "although the Korean War was blamed more on Mao than Stalin, Communism everywhere was now viewed as an imminently threatening force" (Malia 1994, 310).

Both the fall of China to the Communists and the invasion of South Korea by the Communist North occurred against the backdrop of an event that would forever change the strategic nature of the cold war. An American reconnaissance aircraft taking air samples off the northeastern coast of the Soviet Union would uncover evidence that the Soviets had tested a nuclear device sometime during August of 1949. Western experts had predicted that the Soviets would develop the capability for conducting such a test, but they doubted it could happen before the mid-1950s; it would not be the last surprise Soviet scientists would pull on the West. The reality now was that the United States no longer possessed a monopoly of nuclear weapons, the one thing that balanced Soviet superiority in conventional weapons. For his part Truman would remain skeptical that the Soviets actually had "a real atomic bomb"; he refused to credit "the Soviets with the technological skills to produce an atomic bomb as soon as they did" (Donovan 1982, 101). A partial explanation was provided a few months later when Klaus Fuchs, a British physicist who had worked at Los Alamos, revealed he had passed atomic secrets to the Soviets. His admission, however, only increased America's anxieties because it implied the Soviet Union had the capacity to penetrate America's most secure military installations.

The Soviet nuclear test, combined with the revelations of Fuchs's treachery, was all that was needed to convince Truman and his advisers that the United States must proceed with the development of the so-called super bomb, or hydrogen bomb. That the Soviet Union might already be ahead of the United States in developing such a weapon only made Truman's decision easier: "There could be no assurance that the Russians would refrain from practicing thermonuclear diplomacy if they possessed thermonuclear weapons and the Americans did not" (Gaddis 1997, 100).

The combination of the successful Soviet nuclear test and the so-called loss of China led Truman to establish a committee under the chairmanship of Paul Nitze, the State Department's new head of policy planning, to reassess America's defense policies. The committee's report, completed in April 1950 and designated NSC-68, declared that America was in grave danger due to growing Soviet atomic capabilities, which were neutralizing America's nuclear edge "more rapidly than conventional forces could be created to fill the gap" (Trachtenberg 1994, 112). The United States, therefore, had to be prepared to fight a total war and able "to control the skies, transport troops by air and sea, blunt armor attacks with armor. The minimum price tag was $40–50 billion, three times what the Eisenhower administration currently allotted to defense" (Isaacson and Thomas 1986, 496). Truman reacted to the report's conclusions with his customary caution, but once again events would overtake him. When the armies of North Korea invaded South Korea without warning in June 1950, Truman moved quickly to implement NSC-68's recommendations. As a result the "total budget for defense and international affairs [would] rise from $17.7 billion for the fiscal year 1950 to $53.4 billion in fiscal 1951" (McCullough 1992, 247).

For the United States the cold war had taken a dangerous turn, and the initiative appeared to be in the hands of the Soviets. The United States constantly found itself responding to events for which it had little to no advance warning: the Berlin blockade, the Soviet atom bomb, and the invasion of South Korea. Washington policymakers, not to mention military planners, needed better information. They were not dealing now "with an ordinary adversary, but with a ruthless enemy intent on world domination and ultimately on the destruction of the United States" (Trachtenberg 1994, 112). Could, for example, the invasion of South Korea be a prelude to the invasion of Germany, or at least to the incorporation of West Berlin into the German Democratic Republic? Were Soviet troops in Eastern Europe and western Russia being mobilized for a possible invasion?

On 15 November 1950, the new Office of National Estimates produced its first Estimate of Soviet Capabilities and Intentions (NIE-3). The authors introduced their report by claiming that the ultimate objective of

Soviet leaders was a Communist-dominated world but that such an objective could not be attained without recourse to military conflict with the United States and its NATO allies. The NIE suggested that Soviet leaders might well provoke the West when they felt the Soviet Union had reached maximum military strength relative to the West; "such a period will exist from now through 1954, with the peak of Soviet strength relative to the Western Powers being reached about 1952" (NIE-3, 1, 2, in Koch 1993, 169–70).

In their discussion of Soviet capabilities, the authors of NIE-3 made clear their belief that the United States enjoyed a considerable margin of superiority in numbers of atomic weapons; as of mid-1950 the USSR was estimated to possess only twenty-two atomic bombs, although this number was expected to reach about one hundred sometime during 1952. As for its ability to deliver such weapons, the NIE concluded that the Soviet Union possessed sufficient aircraft, trained crews, and bases from which to launch its aircraft, though the report's authors admitted also that "definite information is lacking" (NIE-3, 5, in Koch 1993, 173). There was speculation that the Soviet air force might possess jet medium bombers by 1952 and heavy bombers by 1953, but again there were few hard data on which to base any of these assumptions.

Ever since the end of the war the United States and its allies had been sending agents into the Soviet Union. Most of the agents were displaced persons or émigrés—Latvians, Lithuanians, and Ukrainians—who were sent back to their native republics. While some were sent for the purpose of organizing armed resistance to the establishment of Soviet control over the Baltic states and western Ukraine, others were sent to watch military facilities to report back to the West any unusual activity. Few of the agents lasted very long; most were captured and executed—or doubled to lure back more agents. The émigré organizations from which most of the volunteers were drawn were thoroughly penetrated by Soviet counterintelligence. In addition, agents working for the Soviet Union, including the infamous Donald Maclean, Guy Burgess, and Kim Philby, were operating at the highest levels of the British diplomatic and intelligence services. These individuals had access to their government's most sensitive secrets, which allowed them to tip off the Soviets when agents were to be parachuted into the country or slipped across the border.

As for the few British and American intelligence officers operating in Moscow under diplomatic cover, they could achieve little because their movements were so carefully monitored: "The Soviet Union's all pervasive internal security system made the recruitment of agents and the running of clandestine operations almost impossible" (Marchetti and Marks 1974, 24). Former U.S. ambassador Charles Bohlen described the Stalin years as a time when "any attempt by a foreigner to get in touch with a Soviet citizen was the equivalent of signing an order for his arrest if not his execution" (Bohlen 1973, 45). Traditional espionage turned out to be an ineffective means of gathering intelligence on the Soviet Union; technical collection efforts were the only available option.

Unfortunately, America's technical capabilities were hard pressed to acquire the kinds of information required by American and British policymakers. This is especially surprising in light of America's experience during World War II, when "60 to 90 percent of Allied intelligence was derived from aerial photography of enemy-held areas" (American Society for Photogrammetry and Remote Sensing 1997, 15). Following a costly pattern established after World War I, however, the U.S. government proceeded to eliminate virtually all of its photoreconnaissance capabilities. The bulk of the military personnel responsible for photointerpretation activities were either discharged or reassigned, and photo laboratories and equipment were sold for surplus (Boyne 1997, 88). What had been painstakingly built up over several years was dismantled literally overnight.

Further complicating the task of gathering information on the Soviet Union was the country's vast size—its eight million square miles made it twice as large as China and nearly three times the size of the continental United States—which enabled many of its most sensitive military facilities to be hidden deep within its interior. During the 1930s Stalin had constructed many of his defense industries in the Urals (Magnitogorsk, Nizhny Tagil, Sverdlovsk, and Chelyabinsk) and the Kuznetsk Basin of eastern Siberia (Kemerovo and Tomsk). These industrial centers grew larger in the early months of World War II, when hundreds of factories were relocated from vulnerable sites in the western regions of the country. Although SAC needed to know exactly where these factories were located and how they were defended, its knowledge of these potential targets was virtually nonexistent. Even the most basic information on Soviet railroads, highways, and airfields was unavailable. Air force personnel were left with compiling "Soviet bombing target dossiers from out-of-date materials in the Library of Congress" (Rositzke 1977, 20). In desperation the United States began to rebuild its photoreconnaissance capabilities.

Until the arrival of the U-2 reconnaissance aircraft in 1955, the United States had to depend upon a variety of modified bombers for reconnaissance missions. The first of these was the RB-29, which was stripped of much of its protective weaponry to make room for the aerial cameras, radio receivers, and air sampling devices it had to carry. From the start, however, the inadequacies of this aircraft were apparent, and it was soon replaced by the larger and more powerful RB-50, the first aircraft suitable for the high-altitude, long-range missions required by SAC planners. It would remain the reconnaissance workhorse until jet aircraft appeared on the scene.

Over time the RB-50 would itself be replaced by the Convair RB-36D. With a combination of six propeller-driven engines and four jet engines, the RB-36 had a greater range than any previous aircraft. Unfortunately, as it turned out, it lacked the speed to successfully penetrate the heavily defended Iron Curtain countries. It was simply "much too big and much too slow for any covert missions in such areas" (Infield 1970, 7). The RB-36D would, therefore, be forced to share its reconnaissance responsibilities with Boeing's swept-winged RB-47. This faster, medium-range aircraft could be used for long range by means of in-flight refueling. The RB-47 could carry seven precision cameras and, operating at an altitude of forty thousand feet, "could photograph one million square miles of territory during a three-hour flight, recording a strip 490 miles wide by 2700 miles long" (Volkman 1985, 138).

Unfortunately, modified bombers proved ineffective for reconnaissance missions over the Soviet Union. A typical mission, even one originating from an airfield in close proximity to the Soviet border, required a flight of one or two thousand miles, most of which was spent within Soviet airspace. Without an armed escort, a lone reconnaissance aircraft stood little chance against Soviet air defenses. On the other hand, an overflight of Soviet territory by a reconnaissance aircraft accompanied by a protective cover of fighter aircraft (even assuming the fighters had sufficient range to do so) was provocative at best and in the worst-case scenario could conceivably ignite World War III. Thus photographic missions were generally limited to incursions of two hundred miles or less, whenever possible taking advantage of bodies of water (such as the Barents, Baltic, and Black Seas) to fly under Soviet radar coverage.

Photoreconnaissance flights began in Asia as early as 1945 under a Post-Hostilities Mapping Program sponsored by the War Department. The program had two objectives. The first was to acquire complete photo coverage of the entire Japanese archipelago; the War Department was only too well aware of the problems it had recently faced in planning military campaigns in the absence of adequate photo coverage. Second, the program sought to acquire aerial photos of airfields and naval bases along the Asian coast to determine whether the Soviet Union might be marshaling its forces for an invasion of Japan or China for an invasion of Formosa. The missions, generally conducted out of Yokota, Japan, involved both RB-29s and RB-50s. The aircraft carried twelve-, twenty-four-, and thirty-six-inch focal length cameras and acquired high-resolution stereo photos that enabled photointerpreters to identify the number and types of aircraft and naval vessels stationed there.

These flights were extremely risky, however. To begin with, they were flown in broad daylight and the crews knew they were being tracked by radar. Furthermore, the question of sovereignty over the air space adjacent to the high seas had yet to be resolved. The generally accepted principle was that a nation's sovereign airspace extended as far offshore as the limit of its territorial waters, but while the United States claimed only a three-mile limit to its territorial waters, other nations were already claiming twelve miles and, in a few cases, two hundred miles. As a compromise it "appeared that reconnaissance aircraft could, if they didn't pose a military threat to another nation, fly within twelve miles of that nation's border and still be in international air" (Infield 1970, 197). American pilots, however, could never be certain that Soviet fighter pilots would honor this principle.

Not all flights, however, were conducted along the Soviet Union's periphery. In early 1952 U.S. intelligence learned that the Soviets were moving large numbers of Tu-4 bombers, similar in appearance to the B-29, to air bases in eastern Siberia. The Tu-4 was thought capable of carrying atomic weapons, so from bases located just across the Bering Sea they could strike the United States. The air force requested the permission of President Truman to conduct overflights of the suspected airfields. Fearful

26

of provoking the Soviets, Truman authorized a single overflight. In October, SAC successfully conducted the mission using an RB-47. The resulting photography failed to show any massing of Tu-4 bombers and the threat receded (Day, Logsdon, and Latell 1998, 96). No further overflights were authorized during Truman's presidency.

Flights along the Soviet Union's borders continued, and on more than one occasion they met with tragic results. During the same month that SAC was overflying eastern Siberia, a Russian fighter downed a USAF RB-29 on a photoreconnaissance mission off northern Hokkaido. The crew of eight was never found. The Soviet government claimed the incident took place near the Island of Yuri, which it contended had become Soviet territory by virtue of the Yalta agreement. The U.S. government repudiated the Soviet claim and, in fact, demanded the Soviet government compensate the United States for the loss of the aircraft, for death benefits to the crew's families, and for the costs of training a new crew. While the incident did not stop the United States from continuing its aggressive policy of intelligence gathering, neither did it moderate the Soviet response.

Just nine months later, on 29 July 1953, a MiG-15 downed an RB-50 over the Sea of Japan. The crew, assigned to the 55th Strategic Reconnaissance Wing at Yokota, returned fire, but to no effect. Only a single member of the crew survived. Another RB-29 was lost over Japanese territory on 7 November 1954. The aircraft was armed but chose not to return fire. The aggressiveness of the Soviets made it clear they saw these flights as a threat to their national security.

Photoreconnaissance missions were also directed at naval and air bases on the Kola Peninsula, along the Baltic coast, and along the coast of the Black Sea. Missions directed at the Kola and Baltic coastlines typically originated from bases in England—Brize Norton, Lakenheath, Manston, and Burtonwood; missions over the Black Sea and Caucasus Mountains originated from Adana, Turkey, and Port Lyauty, Morocco. Whatever their origin, they seldom surprised the Soviets, even those conducted at night using photo flash bombs. Soviet radars were simply too good; they picked up reconnaissance aircraft early and could track them for long distances. In addition, over extremely sensitive areas like the Kola Peninsula, Russian fighters were in the air twenty-four hours a day.

In fact, most reconnaissance missions flown along Soviet borders were not for photographic purposes but to acquire electronic intelligence, or ELINT. These flights, referred to as "ferret flights," had as their primary mission to detect the precise location and characteristics of Soviet air defense radar systems, information that would be critical should America's strategic bomber force be ordered to strike at targets within the Soviet Union. These missions were conducted in deepest secrecy, though clearly not to the Soviets. Between the late 1940s and late 1960s perhaps as many as twenty thousand such missions were undertaken. They became so frequent that Soviet radar operators grew reluctant to turn on their systems so as not to give away critical information on their operating characteristics. To force the issue, ferret pilots would provoke operators by flying straight into Soviet airspace; while a very effective tactic, it was also an extremely risky one because ferret aircraft were neither fast nor armed.

In the twenty or so years that these missions were conducted at least thirty aircraft were downed and over 150 crewmen killed or unaccounted for (*USN&WR* 1993, 34). These ELINT missions provided a vast storehouse of data on Soviet air defenses but none more significant than what they discovered along much of the Soviet Union's northern periphery: there were no early warning radars there. It was not until the late 1950s that the Soviets began developing an early warning system in northern Siberia. Clearly, it was in the best interests of the United States to keep its knowledge of this gap highly secret. If the United States were to have launched a B-52 strike across the North Pole, the Soviets would not have detected it until it was too late (Andrew 1995, 220).

Though the data provided by the photoreconnaissance and ferret flights remained fragmentary, they nevertheless provided a moderating effect upon the intelligence community's assessment of the likelihood that the Soviet Union would initiate a general war. Published on 8 January 1952, NIE-25 suggested that Soviet leaders might already have concluded that the strategic military balance had shifted to the advantage of the West. A war was, therefore, a hazardous gamble in that it would involve widespread destruction in the Soviet Union and "with it the risk that the Soviet system itself would be destroyed" (NIE-25, 4, in Koch 1993, 195). Accordingly, there was little chance that the Soviets would deliberately initiate a war in 1952. However, if a war did take place, the authors believed the Soviet Union could survive a U.S. nuclear attack and "maintain sufficient strength to carry on the war" (NIE-25, 3, in Koch 1993, 194).

By the time the Truman presidency came to an end in early 1953, the cold war was at its height. For his part Truman had done seemingly everything possible to contain the spread of communism, although his critics did not share this view. Nevertheless, in the span of just over seven years he had instituted a plan to create a prosperous, non-Communist Europe, and to guarantee its security he had created NATO, the core of which included the permanent stationing of American troops on the European continent. In Asia, where he was blamed for "losing China," Truman guaranteed Japan's security while waging a limited war in Korea as part of his global containment policy. All the while he continued to build up the United States's nuclear stockpile, expanded the Strategic Air Command, and constructed nearly one hundred overseas bases from which America's strategic bomber fleet could strike the Soviet industrial heartland.

Yet for all Truman's success in responding to the Soviet challenge, policymakers in Washington possessed little direct information on which to determine Soviet military capabilities and intentions. Much of what they did possess, in fact, was derived from captured German documents. The combined efforts of military attachés and intelligence agents in Moscow, along with the pilots and crews who conducted ferret flights along the periphery of the Soviet Union, were inadequate for strategic planning purposes. At a time when the threat of nuclear war appeared a real possibility, America's reconnaissance efforts not only provided little information but also remained highly provocative.

# 2

## An Interim Solution

When Dwight Eisenhower succeeded Truman as president in early 1953, he was viewed by many as the one man who could effectively deal with the Soviet Union. While Eisenhower himself supported the strong stand taken by Truman to contain Soviet expansionism, he nevertheless pledged to wage the cold war "more efficiently and successfully" (LaFeber 1991, 146). Eisenhower believed firmly that America's greatest asset in its competition with the Soviet system lay in its economic productivity, not in its military strength, and as a fiscal conservative, he believed that the essential ingredients for economic growth were balanced federal budgets and low inflation. The only way these conditions could be met, Eisenhower contended, was through a reduction in defense spending.

In fact, Eisenhower was able to accomplish all of these things to some degree. He was able to reduce defense spending, for most of his eight years he balanced his budgets, and he was able to keep the average annual rate of inflation at about 1.15 percent (Ambrose 1981, 275). Unfortunately for Eisenhower, a series of Soviet actions, including the surprise launch of *Sputnik* in 1957, would lead his Democratic critics to charge that his defense cuts were imperiling America's national security. Spurious claims about "bomber gaps" and "missile gaps" would help the Democrats regain the White House in 1960. However, in his quest for better information to refute these claims, Eisenhower would be responsible for developing three of the nation's most sophisticated photoreconnaissance systems—the U-2 and SR-71 aircraft and the photographic reconnaissance satellite.

The first step toward his goal of cutting defense spending was to find a way of halting the Korean War, and to this end Eisenhower was helped immeasurably by the unexpected death of Stalin in March 1953. Neither the North Koreans, who had suffered the most from this conflict, nor their Chinese allies were inclined to prolong the war; unsettled claims could be better settled at the negotiating table than on the battlefield. Talks on ending the conflict began in April, and although at one time or another all parties attempted to obstruct negotiations, an armistice was finally hammered out and signed on 27 July 1953.

Another consequence of Stalin's death was the succession crisis it provoked within the Soviet Union. Georgi Malenkov initially assumed Stalin's leadership position, but he made the costly mistake of becoming premier, which made him the head of government, while turning over to Nikita Khrushchev the more important post of party secretary. Khrushchev would move quickly to fill party administrative positions with his own people. By February 1955 Malenkov would be ousted (he was named minister of electric power) and Khrushchev's man, Nikolai Bulganin, would be named premier. In the interim, however, the Soviet Union was ruled collectively, and domestic concerns tended to take precedence over foreign affairs. Still, Malenkov made one announcement that reverberated throughout Washington: on 12 August 1953, he stated, the Soviet Union had successfully tested a thermonuclear device (a hydrogen bomb).

In spite of the fact that the Soviets now possessed the H-bomb, Eisenhower pressed ahead with his pledge to reduce defense spending. In the budget for fiscal 1953, which Eisenhower had inherited from President Truman, $50 billion was authorized for defense. Over the next two years Eisenhower, in what he would call his New Look defense policy, would reduce that amount by nearly one-third to about $34 billion. His approach for making such cuts, without drastically weakening America's defense posture, was to rely increasingly upon nuclear weapons. Between 1953 and 1955 America's nuclear stockpile would nearly double while its fleet of B-52 bombers would grow steadily from year to year (LaFeber 1991, 155). Eisenhower would also make clear his intention to use such weapons against Soviet cities if it became absolutely necessary. His strategy would become known as "massive retaliation."

The rapid development of America's nuclear delivery capability was not lost on the Soviet leadership. Their awareness was never greater than during the early months of 1954, when the United States undertook Operation Bravo, a series of thermonuclear tests conducted at its Pacific Ocean atomic test site. In the very first test of this series on 1 March the United States detonated a 15-megaton hydrogen bomb, not only the most powerful explosion created to that point by human beings but one three times more powerful than its designers had predicted (Smirnov and Zubok 1994, 15). Under these circumstances Khrushchev felt compelled to reach some kind of accommodation with the United States, but he did not want to do it from a position of nuclear inferiority. Unfortunately, for the immediate future the Soviets would possess neither the capacity to catch up to the United States in nuclear warhead production nor the ability to produce long-range bombers capable of reaching the United States. Lacking a credible response to America's "massive retaliation" strategy, Khrushchev would choose instead a combination of intimidation and "strategic deception" to mask his country's vulnerability.

To this day it remains unclear whether Khrushchev's "strategic deception" strategy was a unified plan or simply a series of ad hoc responses to events as they occurred. At any rate, in practice it involved a number of well-publicized events conducted over a several-year period, including atmospheric tests of extremely powerful nuclear devices, public flyovers of what appeared to observers on the ground as endless numbers of strategic aircraft, and, of course, an entire series of spectacular missile launchings beginning with *Sputnik* (Malia 1994, 345). In combination these events helped to create the impression that the Soviet Union possessed a strategic nuclear capability comparable to SAC's. It was Khrushchev's hope that the deception would last long enough for the Soviet Union to at least approach nuclear parity with the United States.

In fact, Khrushchev's "strategic deception" may have worked only too well. With no means of disproving Khrushchev's boasts, Americans for the first time began to fear the possibility of a surprise Soviet nuclear attack. The United States simply had no way of knowing if at that very moment the Soviets were preparing their aircraft or missiles for such a mission. Intelligence agents in the field had already demonstrated they could not acquire this kind of information in any timely manner. Thus a surprise attack would probably go undetected until incoming Soviet bombers were picked up "by American air-defense radars on the North American continent" (Volkman 1985, 143). This fear, then, would provide the main impetus for Eisenhower's decision to develop a reconnaissance system capable of providing at least some warning of Soviet intentions.

Eisenhower had long been intrigued by the concept of a space-based reconnaissance system. This idea had been around for nearly a decade. As early as 1945 RAND Corporation was studying the technical feasibility of earth-orbiting satellites for the U.S. Army Air Force, and by 1954 it had identified literally all of the missions that would later form the air force's military satellite program (Peebles 1997, 5). Unfortunately, the boost capability for placing a space vehicle in orbit had not yet been achieved, and research suggested it would not be available until 1960 at the earliest. Eisenhower decided, therefore, that another approach would have to be found since the threat to America's national security posed by the Soviet Union appeared to be growing.

So it was in 1954 that Eisenhower appointed a special committee, the Technological Capabilities Panel, chaired by James Killian Jr., president of the Massachusetts Institute of Technology, and comprised of representatives of the military, industrial, and academic communities, to examine the surprise attack issue. Killian in turn created a subcommittee, under the direction of Edwin "Din" Land of Polaroid Corporation, to come up with methods for monitoring Soviet military capabilities. At one of its earliest meetings members of the subcommittee were briefed on a proposal for a high-altitude reconnaissance aircraft that Lockheed Corporation had sent to the air force. The proposal, the work of Lockheed's chief designer, Clarence "Kelly" Johnson, called for an aircraft that could fly over two thousand miles at an altitude of seventy thousand feet. Committee members quickly became sold on the design, seeing in it the interim solution for which they were looking. Their recommendation for an integrated aerial reconnaissance system was approved by the Intelligence Advisory Board, which sent it along to the president. When Eisenhower gave his go-ahead to their proposal on 1 December 1954, the U-2 program was born.

In authorizing the U-2, Eisenhower was well aware of the program's risks and limitations; he saw it at best as a stopgap measure. For one, aircraft overflights of Soviet territory would be in clear violation of international law and the Soviet government would be certain to protest loudly. Then, too, the flights were provocative. The aircraft could be downed and the pilot captured or killed. Even best estimates gave the program only two to three years before such an eventuality. Perhaps more worrisome, the aircraft could be mistaken for a SAC bomber, with even greater repercussions thus a possibility. While the U-2 would clearly not be mistaken for a B-52 under most circumstances, it was uncertain how it might appear on a Soviet radar screen. Given the fact that SAC bombers frequently skirted Soviet airspace, it was entirely possible that an anxious air defense commander might interpret such a blip as the initial phase of a surprise nuclear attack (Beschloss 1986, 158), and if the risks were not great enough, the overflights could be expected to cover only a small portion of the country. Still, the desperate need for information outweighed all of these concerns.

In response to at least some of his concerns, Eisenhower imposed several conditions on the program. He was, for example, adamant that uniformed air force personnel would not be allowed to overfly Soviet territory; pilots of U-2 aircraft would be CIA employees, though the air force would recruit and train them. Eisenhower felt that the political fallout from the downing of a U-2 in Soviet airspace would be less if the program could credibly be demonstrated to be a civilian one. But there were other reasons for wanting the CIA to manage the U-2 program, not least of which was to minimize interservice rivalries. Eisenhower had good reason to believe that if the Pentagon were in charge of gathering information on Soviet military capabilities, it might use what was found to enhance its own interests. He suspected the air force was already using exaggerated estimates of Soviet bomber production as a means of pressuring Congress to enlarge its fleet of B-52s. In the absence of more reliable data, there was little Eisenhower could do to restrain Congress, but he could make the air force pay in other ways.

The story of the U-2's actual development has been well documented over the years. Suffice it to say that in a remarkably successful collaboration, the CIA and Lockheed Corporation were able to bring forth the U-2 under budget and ahead of schedule. Richard Bissell, a former professor of economics at Yale, was hired by the CIA, under the title special assistant for planning and coordination, to direct overall program management of Project Aquatone. The Lockheed team, which consisted of two dozen aircraft designers, was headed by Kelly Johnson himself. Their work was done under deepest secrecy at a large hangar, known as the Skunk Works, at Lockheed's Burbank facility. Johnson's Skunk Works had already established a reputation for itself, having built the P-38 fighter-bomber, the F-80 jet fighter, and the world's fastest jet, the F-104 (Beschloss 1986, 91). The U-2, however, would become the team's most famous aircraft, though it would take only eight months to design and produce the first prototype. Johnson and his crew would build another twenty for a mere $22 million, in part because "the U-2, from nose to cockpit, was basically the front half of the F-104, but with an extended body from cockpit to tail" (Rich and Janos 1994, 131).

The U-2 was an engineering marvel, though it looked like nothing more than "a glider with a jet engine attached" (Infield 1970, 167). It had an eighty-foot wingspan, which gave the aircraft an ungainly appearance on the ground, but these same wings made the U-2 extremely stable at high altitudes. It could also fly great distances without refueling since the wings could carry over thirteen thousand gallons of fuel. Furthermore, once airborne, the jet engine only had to be used intermittently; the rest of the time it simply glided silently along its flight path. In total the U-2 could fly for nine hours, travel approximately 5,000 nautical miles, and glide for another 350 nautical miles if it lost power. But most important, the U-2 could cruise at altitudes of nearly seventy-five thousand feet, which intelligence experts at the time believed would put it beyond the range of Soviet radar. This notion was dashed, however, with the very first flight over Soviet territory, although for four years the aircraft would prove to be invulnerable to Soviet fighters and surface-to-air missiles (Rich and Janos 1994, 125).

U-2 missions over the Soviet Union were stressful for everyone involved, though most of all for the pilots themselves. Not only would a pilot be jammed into his tiny cockpit for over eight hours, but he was subject to attack by Soviet air defenses for most of the time spent over enemy territory. Even takeoffs and landings were not without hazards. On take-off there was always the danger that one of the long, flexible wings would strike the runway. To guard against this possibility a small wheel, or "pogo," as it was called, was attached to each wing tip. But how to release these pogos once airborne? An early method was to have a crewman sit on each wing tip until sufficient speed was reached to stabilize the aircraft. The crewman would then "leap off the wings, pull the pins attaching the 'pogos' to the wing tips, and the wheels would fall free" (Infield 1970, 171). Landings were no easier. Exhausted after hours in the air, pilots would have to land the U-2 on two small wheels, one at the front, the other at the rear. The aircraft would then taxi to a grassy strip adjacent to the runway, where one of the wing tips would be allowed to touch down.

It was the pilot, of course, who presented the most serious diplomatic problem if a U-2 were downed over Soviet territory. Many officials in Washington, including President Eisenhower, were led to believe, however, that a pilot would not survive the crash of a U-2 because of the aircraft's fragile frame and the altitude from which it was expected to fall; the aircraft would simply disintegrate. To save weight, ejection seats were not built into U-2s, though parachutes and survival kits were issued to every pilot; most felt they were intended more for pilot morale than pilot survival since if the U-2 were to be struck by a surface-to-air missile (SAM), it would disintegrate "before the pilot had a chance to even think about bailing out" (Beschloss 1986, 15).

Simultaneous with the development of the U-2, the White House had requested that the CIA establish a photointelligence component capable of planning U-2 missions as well as exploiting the resulting photography. The person charged with this responsibility was Arthur "Art" Lundahl, a former naval intelligence officer who had been brought to the CIA in 1952 to develop and head the agency's first photointerpretation group, the Photo Intelligence Division (PID), forerunner of the Office of Imagery Analysis. Lundahl proved perfect for his new assignment, and by the time the first rolls of film acquired over the Soviet Union arrived in July 1956, Lundahl had the Photographic Interpretation Center (PIC) prepared to handle them. Housed in the old Steuart Building at the corner of Fifth and K Streets in downtown Washington, D.C., PIC was comprised of more than two hundred photointerpreters drawn from the CIA, army, navy, and air force (NPIC 1991, 6).

Gratified as Eisenhower was by the pace of these development, by early 1956 the need for information on Soviet military activities had become intense. One issue in particular overshadowed all others: Had the Soviets developed an intercontinental-range bomber capable of reaching the United States? The issue had been around since the end of the war, but it was revived in 1948 when military attachés in Moscow saw the Tu-4 Bull for the first time as it flew over the May Day parade. Intelligence suggested that the Soviets were producing the Tu-4 at a rate of ten to twenty-five aircraft per month, but it also became clear that it lacked the range to reach the U.S. mainland in the absence of an aerial refueling capacity. A turboprop version of this aircraft, designated the Barge, was sighted at a Soviet air show in 1951, though it apparently had never gone into production (Brugioni 1991, 5).

The bomber issue intensified in 1954 when Col. Charles Taylor, an air force attaché assigned to Moscow, witnessed a new four-engine swept-wing jet bomber, somewhat similar to the American B-52, overfly that year's May Day parade. The M-4 Bison, as it became designated, was in time estimated to fly at over five hundred miles per hour and carry a load of ten 1,000-pound bombs seven thousand nautical miles. The NIE for that year predicted that a few Bison aircraft would become operational by mid-1957, with the number rising to about one hundred by mid-1959. Significantly, the report's authors admitted they had underestimated Soviet progress in the past, so they added the statement that "substantial numbers of jet heavy bombers may appear in operational units prior to mid-1959 and possibly by mid-1957" (NIE 11-5-54, 8, in Koch 1993, 210).

The following year Colonel Taylor reported witnessing an entire squadron of these aircraft fly past the reviewing stand, and a few weeks later, on Red Air Force Day, he "counted fully twice the number of Bison bombers as had flown past the May Day parade earlier that year" (Burrows 1986, 68). But the Bison was not the only new aircraft to be seen at this time. There was also the Tu-16 Badger, a smaller version of the Bison, and a larger, turboprop heavy bomber, the Tu-95 Bear, which was reported to be capable of carrying a 25,000-pound bomb load nearly eight thousand nautical miles.

These sightings had a major impact on NIE 11-7-55, which projected that by mid-1959 the Soviet bomber fleet could contain as many as three hundred Bears, four hundred Bisons, and nearly seven hundred Badgers, which would give Soviet Long Range Aviation a greater number of bombers than SAC. The report added that the Soviets could launch a force of up to seven hundred heavy bombers against the United States from interior bases "and, with inflight refueling where necessary, could reach any target in the United States on two-way missions." The Soviets could enhance their success in striking heavily defended targets by using air-to-surface missiles armed with nuclear warheads (NIE 11-10-55, 6, in Koch 1993, 222). When these estimates were leaked to the press, very possibly by the air force, the "bomber gap" myth, which would become a major political issue for Eisenhower, was born. The air force would use the bomber gap to pressure Eisenhower into authorizing the production of more B-52s than he thought necessary, but he too would take advantage of the issue to bring the CIA into the process of estimating Soviet strategic weapons production.

It was against this backdrop that Eisenhower agreed to meet in Geneva in July 1955 with representatives of Britain, France, and the Soviet Union in the first four-power summit of the postwar period. Charles Bohlen, the U.S. ambassador in Moscow, advised the White House that "the Kremlin genuinely wished to relax tensions" (Isaacson and Thomas 1986, 577), though, in fact, there were ulterior motives to this desire. For one thing, Soviet leaders hoped to lull the West into complacency and, in particular, "allay anxiety concerning the Soviet maneuvers in Asia, the Middle East, and Africa"; in addition, they hoped to encourage the West to cut defense spending in order that they might close the weapons gap (Rostow 1982, chap. 4, p. 21). However, in the weeks immediately preceding the conference, West Germany, one of the main issues on the Geneva agenda, was accepted into NATO and immediately began the process of rearming. Soviet leaders were extremely angered by this move and were, therefore, in no mood to consider any new Western proposals. This proved unfortunate because Eisenhower introduced his Open Skies plan, which, had it been approved, might have altered the course of the cold war.

Eisenhower's Open Skies plan called for the United States and the Soviet Union to exchange detailed blueprints of each other's military facilities and to allow the other side to regularly photograph these facilities from the air as a means of preventing the possibility of a surprise attack. To demonstrate just how far he was willing to go in pursuit of peace, Eisenhower was prepared to allow the Soviet Union to construct airfields in the United States from which these overflights would be conducted. The only conditions Eisenhower set were, first, that each Soviet overflight would have an American representative on board the aircraft, and second, that whatever privileges were granted to the Soviets in the United States be granted to Americans in the Soviet Union (Ambrose 1981, 217). The prime minister of Britain and the premier of France expressed immediate approval of the idea; Bulganin, the nominal head of the Soviet delegation, responded that the plan had merit and that the Soviets would give it careful study. This encouraging statement, however, was soon rejected by Nikita Khrushchev, the real leader of the delegation, who termed the Open Skies plan as nothing more than a bald plot by the West to conduct espionage against the Soviet Union. In a sense, Khrushchev was correct. The United States had far more to gain from such a plan than the Soviet Union, which had access to a vast quantity of information on U.S. military affairs through newspapers, magazines, maps, and even U.S. government aerial photographs. Most important, the United States would discover the Soviet Union's military shortcomings and by so doing undermine Khrushchev's policy of "strategic deception."

Although the Open Skies plan was rejected, Eisenhower's initiative was generally regarded as a great success; he was lauded for attempting to push open the door to arms control. His critics, on the other hand, saw his plan as political grandstanding, especially since it was against the law to exchange blueprints and aerial photos of defense plants. In fact, Eisenhower's motivations were far more complex than that. First and foremost a committed advocate of arms control, Eisenhower saw in the Open Skies scheme a potential stabilizing device in a nuclear age which might, indeed, open the way for serious arms control agreements" (Rostow 1982, chap. 4, p. 75). But there was also an element of desperation in the Open Skies plan. During the 1950s American political leaders were deeply frustrated by their almost total lack of information on the Soviet nuclear weapons program. It was assumed that the United States was ahead technologically in the development of nuclear weapons, but the question of whether the Soviets were catching up, had already reached parity, or were developing a first-strike capability could not be adequately answered. At stake was the security of the nation, and if this information could not be acquired through a mutually agreed-upon aerial inspection plan, a unilateral plan would have to be undertaken. In such an instance, the U.S. position in the international community would be stronger "if the Open Skies offer were made before U.S. flights over the USSR began" (Rostow 1982, chap. 4, p. 9a).

As it turned out the air force had long been testing a very different type of reconnaissance system, and with the U-2 still several months away from becoming operational, Eisenhower now gave in to air force pressure to employ it. Code-named Genetrix (119L), the system involved the use of high-altitude weather balloons fitted out with aerial cameras to acquire photographs of Soviet territory. The inspiration for Genetrix was a Japanese operation that attempted to drop incendiary bombs on the continental United States during World War II. The bombs were attached to balloons in Japan, where they were sent aloft and carried six thousand miles to the United States by the prevailing westerly winds. This operation, code-named Tu Go, lasted for about six months. By the time it ended in April 1945, a total of 285 balloons either had been intercepted by U.S. military forces or had dropped harmlessly into the Pacific (Volkman 1985, 139). Few made it to the mainland, although ironically one made it through U.S. air defenses and successfully released its incendiary device on a home in Oregon; the ensuing fire killed one of the house's occupants.

Operation Genetrix was made possible because of a meteorological research program being conducted jointly by the air force and the navy's Office of Naval Research. This program was employing huge gas-filled balloons called Skyhooks to acquire information on the upper levels of the earth's atmosphere, where future aircraft and missiles were expected to operate. As a part of Genetrix, these balloons were fitted out with specially designed wide-area search cameras capable of acquiring photographs at about fifty thousand feet. The plan was to launch them from bases in Western Europe, from where they would drift across Soviet territory under the influence of the prevailing westerly winds. If they actually made it to the Pacific, they would be caught in midair by modified C-119 transports or recovered from the ocean's surface—techniques later used to recover Corona payloads (Day, Logsdon, and Latell 1998, 103).

On 10 January 1956 President Eisenhower gave his approval for the launch of the first balloons. Over the next three to four weeks a total of 516 balloons were launched from bases in England, Norway, Turkey, and West Germany, of which 44 were ultimately recovered. When, however,

40

the Soviets protested the use of such balloons, many of which landed in Soviet territory, Eisenhower ordered the program to be halted. While several thousand photos of Soviet territory were acquired in this manner, most possessed very little of intelligence value (Peebles 1997, 3). The program's chief impact, in fact, was to trigger a UFO scare in both the United States and Europe. The huge weather balloons, which became saucer-shaped under the influence of the upper atmosphere's wind system, appeared to many observers to be spacecraft of unknown origin.

The failure of Genetrix did not entirely dash the idea of using balloons for reconnaissance purposes. A second series of balloon launchings was initiated in July 1958 under a program designated WS-461L. These balloons were intended to be launched from ships in the Gulf of Alaska, rising to an altitude of one hundred thousand feet, where they would encounter an east-west jet stream that would propel them across the Soviet Union. They would carry a twelve-inch panoramic camera especially designed for the program by Boston University. As it turned out only three balloons were ever launched in this series, all of which ended up landing in Polish territory. The Soviets thus gained access to America's most sophisticated camera system, a twenty-four-inch version of which would be employed in the first Corona satellites (Anselmo 1994, 6). As for President Eisenhower, he became so furious when he was told what happened that he summarily ordered an end to all balloon reconnaissance programs.

Fortunately, by mid-June flight testing of the U-2 at the air force's highly secret Groom Lake facility in Nevada was completed and Eisenhower promptly gave his authorization for the first overflights of the Soviet Union. Ironically, however, General Nathan Twining, the air force chief of staff, was visiting Moscow just at this moment so the first U-2 overflight had to be delayed. It finally took place on 4 July 1956. For its inaugural overflight, the aircraft took off from Wiesbaden, where it proceeded to follow a flight path that took it over northern Poland and the Soviet republic of Byelorussia before reaching Moscow. The pilot then overflew the Soviet capital twice before heading northwest to the city of Leningrad. After photographing the most important military targets around Leningrad, the U-2 flew safely back to Wiesbaden via the Baltic Sea. The aircraft has spent a total of two and one-half hours over Soviet territory. It had also been tracked nearly the entire way by Soviet and

Warsaw Pact radars, and a host of fighter aircraft had tried in vain to reach the U-2, "but the fighters ceilings were below U-2 altitudes by several kilometers" (Orlov 1998–99, 8).

The next day two separate overflights were undertaken. One acquired coverage of targets to the south in the Ukrainian Republic; the other, as it turned out, became the only U-2 mission to ever acquire photography of the Moscow area. Both missions had military airfields as their primary targets. The most productive of these early flights, however, took place three days later, on 8 July, when a U-2 flying over Engels Airfield outside of Leningrad photographed thirty Bison bombers sitting wing-to-wing on the tarmac. While initially these aircraft appeared to confirm the rumors of an alleged bomber gap, subsequent overflights of other long-range airfields failed to discover any additional Bisons; the Engels aircraft turned out to be the entire Bison fleet (Rich and Janos 1994, 148).

For these missions U-2s were fitted out with massive camera systems weighing several hundred pounds. The most commonly employed system was a panoramic camera with either a twenty-four- or a thirty-six-inch focal length; as the camera swung from horizon to horizon it took photographs at several different stations. At nadir the spatial resolution of these photographs was two to three feet from an altitude of seventy thousand feet. These cameras also carried nearly twelve thousand feet of film, which meant they could photograph the equivalent of a 750-mile-wide swath of terrain stretching "from Washington to Phoenix in one flight" (Beschloss 1986, 92). When the missions were completed the film was flown to the United States, where in a matter of two or three days, it was developed into transparent positives, duplicated, and distributed to photointerpreters at SAC's targeting section in Omaha, Nebraska, and the CIA's Photographic Interpretation Center in Washington. Once PIC's photointerpreters had completed their analysis, Art Lundahl, the center's director, would take enlargements of some of the best photos over to the White House, where he would brief President Eisenhower on the latest mission. With the possible exception of John Kennedy during the Cuban missile crisis, no president ever displayed a deeper appreciation of reconnaissance photos than Eisenhower. The president would never forget the Battle of the Bulge, where the lack of good intelligence on German troop movements allowed them to surprise Allied forces and nearly turn the tide on the western front.

42

From the beginning the U-2 program was so heavily classified that only a few hundred individuals received clearances to use the photos and photo-derived products (code-named Talent). Over time, it became necessary to increase the numbers of analysts having access to Talent materials. After a few years the Steuart Building became so overcrowded that a new home had to be found. On 1 January 1963, PIC, now known as the National Photographic Interpretation Center, moved to Building 213, a renovated naval gun factory in the Washington Navy Yard, where it has remained ever since.

As unaware as most of the American public was of the U-2 program, at least until the downing of Francis Gary Powers's aircraft in May 1960, the program was no secret to Soviet leaders. Among the photo enlargements shown to President Eisenhower after the very first mission were those "of MIG fighters trying desperately to reach the U-2, then falling back as their engines cut out at high altitude" (Andrew 1995, 224); in all the Soviets had attempted twenty intercepts. Part of the confusion arose from the fact that Soviet air defenses were designed to attack waves of bombers, not a single aircraft. Just as ominous to Eisenhower was the formal diplomatic protest handed to Secretary of State John Foster Dulles by the Soviet ambassador six days after the first overflight. The note claimed that a twin-engine air force bomber had intentionally violated Soviet airspace. So the flights were going to go neither undetected nor unprotested. The State Department waited several more days before responding, by which time additional missions had been completed. The U.S. response simply noted that an inquiry had turned up no evidence of a military aircraft violating Soviet airspace. On the assumption that the U-2 was a civilian aircraft, the response could technically be considered true (Brugioni 1991, 32).

President Eisenhower was concerned nevertheless that the Soviet Union would use these overflights as an excuse to create a major international incident. For this reason he was inclined to call at least a temporary moratorium on future flights. As it turned out, however, Soviet protests were made privately, and in time they ceased entirely. The Soviets did not want to publicize to the whole world that they were technologically incapable of protecting their airspace. But more important, the existence of these overflights could have undermined "the authority of the regime: How would the Soviet people respond if they knew their government could not perform the most fundamental task of protecting against foreign invaders" (Beschloss 1986, 157). Many Soviets remembered the Luftwaffe overflights that had preceded the German invasion of June 1941 and wouldn't they now wonder whether the U-2 overflights might not augur a similar attack?

Eisenhower's reluctance to authorize additional overflights of the Soviet Union, though not elsewhere, was reinforced by events in the Middle East, where Egypt's Nasser had seized the Suez Canal in July and had nationalized the British-controlled Universal Suez Canal Company (LaFeber 1991, 185). Although he promised to keep the canal open to all former users, the British and French wanted military action to overthrow Nasser and take back control. Eisenhower would have none of that, though he agreed to covert action to undermine Nasser. Enlisting the aid of the Israelis, the British and French attacked Egypt on 29 October, and one week later Khrushchev took advantage of the crisis to order Soviet tanks into Budapest to crush a "counter revolution." Meanwhile, Khrushchev reminded French and British leaders of their nations' vulnerability to Soviet missiles if they did not withdraw their forces from Egypt. In response to Khrushchev's warning, President Eisenhower placed American military forces on alert, hoping to forestall any Soviet intervention in the Middle East. Both crises faded, but tensions between the United States and the Soviet Union remained high. Under these circumstances Eisenhower felt it prudent to temporarily suspend U-2 overflights of the Soviet Union for the remainder of the year.

Bissell was constantly pressuring Eisenhower to authorize more flights, and in early 1957 he did so. By this time there were three operational U-2 squadrons: Detachment A was based in Wiesbaden (later transferred to Giebelstadt), West Germany, where it was designated the 1st Provisional Weather Reconnaissance Squadron; Detachment B, or 10-10 as it was called, was assigned to Incirlik Air Base in Adana, Turkey; Detachment C was sent to the U.S. Marine base in Atsugi, Japan. In addition, U-2s also flew from air bases in Iran, Pakistan, Norway, and even on occasion from bases in Alaska. Incirlik, however, was considered the most attractive base of operations for the U-2, due in large part to the fact that Soviet air defenses were considerably weaker there than along other portions of the Soviet border.

The U-2s were now bringing back more and more film coverage of Soviet military bases, defense industries, missile test facilities, and nuclear, biological, and chemical warfare test sites. Many of these targets had never before been photographed, and, fortunately for U.S. photointerpreters, the Soviets appeared to be employing no concealment or camouflage techniques (Brugioni 1991, 31). The most immediate impact of these photos was to improve the targeting data required by SAC mission planners, who until now had depended upon captured German documents, defector reports, and ELINT data; the list of potential targets now increased from three thousand to nearly twenty thousand (Beschloss 1986, 156). As these sites became the object of repeat coverage, additional information could be derived: preliminary order-of-battle, production rates for defense plants, and specifications for new weapons systems. Compared to some of the more sophisticated methodologies employed by imagery analysts today, the early techniques appear crude, but they were a significant improvement over many of the partisan statistical techniques used by the military.

One thing was definitely becoming more obvious with each mission— there was no bomber gap; U-2 photographs revealed far fewer bombers at forward air bases than expected. In response a Special NIE (SNIE 11-7-58) was produced which concluded that the Soviets were apparently foregoing a rapid buildup of their heavy bomber forces, probably because of dissatisfaction with both the Bison and the Bear aircraft, and were instead concentrating on developing an operational ICBM capability. The SNIE estimated that as of 1 April 1958 there were only about 100 to 125 operational Bison and Bear heavy bombers, though there were nearly 900 Badger medium bombers. As for the Bison, less than 100 would ever be produced and many of them would be converted to tankers. The Bear would ultimately go on to become the mainstay of Soviet Long Range Aviation, but in 1958 only 50 to 60 appeared operational and there was evidence the program had been at least temporarily suspended. These heavy bomber totals, however, represented a fraction of the nearly seven hundred Bison and Bears projected to be operational in mid-1959 by NIE 11-56. The value of U-2 photos was proving to be enormous. The photos were providing not only accurate estimates of operational aircraft but also evidence that "the Soviets were building [aircraft] at a rate considerably short of capacity, and there was nothing in the pipeline, such as the movement of basic supplies to construction sites, that suggested they intended to speed up" (Ambrose 1981, 277).

Among the individual sites accorded highest priority coverage were the known missile test facilities at Kapustin Yar–Vladimirovka (on the lower Volga) and Sary Shagan (west of the Aral Sea), where MRBMs (medium-range ballistic missiles), IRBMs (intermediate-range ballistic missiles), and SAMs were developed. In 1955 the United States had built a ground station at Samsun, Turkey, for the specific purpose of acquiring telemetric intelligence (TELINT) on the missiles being launched there. The station had become operational "just in time to track the first Soviet IRBM launches from the testing ground at Kapustin Yar" (Andrew 1995, 220). But the question had remained: Were there missile test facilities in the interior of the country beyond the range of ground stations? The not-unexpected answer came in early 1957 when a U-2 flying over the Soviet republic of Kazakhstan photographed the Tyuratam missile test center. Analyses of the photographs revealed only one completed rail-served launch pad. The dimensions of the pad were so large, however, that missile specialists doubted it was designed for operational purposes (Brugioni 1991, 35).

Once the Tyuratam missile test center was discovered, it was monitored on a regular basis and photointerpreters were able to acquire considerable data on Soviet missile capabilities. Among the techniques they now developed was one that enabled them to "determine the size and power of Soviet rockets based on burn marks and the configurations of the pads for exhaust gases" (Bissell 1996, 119).

In June 1957 a U-2 mission brought back photos of an SS-6 on an erector at the one completed launch pad. At the time the SS-6 was the largest ICBM by far in the Soviet arsenal with an estimated maximum operational range of from five thousand to seven thousand nautical miles. In August the United States detected the first successful launch of an ICBM, possibly the SS-6 photographed in June. The significance of the Soviet launch was enhanced by the failure of four well-publicized test flights of America's Thor missile (Brugioni 1991, 34), and when, on 4 October 1957, the Soviets successfully launched the world's first artificial earth satellite, the 184-pound *Sputnik*, most Americans were stunned. How was it possible that the Soviet Union had beaten the United States into space?

President Eisenhower was totally unprepared for the public's reaction to *Sputnik*, a reaction that would be politically costly both to Eisenhower himself and to the Republicans in general. Newspapers claimed the United States had suffered the scientific equivalent of a Pearl Harbor and was now wide open to a surprise nuclear attack by the Soviet Union (Andrew 1995, 240). Public opinion polls recorded a dramatic drop in confidence in the policies of the Eisenhower administration. The Democrats took full advantage of the event to charge the president with complacency. They claimed that as a result of Eisenhower's defense cuts, the Soviet Union had overtaken the United States in missile technology. A report prepared at Eisenhower's request by his science advisor, George Kistiakowsky, concluded that the United States was ahead of the Soviet Union in both strategic weapons research and missile deployment (Brugioni 1991, 37), but it was probably also true that Eisenhower's efforts to head off an arms race had restrained the United States from being first in space. Totally forgotten amidst all this furor, however, was the ironic fact that the United States had developed an aircraft capable of flying with impunity over the Soviet Union's most highly secret military installations (Bissell 1996, 119).

But the political situation only continued to worsen for President Eisenhower. On 3 November the Soviets successfully launched a second, larger satellite; this one carried a dog into space. About the same time a supposedly top secret report was leaked to the press that presented an ominous view of America's military capabilities. The Gaither Report, named for its author, H. Rowan Gaither Jr. of the Ford Foundation, was prepared by a commission established by Eisenhower's NSC to evaluate the status of the U.S. military; however, members of the commission were not given access to Talent materials, nor were they even apprised of their existence. Based on information provided by the military, the report projected that by 1959 and for a period of at least two years the Soviets might have the capacity to launch an ICBM attack, against which SAC would be defenseless because it had neither a ballistic missile early warning system nor an antimissile defense (Prados 1982, 71). The next two years were seen as especially critical; commission members recommended increasing defense spending by 25 percent (Andrews 1995, 241).

Eisenhower dismissed the Gaither Report as misguided and vowed never again to have outsiders conduct such an assessment. He was also determined not to increase defense spending dramatically. The economy was in the midst of a recession at that moment, and he was going to do nothing to exacerbate it. However, while he believed America's nuclear capability was superior to that of the Soviet Union, he approved a supplemental appropriation of $1.37 billion, "the major part of which was intended for SAC alert and dispersal, ballistic missile warning radars, and an acceleration of the ICBM program" (Prados 1982, 75). Three months later he would approve an additional supplemental request for $1.45 billion.

Among the measures introduced by Eisenhower to counter the public clamor for action was the decision to station American IRBM and MRBM missiles in Europe, from which they could reach targets in the Soviet Union. England was persuaded to take intermediate-range Thor missiles, and Italy and Turkey agreed to medium-range Jupiter missiles. Khrushchev "was deeply offended by the prospect of nuclear-tipped missiles" so close to his borders (Lebow and Stein 1994, 42). Eisenhower was not comfortable with the policy, either. The missiles, as it turned out, were extremely vulnerable and of use only as a first-strike weapon. Although Eisenhower found it politically impossible to annul his decision, when he left the White House in early 1961 the missiles had yet to be deployed.

In early 1958 Eisenhower received a report stating that the follow-on satellite reconnaissance system was falling behind schedule, and there was little prospect it would be ready before mid-1959. This placed enormous pressure on Eisenhower to authorize additional overflights of Soviet territory. *Sputnik 2* had weighed over eleven hundred pounds, which was warhead size (Burrows 1986, 95). The Soviet Union had demonstrated to the world that it had the technological capability to build ICBMs; the only question now was whether they had deployed any. Eisenhower was growing increasingly worried about the overflights. He wondered whether the intelligence was worth "the exacerbation of international tensions" (Beschloss 1986, 161).

The concerns about the growing vulnerability of the U-2 were legitimate. American agents in Moscow were reporting that the Soviets had compiled an impressive data base on the aircraft's capabilities and were developing an array of weapons to counter it. Already they were augmenting their air defense regiments with the new SU-9 high-altitude interceptor aircraft. Even more ominous was their deployment of the new

SA-2 Guideline missile, a far more dangerous system than its immediate predecessor, the SA-1. From the beginning, when U-2 pilots had first spotted the ubiquitous SA-1 complexes with their telltale Star-of-David pattern, they had come to recognize that these missiles had been designed for attacking bombers and did not operate effectively above fifty-five thousand feet. The SA-2, however, was another matter. First seen on parade in Moscow in November 1957, these new missile systems were given wide berth by the U-2 pilots since they were considered effective up to an altitude of nearly seventy thousand feet. Clearly it was only a matter of time before a U-2 was downed.

In mid-1958 the conclusions of NIE 11-10-57 were leaked to the press. The NIE predicted the Soviets would have an operational capability of about ten ICBMs by mid-1958 to mid-1959. After that, stated the report, they could probably build ICBMs, along with the necessary launch facilities, at a rate of about one hundred per year, attaining an operational capability of five hundred ICBMs within two to three years of the first missiles becoming operational (Steury 1996, 63–64). Again suspecting the air force of using the media to pressure Congress into authorizing additional funds for more B-52 bombers and ICBMs, Eisenhower found his suspicions only strengthened when an air force general was quoted as saying that "the reason the Soviets did not appear to be building so many bombers was precisely because they had chosen to accelerate their missile program" (Prados 1982, 81). Meanwhile, Khrushchev himself was doing nothing to dispel the notion of a missile gap. In December 1958 Khrushchev claimed that "the Soviet Union had an ICBM capability of carrying a 5-megaton nuclear warhead 8,000 miles" (McDonald 1995, 700), and he later boasted he had all the rockets he needed and that Soviet factories were cranking out missiles "like sausages" (Beschloss 1986, 152). Eisenhower felt trapped; while he doubted such a gap existed, he needed more empirical data to be certain.

The search for deployed ICBMs was a far more difficult process than monitoring known facilities. In the first place, the Soviet Union covered an area of over eight million square miles and any single U-2 overflight provided cloud-free photography of an area less than 1 percent of that. Therefore, some assumptions had to be made about where the Soviets were most likely to deploy these missiles. Because of their limited range (seven hundred to eleven hundred nautical miles), MRBMs were largely deployed along the western border areas, within range of NATO targets in Europe; a small number were located in the southern USSR and the Soviet Far East. Longer-range IRBMs (two thousand nautical miles) tended to be concentrated in the south where they could cover the Middle East and North Africa, while others were deployed in the Far East to threaten Taiwan, the Philippines, and China. ICBMs, however, with their vastly greater range (sixty-five hundred nautical miles), could be dispersed widely throughout the Soviet Union.

One assumption was to exclude from the search the vast area of northeastern Siberia, representing nearly half the country, because of rugged terrain, continuous permafrost, and an almost total absence of the infrastructure required to support an ICBM launch complex. A second assumption was that in the absence of a well-developed highway network, ICBM launch complexes would be rail-served. Thus U-2 flight paths were planned whenever possible to parallel major rail lines. If, in fact, a U-2 flew directly over a rail line, an area stretching twenty-five miles on either side of the track would be photographed. As of mid-1958 the only known Soviet ICBM launch sites were those at the Tyuratam Test Center and what appeared to be a launch site in the early stages of construction at Plesetsk (just south of the White Sea). No operational ICBMs would be located, however, and there had been only six ICBM test flights, "a trivial number if they were to deploy a hundred by 1959 or 1960" (Beschloss 1986, 152). In spite of this evidence, the 1958 NIE continued to project one hundred ICBMs by 1960, three hundred by 1961, and as many as five hundred by 1962 (Prados 1982, 83).

As the U-2 program entered its third year Eisenhower wanted to bring it to a halt. The program's designers had predicted it would last possibly two years, three years at a maximum. With the deployment of SA-2s, which the CIA estimated could strike a target as high as seventy thousand feet (Beschloss 1986, 238), the risk of a U-2 being downed was increasing sharply with each mission. The fact that the U-2 had been experiencing mechanical failures only exacerbated the problem. There had been several crashes between 1956 and 1958, and SAC actually grounded all its U-2s in July 1958 "after two fatal crashes had occurred in a twenty-four hour period" (Prados 1982, 85). Adding to Eisenhower's concerns were

trust
but
verify

the reconnaissance activities of the air force. For over a decade their "ferret flights" had been probing the Soviet Union along its periphery. In June 1958 the Soviets protested a violation of their airspace in the Far East by a ferret aircraft. In July an RB-47 was nearly downed by Soviet aircraft over the Caspian Sea. Still, Eisenhower could never quite order Dulles to shut down the program (Beschloss 1986, 160).

It was about this time that President Eisenhower received a briefing on the reconnaissance aircraft planned as a successor to the U-2. Officially designated the A-12 (Project Oxcart), but better known as the SR-71, this aircraft grew out of discussions between Richard Bissell and Kelly Johnson that had begun as early as 1956. What was needed was an aircraft that could fly higher and faster than the U-2 since it would be expected to overfly areas like the Soviet Union that were studded with SAM sites. The aircraft described to Eisenhower would be capable of operating at altitudes of over eighty thousand feet and would travel at a maximum speed of Mach 3, or about thirty miles per minute. The president was clearly impressed by what he heard, but his highest priority remained a satellite reconnaissance system. As a result it would be another year before he would make the decision to proceed with production of the SR-71.

In the meantime the issue of the "missile gap" would not go away, and because Talent materials were held at such a high level of security, Eisenhower could not reveal what he knew about Soviet missile deployments. Furthermore, a satellite reconnaissance system was still a year or so away. Though no one was willing to admit it, the U.S. nuclear deterrent program was at the height of its effectiveness. At that moment there were no Soviet long-range bombers or ICBMs that could threaten the United States. Yet Bissell continued to urge Eisenhower to authorize additional flights. To get more overflights Bissell even went so far as to have Britain enter the U-2 program with the United States; Prime Minister Macmillan authorized his first U-2 flight using RAF pilots on 24 August 1958 (Andrew 1995, 243).

The program's last year and a half before the fateful 1 May overflight was a busy one. More frequent coverage allowed photointerpreters to detect new SA-2 sites, monitor the expansion of missile test facilities, and derive estimates for the production of tanks, trucks, ships, and aircraft. The myth of the bomber gap had been refuted, but the so-called missile gap was more difficult to dispel. For one thing, Eisenhower remained unwilling to make public the U-2 program by providing the necessary evidence to silence his critics: "Those outside the small U-2 circle could scarcely have imagined without seeing the unprecedented imagery skillfully interpreted by Lundahl's analysts, the astonishing precision and detail of the intelligence it provided" (Andrew 1995, 243). In addition, as the intelligence community downgraded the Soviet missile threat, the Democrats accused the Eisenhower administration of juggling the data (McDougall 1985, 219).

There was one final factor that bothered even Lundahl's analysts. While they were perfectly certain they had missed nothing on the photos, there was the nagging issue about their assumptions. Were they looking in the right places? To an imagery analyst what is seen is less worrisome than what is not seen, and the U-2 photos, after all, covered only a small portion of Soviet territory. In a recently declassified document summarizing Talent coverage of the Soviet Union for the period January 1959 to May 1960 it was stated in reference to the search for deployed ICBMs that "more than 85% of suitable area, 95% of priority areas, and 85% of rail route mileage in priority areas have not been observed or covered by useable TALENT during the period" (Ruffner 1995, 107). The issue of photo coverage would not be adequately resolved until the advent of reconnaissance satellites; Eisenhower was assured the United States would have such a system by mid-1960. In the meantime Eisenhower would authorize as few flights as possible, a determination strengthened even more by his decision to attend a four-power conference scheduled for June 1960 in Paris.

In late 1959 a new NIE (11-8-59) appeared that reported no operational ICBMs had yet been identified on U-2 photographs, although it added that series production of ICBMs was almost certainly under way. The report went on to project that the Soviets would have a small number of missiles, perhaps thirty-five, on launcher by mid-1960; after that the numbers of ICBMs on launcher would increase rapidly to an estimated 140–200 by mid-1961 and 350–450 by mid-1963. It would be very important, therefore, to conduct several missions prior to the Paris Summit so that Eisenhower would have in his possession the most timely information on Soviet missile deployments when he met Khrushchev. Eisenhower agreed to authorize another overflight. It took place on 9 April and would be the last successful U-2 mission over the Soviet Union.

It was one of the many unfortunate aspects of the high degree of secrecy surrounding Moscow's actions that the United States never understood how angered and frustrated Soviet leaders were made by the U-2 overflights. It was generally assumed by American policymakers that since the Soviets had made few diplomatic protests they must have resigned themselves to these intrusions at least until they had the capability to down the aircraft. Indeed, when Khrushchev visited the United States in 1959 for private talks with Eisenhower, the issue of U-2 flights was never raised (Beschloss 1986, 215)! In any case, were the Soviets able to overfly U.S. territory with relative impunity, they certainly would be doing so. But, in fact, Khrushchev was outraged by the overflights and especially by the resumption of flights in April. Only a few months before he had publicly asked that the West do nothing prior to the Paris Summit to "worsen the atmosphere," and now this. Khrushchev took it as a personal insult, but it probably also undermined his authority with members of the Politburo (Beschloss 1986, 239).

The 9 April mission was directed at target-rich central Asia. The flight path took the U-2 over the Semipalatinsk nuclear test site, the Sary Shagan SAM test area, and, finally, over the Tyuratam strategic missile test center. The overflight had lasted six hours. When told of this, Khrushchev became enraged. How was it, he demanded to know, that his air defense forces found it impossible to bring down an unarmed, slow-moving aircraft like the U-2? It must not happen again, ever again!

From the United States' point of view the flight had gone perfectly. Now the CIA requested one more, this one to cover the Plesetsk ICBM complex, where the first operational ICBMs were being deployed. Agency officials wanted to photograph the missile construction activities there before the Soviets began to camouflage them, but Eisenhower was hesitant. He was eager to build a more stable relationship with Moscow, and he knew the overflights were only undermining his efforts. Yet for all his concerns, Eisenhower once again gave in to his advisers.

Ironically, the overflight took place on 1 May, May Day, the occasion when Moscow demonstrated to the world its military prowess. The mission, code-named Operation Grand Slam and planned as the longest ever attempted (flying time would be nine hours), would be flown by Francis

Gary Powers. It would originate in Peshawar, Pakistan, transverse nearly four thousand miles of Soviet territory, and end in Bodo, Norway. The flight path of the U-2 would take it over the Tyuratam missile test center, the military-industrial complex around Sverdlovsk, the suspected ICBM deployment complex at Plesetsk, and the shipyards and naval bases along the northern coast of the Kola Peninsula. "All," note Rich and Janos (1994), "were heavily defended" (158).

Though the details of what exactly happened to Powers on that day have remained clouded in controversy, the truth has begun to emerge as Soviet participants have stepped forward to give their side of the story. Apparently, the missile battalion whose zone Powers initially entered was not on alert, though the aircraft had been detected on radar. A fighter aircraft in the area was ordered to ram the U-2, but the pilot could not find it. Finally, as Power's aircraft entered the engagement zone of a SAM battalion near Sverdlovsk (now Yekaterinberg), the commander ordered a barrage of SAMs to be fired. Although none initially struck the aircraft, one exploded sufficiently close that fragments destroyed much of the tail section. Unable to control the aircraft, Powers ejected and landed relatively unharmed. The U-2 was now struck by a SAM as it descended, scattering sections of the aircraft over a fairly wide area. In spite of this, "investigators found large, wide rolls of exposed film, much of which was developed later almost without losses, enabling the Soviets to see what targets had been photographed and with what quality" (Orlov 1998–99, 11). In his memoirs, Richard Bissell could only lament, "The mission was well within the range capability of the U-2, and all the usual safety factors had been considered. Our luck just ran out" (Bissell 1996, 127).

Luck may certainly have played its role, but it also appears mission planners had become supremely overconfident. Bissell admits they continued to depend upon an intelligence estimate that described the SA-2's optimum range to be sixty thousand feet. Above that height, the report concluded, the Soviets could not control the missile. In the same vein, he concedes that they never gave sufficient consideration to the possibility that a near miss might make the aircraft inoperable but at the same time allow the pilot to survive and successfully bail out (Bissell 1996, 122).

Although there was considerable disquiet in Washington over the loss of the U-2, it was decided that NASA should release a statement that had been prearranged; it was assumed both pilot and aircraft had been destroyed. The NASA statement simply noted that an unarmed NASA U-2 aircraft operating over Turkey on a joint NASA–U.S. Air Force mission had gone down near Lake Van and a search was under way for the missing aircraft. The pilot was a Lockheed employee under contract to NASA.

To this point Khrushchev had said nothing and, in fact, had apparently even "considered sweeping the matter under the rug" and moving ahead with the summit (Beschloss 1986, 40). He ultimately concluded that his enemies within the party would accuse him of being intimidated by Eisenhower, and so, on the evening of 4 May, he passed along word to diplomats in Moscow that he would be making an important announcement at the opening session of the Supreme Soviet on 5 May. For the first two hours of that session Khrushchev provided little more than the usual monotonous litany of Soviet successes. Then suddenly his tone changed as he began his report of the downing of a U.S. reconnaissance aircraft deep within Soviet territory on May Day (Andrew 1995, 245). He went on to suggest that perhaps this was an attempt to "torpedo" the Paris Summit. Significantly, there was no mention of the aircraft or pilot. The next day, however, a photograph purporting to be the wreckage of the U-2 appeared in the Soviet newspaper *Trud;* the twisted metal was almost certainly meant to imply the pilot had been killed (Beschloss 1986, 253). Designers of the U-2, upon examining the photo, declared it a fake; the aircraft in the photo was not a U-2. At the White House, advisers to President Eisenhower insisted that someone should refute Khrushchev's charges. Reluctantly, he agreed to have a NASA spokesman provide additional information. It was already too late; the U.S. government was walking directly into Khrushchev's trap, which he sprung at another session of the Supreme Soviet on 7 May. We have the pilot of the U-2, Khrushchev announced, and he is in good health. Interestingly, he suggested the CIA and Pentagon may have ordered the overflight without Eisenhower's authorization. He was, in fact, giving Eisenhower an out; all Eisenhower now had to do was to blame some CIA or Pentagon official, apologize for the overflights, and they could all get on with the Paris Summit.

To a degree this was the option chosen: "Eisenhower opted for implausible denial" (Andrew 1995, 246). On the evening of 7 May the State Department issued a statement suggesting that a U-2, without authorization from Washington, may have overflown Soviet territory in an attempt to acquire critical military intelligence. This time the reaction came from the American news organizations, which felt they had been participants in a gigantic lie. Eisenhower was alternately described as "uncertain, absentminded, and incompetent"; his credibility was clearly on trial. Something had to be said to calm his legion of critics. Even his vice president, Richard Nixon, who would be the Republican candidate for president in the upcoming fall election, found it necessary to distance himself from Eisenhower's actions.

On 9 May Art Lundahl provided a classified briefing on Capitol Hill to a small group of senators on the achievements of the U-2 missions over the Soviet Union. When he completed his presentation, the senators gave him "a standing ovation" (Andrew 1995, 247). At about the same time, across town, Secretary of State Christian Herter was making another statement, the fourth in five days. This one claimed that indeed the United States had been conducting unarmed overflights of the Soviet Union as a means of guarding against a surprise attack, and while, yes, the president knew about the U-2 program, he was not required to authorize individual missions.

When Khrushchev received word of Herter's comments, he was "apoplectic" (Beschloss 1986, 259). He had done his best not to accuse Eisenhower directly and now it appeared Eisenhower was actually "boasting" about the overflights. Two days later, when an exhibition featuring the U-2 opened at Gorky Park, Khrushchev continued his tirade against the United States. If its war that the United States wants, he exclaimed, "we will fire rockets and hit their territory a few minutes later" (Beschloss 1986, 262). Eisenhower was caught squarely in the middle, and his policies were being criticized as harshly in the American newspapers as in the Soviet. Furthermore, the Paris Summit was only a few days away.

On the same day Khrushchev appeared at the Gorky Park exhibition, President Eisenhower held a press conference at which he made his first public comments about the U-2 incident. No one, he stated, wants another Pearl Harbor, and we must have some means of gathering military intelligence on the Soviet Union. He added, the United States and its allies "have engaged in nothing that can be considered honestly provocative" (Beschloss 1986, 265). Eisenhower was not going to make it easy for

Khrushchev, and he certainly intended to say nothing that could be inter-preted as an apology.

Both Khrushchev and Eisenhower arrived in Paris for the 15 May summit, but the U-2 incident posed an insurmountable obstacle. Khrushchev was under great pressure at home for his domestic policies, his defense cuts especially, and for his handling of relations with China. He needed a major propaganda victory of some kind to restore his authority in the Politburo. Khrushchev had little choice but to appear tough. As for Eisenhower, his position was strangely similar. He, too, was receiving intense criticism at home, and he was determined to appear neither apologetic nor to be strengthening Khrushchev's political situation. Still, Eisenhower was prepared to make some concessions; he wanted a test ban treaty with the Soviet Union, and even if that proved impossible to achieve at the Paris Summit, he hoped to have one before his term ended. Eisenhower was optimistic about the Soviets agreeing to such a treaty because he knew how eager they were to keep Japan and Germany from getting nuclear weapons. But a test-ban treaty was never discussed, nor was any other issue. The summit meeting collapsed, along with a proposed visit Eisenhower was scheduled to make to the Soviet Union.

It appears that while the Politburo gave its consent to Khrushchev's attending the Paris Summit, "a price was imposed" (Beschloss 1986, 367). The price was a set of conditions to which Eisenhower would have to agree in order for the summit to take place. First, he would have to apologize for the overflights; second, he would have to guarantee that no further overflights of Soviet territory would occur; and third, Eisenhower would have to punish those responsible for authorizing the overflights. There was simply no way in good conscience Eisenhower could agree to these demands since it was he who had authorized each and every flight.

For Khrushchev the collapse of the summit was costly since he was forced to walk away empty-handed. Once again he felt he had been personally humiliated. During Khrushchev's remaining four years the cold war would perceptibly intensify. In 1961 a crisis would occur over the construction of the Berlin Wall; the following year would witness the Cuban missile crisis. There are those who believe to this day that the impossible demands imposed on Khrushchev's participation were directed more at canceling Eisenhower's planned visit to the Soviet Union than at causing the collapse of the summit. Hard-liners among the Soviet leadership were genuinely concerned about the impact Eisenhower's visit would have upon the Soviet public. Eisenhower remained a wartime hero to most Russians, and in all probability they would have received him with unabashed enthusiasm. Were Soviet leaders already planning to adopt a tougher line with the West, such a welcome for Eisenhower would undermine their efforts.

But there was an even better reason for canceling Eisenhower's visit had Soviet leaders only known; technicians had modified *Air Force One* to handle aerial cameras. *Air Force One* was to be a spy plane! Eisenhower had received permission from Khrushchev to use his personal aircraft to fly within the Soviet Union, and since the aircraft would be flying at perhaps half the altitude of a U-2, the photos of the route into Moscow were expected to be superb. This was all being done with Eisenhower's full knowledge, although it was understood that he did not want the flight path established with intelligence targets in mind (Beschloss 1986, 229).

Within several days of the failed summit President Eisenhower went on television to explain to the American people what had happened in Paris. In making his remarks Eisenhower had planned to use enlargements of U-2 photos prepared for him by the CIA. The photos were to have displayed Soviet airfields, missile launch sites, and naval bases, but once again Eisenhower vetoed their use at the last moment. Instead, Eisenhower displayed only a single U-2 photo, of the North Island Naval Air Station in San Diego. In his prepared comments Eisenhower reported that he had gone to Paris in an attempt to reduce tensions with the Soviet Union, but the U-2 incident had occurred. He went on to describe the importance of the U-2 flights and to stress that Khrushchev had known about them from the outset (Brugioni 1991, 51). While the president's address laid to rest some of the issues raised by the U-2 incident, his remarks lost much of their force because of his continued reluctance to publicly display U-2 photographs. By failing to show viewers similar U-2 photographs of Russian airfields, Eisenhower missed a golden opportunity to demonstrate how successfully the Soviet nuclear strike force had been monitored (Andrew 1995, 249).

Eisenhower next passed the word to officials in the intelligence community that there would be no more U-2 overflights of Soviet territory;

he also closed down the secret overseas bases at the request of the Japanese and Turkish governments. The increasing numbers of SA-2 missiles combined with the imminent deployment of a satellite reconnaissance system had rendered the Soviet portion of the U-2 program obsolete. U-2's would continue to fly along the periphery of Soviet territory, but they never deliberately overflew Soviet territory again. In 1962, when a U-2 inadvertently overflew Sakhalin Island, the Soviets chose not to down the aircraft but to lodge a diplomatic protest instead. President Kennedy apologized for the intrusion and reasserted the claim that U.S. aircraft were under orders not to penetrate into Soviet airspace. Other aircraft were not always so lucky. Several military aircraft would be downed in ensuing years over allegedly international waters. The most publicized incident, of course, occurred in 1983, when the Soviets downed a Korean commercial jetliner (KAL 007) that had strayed into Soviet airspace over the Sea of Okhotsk.

The U-2 program had lasted less than four years and had totaled only twenty-four overflights of Soviet territory, yet its impact exceeded the most exaggerated expectations of program designers. Perhaps its greatest contribution lay in providing President Eisenhower with sufficient information to resist congressional pressures to increase defense spending. In spite of documents like NSC-68 and the Gaither Report and political issues like the bomber gap, *Sputnik*, and the missile gap, Eisenhower's budget for FY1960 projected a surplus of $1 billion; during his seven years in office his budgets increased only 20 percent, while gross national product was increasing nearly 25 percent in constant dollars (MacDougall 1985, 137). As for his defense budgets, they averaged about $40 billion annually during his two terms, a figure "about some US$10 billion under what Truman had proposed, and what the Democrats were advocating be spent" (Ambrose 1981, 275).

The issue, however, was not only the amount of money spent on defense but how well the money was spent. Information provided by the U-2 overflights enabled Eisenhower to make informed decisions on what weapons were most needed. The U-2 photos revealed no crash program to produce long-range bombers, ICBMs, submarines, or tanks. The Soviet military buildup was steady but modest; the United States was more than keeping pace even with Eisenhower's New Look defense budgets. The one time Eisenhower gave into pressure to authorize additional spending, during the height of the "bomber gap," he was deeply angered and never forgave the air force for making him do it. Nevertheless, without the information provided by the U-2s on Soviet hardware, there would have been many more such examples of unnecessary defense spending.

The U-2 overflights played as well a significant role in reducing the fear of a surprise attack. Although the flights did not occur with sufficient frequency to act as an early warning system, they revealed nevertheless that the Soviets lacked the long-range heavy bombers and ICBMs to make such a threat credible. During the entire period the U-2 program was operational, the United States enjoyed an overwhelming numerical superiority in both strategic bombers and ICBMs. Similarly, by informing the public of impending nuclear tests and space launches, Americans became reassured, at least after *Sputnik*, that the White House was formulating policy on the basis of solid intelligence.

On a more practical level, the U-2 program vastly improved the targeting data available to SAC's mission planners. Prior to the overflights America's knowledge of Soviet military and defense-related facilities was based upon some of the most flimsy and unreliable data, and even this knowledge was largely restricted to the western regions of the Soviet Union. For the vast expanse of Soviet territory stretching eastward from the Volga River, including especially the heavy industrial centers of the Urals, there was virtually no information available. Each U-2 mission significantly expanded the intelligence community's Soviet data base; according to Richard Helms the U-2 program had produced "fully ninety percent of the hard data on Soviet military developments that was available to the intelligence community" (Prados 1982, 102). In time this data base became sufficiently complete that analysts were able to prepare reports not only on scientific and military matters but on broader economic issues as well (e.g., investment priorities, new plant construction).

Finally, the U-2 played a major role in helping to unveil the shroud of secrecy that had enveloped the Soviet Union during the Stalin years. Khrushchev was already, in fact, attempting to eliminate some of the worst excesses of the Stalinist system, and the inception of the U-2 program coincided with Khrushchev's "thaw," a period of relaxation that anticipated Gorbachev's *perestroika* by twenty years. The overflights would gradually bring to the Soviet leadership the realization that it was no longer possible to conceal from the West the deployment of ICBM systems or the preparations for nuclear tests (even with camouflage). No longer was it possible to ensure national security by engaging in such ploys as Khrushchev's "strategic deception." The U-2 had narrowed the options available to Soviet leaders; they now had to either engage the economically more powerful United States in an arms race of infinite duration or pursue a dialogue with the West with the intent of achieving some kind of arms control.

In retrospect the U-2 program was anything but kind to Khrushchev. It began shortly after he had consolidated his control over the party, and for most of his years in office it would provide a constant reminder of the Soviet Union's technological backwardness compared to the West. Khrushchev tended to take the overflights personally and felt the United States was constantly trying to humiliate him, and when finally he downed a U-2 deep within Soviet territory and trapped the United States into admitting that it had been conducting overflights of the Soviet Union, the incident backfired on him. Instead of scoring a propaganda victory by extracting an apology from President Eisenhower, Khrushchev was forced to "torpedo" the Paris Summit and walk away empty-handed. Years later Khrushchev would admit that after the U-2 incident he would never again exercise full control over the Politburo (Beschloss 1986, 325). Ironically, it would be another incident involving the U-2, the Cuban missile crisis, that would virtually assure his downfall.

In spite of his deep disappointment over the U-2 crisis and the failed summit, President Eisenhower was very active during his final months in office, and this was especially true for matters pertaining to the country's reconnaissance systems. In June Eisenhower ordered Bissell to proceed with Project Oxcart, the development of the SR-71, though on a low-priority basis. The satellite reconnaissance program was on schedule and there appeared to be no need for an aircraft like the SR-71 during peacetime; it certainly wouldn't be overflying the Soviet Union. The SR-71 became operational in 1966, but by this time reconnaissance satellites were providing copious amounts of information without the risk of losing a pilot. By the early 1970s fewer than a dozen of the aircraft were on duty, the rest having been mothballed. Finally, in 1992, even these aircraft were decommissioned. Though recently several SR-71s have been returned to service by the air force, this impressive aircraft has never really been called upon to fill the role for which it was originally designed.

President Eisenhower remained in office long enough to also usher in the satellite reconnaissance era. The Corona program, approved sometime in late 1957, had its first completely successful test in August 1960, after thirteen failures dating back to January 1959. That the program was allowed to continue in spite of the string of failures was due to both Eisenhower's patience and the urgent need for broad area intelligence on the Soviet Union. The August test included the midair "catch" of a film capsule whose contents proved to be of immediate intelligence value. The United States now possessed the capability of photographing the vast areas of the Soviet Union never covered by U-2 overflights. So, in fact, Eisenhower had revolutionized intelligence gathering during his eight years in office with his development of three significant photoreconnaissance systems—the U-2, the SR-71, and the photographic earth-orbiting satellite! It is doubtful such progress could have been made "under Truman or any other president who lacked Eisenhower's enormous enthusiasm for it" (Andrew 1995, 256).

Yet for all Eisenhower's success in developing the means to acquire timely information on the Soviet Union's strategic capabilities, his final months in office were plagued by Democratic charges that he was allowing America's military superiority to be eroded. A change by the intelligence community in the way it derived its estimates had the effect of downgrading the numbers of Soviet ICBMs. While the change in methodology was a rational one, it unfortunately led to the charge that Eisenhower was "juggling the intelligence books" to reduce the missile gap and cover up his misguided defense policies. John Kennedy, the Democratic nominee for president, raised this issue so often that "it became almost the central theme of his campaign" (Ambrose 1981, 278). While labeling the charge nonsense, Eisenhower nevertheless refused to provide the photographic evidence that would have refuted once and for all the missile gap claim. Instead, Eisenhower chose to protect the integrity of his photoreconnaissance assets but in so doing helped pave the way for Kennedy's victory over his own vice president, Richard Nixon.

Eisenhower was deeply hurt by the Democratic victory, interpreting it more as a repudiation of his policies than as a failure of Nixon's campaign.

trust
but
verify

For Nixon, the loss of the presidency was traumatic, and he blamed the CIA in large part for his defeat. Not only did he become convinced that the CIA had deliberately withheld information on the missile gap from him, but he believed that Allen Dulles had secretly provided information on the sensitive issue to Senator Stuart Symington, "whom Kennedy had made head of a special committee on the defense establishment during the election campaign" (Andrew 1995, 350). His mistrust and resentment of the CIA were so great that nine years later as president he continued to suspect the agency of attempting to undermine his policies.

# 3

## The Caribbean Crisis

With the decision by President Eisenhower to ban further overflights of the Soviet Union, it appeared that the U-2 was destined to play a much-reduced role in U.S.-Soviet affairs; henceforth, reconnaissance satellites, which possessed none of the liabilities of aircraft, would be the primary means of acquiring photographic intelligence on Soviet military activities. But, in fact, the U-2 came to play a central role in one of the cold war's most intense dramas—the Cuban missile crisis, or simply "the Caribbean crisis," as the Soviets would refer to it. Due in no small measure to the intelligence gleaned from aerial photography, U-2 as well as low-level reconnaissance aircraft, the crisis was resolved not only peacefully but also in nearly total favor of the United States.

Relations between the Soviet Union and the new Kennedy administration began on an encouraging note. Nikita Khrushchev, under intense pressure at home and eager to improve relations with the new Democratic administration, released two American airmen who had been downed over the Soviet Union the previous summer. President Kennedy was extremely pleased by the gesture, and while he would not call it "a *quid pro quo*, he made clear that U-2 and other aircraft flights over the Soviet Union would not be resumed" (Sorenson 1965, 54). Unfortunately, the cordial atmosphere generated by these early initiatives could not be sustained and relations between the two countries began to deteriorate. By the fall of 1962, with the missile crisis, the United States and the Soviet Union would become engaged in "the most acute confrontation of the Cold War" (Lebow and Stein 1994, 5).

The Kennedy administration's involvement with Cuba began shortly after the November election in 1960, when the president-elect was briefed by Allen Dulles and Richard Bissell on Operation Zapata, a CIA-sponsored operation to overthrow the government of Fidel Castro. Kennedy was told that plans for the operation were largely complete and the invasion force was in Guatemala, where it was being trained by the CIA. At this point Kennedy had not yet been inaugurated, so the decision to proceed with the operation was still Eisenhower's. Later, upon becoming president, he would ultimately give his approval to the operation, though he would admit he understood little of the world of covert operations.

Operation Zapata began on 15 April 1961, when a small force of B-26s, flown by Cuban exiles, struck Cuban airfields with the intent to destroy Castro's air force; the mission failed and Castro's air force was free to attack the small force of Cuban exiles coming ashore at the Bay of Pigs. Poorly planned and executed, the operation was a total disaster. Of the 1,400 men in the invading force, 114 were killed and 1,189 captured (Andrew 1995, 265). Much has been made in the operation's aftermath of Kennedy's refusal to call in adequate air support from U.S. carriers offshore, but had he done so it would have had little impact on the operation's outcome. Even the operation's planners had concluded there was little chance of a popular uprising against Castro without external support, though in their view the landing of a strike force on the island would prove sufficient to trigger one. Unfortunately, "the shock was too ephemeral to damage the Castro regime, let alone threaten its survival" (Warner 1998–99, 26).

Castro was now more firmly entrenched in power than ever. Kennedy had little choice but to accept full responsibility for the disaster, though he demanded the resignations of Dulles and Bissell. In private he would angrily lament, "How could I have been so stupid to let them go ahead?" (Sorensen 1965, 309). Fortunately, he had little time to dwell on the disaster, as he had to prepare for a June summit meeting in Vienna with Khrushchev. Kennedy was hoping to use the meeting to achieve a good working relationship with Khrushchev as a first step toward the negotiation of a nuclear test-ban treaty.

As it turned out, the two-day summit was a sobering experience for Kennedy. Khrushchev proved to be in an especially belligerent mood. Perhaps feeling he could intimidate the young president in the aftermath of the Bay of Pigs fiasco, he demanded an end to the three-power status of West Berlin and a German peace treaty by the end of the year. For his part Kennedy warned Khrushchev not to miscalculate America's intentions, though he left Vienna unsure whether Khrushchev had understood his message. Just to be certain, Kennedy ordered that "National Reserve troops be placed on active duty and announced a dramatic increase of nearly 25 percent in American military strength" (LaFeber 1991, 218). He also decided to move ahead with the deployment of Thor and Jupiter missiles in Europe, hoping "that another demonstration of American resolve would make Khrushchev more cautious in his approach to Berlin" (Lebow and Stein 1994, 45).

But Khrushchev was not about to let Kennedy upstage him. On 13 August, much to the surprise and chagrin of the Kennedy administration, the East Germans suddenly erected a barbed-wire enclosure, "effectively penning East Berliners in their sector of the city" (May and Zelikow 1997, 31). With Soviet help this enclosure was soon reinforced with a massive concrete wall. Kennedy concluded that, short of outright military conflict, there was little he could do to remove the wall, though he may also have interpreted it as an indication that the Soviets were not going to make a move on the Western Sector of the city.

The construction of the Berlin Wall was not to be Khrushchev's only surprise. On 30 August he announced the Soviet Union was about to start a series of nuclear tests that would include the detonation of a 50-megaton device; he also boasted that the Soviets had developed a 100-megaton bomb. Kennedy was livid because Khrushchev had assured him personally in Vienna, just two months earlier, that the Soviets would not be the first to break the moratorium on testing that had been in force since 1958. Nevertheless, between 1 September and 4 November the Soviet Union would conduct thirty nuclear tests, most of them atmospheric (Lebow and Stein 1994, 36). As Khrushchev had claimed, a 50-megaton bomb was detonated on the morning of 31 October over the Soviets' Novaya Zemlya test site in the Arctic. The flash could be seen six hundred miles away. As for the power of the blast, it exceeded by several times the total power of all the explosives used during World War II. The bomb was never meant as a military weapon but rather as "a one-time demonstration of force, part of the superpower game of mutual intimidation" (Adamsky and Smirnov 1994, 19). As Khrushchev explained to a group of visiting British Labour Party officials at the time, it was his hope "to shock the West into concessions on Berlin and disarmament" (Sorensen 1965, 619).

In fact, it had quite the opposite effect. Kennedy now concluded it was time "to disabuse Khrushchev of his illusions regarding the military balance" (Lebow and Stein 1994, 37). First, he authorized his deputy secretary of defense Roswell Gilpatric to publicly describe the superiority the United States had in strategic nuclear capabilities over the Soviet Union. Then, at a November news conference, he followed this up by explaining how he had been misled about the missile gap during the recent presidential campaign. What he found upon entering the White House was, in fact, that the missile gap strongly favored the United States. And, finally, to make certain the Soviets did not miss his point, Kennedy is alleged to have shown Soviet foreign minister Andrei Gromyko satellite photographs of Soviet missile sites to demonstrate that the United States had solid evidence of just how few operational ICBMs the Soviets really had (Lebow and Stein 1994, 38).

The attention of the Kennedy administration meanwhile was beginning to shift to Southeast Asia, where many of its Republican critics were calling for the United States to make a stand against Communist expansion. Well aware of his political vulnerability as a result of both the Bay of Pigs and the Berlin Wall, Kennedy was determined to show his resolve in containing communism. Accordingly, he authorized an increase in the number of American "advisors" in Vietnam—from five hundred to ten thousand—and gave permission to use them in combat operations against the Vietcong.

But neither Berlin nor Vietnam would cause Kennedy to forget Cuba. In fact, within the Kennedy administration there was a near-fixation on Castro. There were those who believed if Castro succeeded with his "socialist revolution" in Cuba, there would be no way of halting communism from taking over the rest of Latin America. There were also more pragmatic reasons for concern. The Republicans had already made it clear they were about to make Cuba "the dominant issue of the 1962 mid-term elections." Kennedy saw Castro as his "heaviest political cross," and he committed himself to Castro's overthrow. The mechanism for doing so would be Operation Mongoose, a covert operation to undermine the Castro government through espionage, sabotage, and assassination. The overall management of this operation was in the hands of Robert Kennedy, the president's brother, who saw it as a "top priority" of the administration (Andrew 1995, 275). Consequently, there would have been a crisis over Cuba even without the issue of Soviet missiles, but Khrushchev's actions may have served Kennedy well by preventing another Bay of Pigs disaster.

While the Kennedy administration was developing the plans for Operation Mongoose, Khrushchev and his advisors were working out the details of Operation Anadyr—the installation of MRBM and IRBM missiles on Cuba. The idea for the operation appears to have been Khrushchev's own and emerged from the Kremlin's recognition that its missile program lagged far behind that of the United States and would require several years at a minimum to attain a strategic balance in forces. During this interval the credibility of the Soviet Union as a superpower would remain in question. However, if the Soviet Union were able to install MRBM and IRBM missiles in the United States' very back yard, a significant portion of the strategic imbalance would be corrected. While these missiles would clearly be inadequate to destroy much of America's strategic strike capability, they might be sufficient to deter Washington from launching a first strike (Burr 1994, 11). After all, Khrushchev would later claim, "we hadn't given the Cubans anything more than the Americans were giving their allies. We had the same rights and opportunities as the Americans" (Khrushchev 1971, 550).

Added to the Soviet Union's nuclear inferiority was Moscow's inability to resolve the annoying issue of Berlin. To this point all of Khrushchev's efforts to pressure the United States into withdrawing its forces from the city had failed. By deploying missiles to Cuba, Khrushchev hoped to finally achieve his objective. With missiles aimed directly at the unprotected midsection of the United States, Khrushchev was certain Kennedy, however reluctantly, would withdraw from Berlin rather than initiate a nuclear conflict. And, if Kennedy instead chose to attack the missile sites in Cuba, the Soviets would have every excuse to march into Berlin.

Finally, there was the issue of Cuba itself. Within the Third World, China's Mao Tse-tung was already beginning to challenge Khrushchev for the leadership in the world Communist movement. If, therefore, Castro were overthrown by the Americans while the Soviets did nothing to aid him, Mao Tse-tung's support would increase dramatically, especially in Latin America. Though Khrushchev never mentioned Mao publicly, he made it clear that if Cuba were to fall, "other Latin American countries would reject us, claiming that for all our might the Soviet Union hadn't been able to do anything for Cuba except to make empty protests to the United Nations" (Khrushchev 1971, 546). The provision of strategic missiles, along with conventional weaponry, should effectively forestall any U.S. actions against Castro and Cuba.

For Operation Anadyr to succeed, the Soviets would first have to install the missiles on Cuba without the knowledge of the United States. Then, once the missiles were made operational, Khrushchev would "dramatically reveal the presence of the Soviet missiles at the moment of his own choosing," demonstrating to the United States that the Soviet Union was serious about resolving the issue of Berlin and to the Chinese that "Russia had not gone soft on imperialism and that therefore they did not need a bomb of their own" (Malia 1994, 347, 346). All of this required secrecy, however, and while many of Khrushchev's advisers warned that the missiles would be detected before they became operational, the Soviet engineers sent to Cuba were overly optimistic in their assessment that the missile construction could be camouflaged (Gribkov and Smith 1994, 16). Khrushchev's major miscalculation would be his failure to formulate a fall-back plan if the missiles were detected before they had become operational; this error, as it turned out, would cost him dearly (Dobrynin 1995, 79).

Initially, Khrushchev requested only defensive weaponry, and on 12 April the Presidium "approved the delivery of about 180 SA-2 missiles to Cuba and a battery of Soviet coastal-defense cruise missiles" (May and Zelikow 1997, 673). Soon after, however, Khrushchev would broach the issue of deploying ballistic missiles to Cuba, first with his most trusted advisers and then, once he had their support, with Castro. Though reluctant, Castro agreed, and in June the Presidium authorized the deployment of forty land-based ballistic missile launchers along with approximately forty-five thousand troops, the latest MiG-21 aircraft, and IL-28 bombers. Cuba was about to become a strategic military base for the Soviet Union, and Washington had not the slightest inkling of it.

By early summer, the pace of Soviet shipments of military equipment to Cuba had increased so dramatically it could not pass unnoticed.

Numerous reports from agents, refugees, and defectors poured into Washington. Whenever CIA analysts concluded a report might be verified (or negated) by aerial photography, it was passed along to NPIC photointerpreters: "Between 31 May and 5 October NPIC examined 138 raw reports referred to it for comment. Of this total, only three cited missile activity that could not be linked directly to the SA-2 and cruise missile deployments. NPIC'S evidence negated those three" (excerpt from Memorandum for DCI, cited in McAuliffe 1992, 100). Yet even as the evidence mounted for this huge arms buildup, Khrushchev continued to assure Washington that his country "had no bases in Cuba and did not intend to establish any" (Burrows 1986, 117). Kennedy, taking no chances, ordered the USIB to make Cuba a high-priority target for reconnaissance purposes. And since coverage by reconnaissance satellites would be too infrequent (there was no satellite in orbit for the period 14 October to 5 November), it was decided that the U-2 would be the most effective method for acquiring systematic, cloud-free photography of the island.

The U-2s employed over Cuba carried a high-resolution panoramic camera, often referred to as the "B" camera. This system held two rolls of panchromatic (black-and-white) film, each nine inches wide and over five thousand feet long. As the U-2 followed along its predetermined path, the camera scanned the terrain below from horizon to horizon, acquiring several photos on each sweep. With a focal length of thirty-six inches, photos taken of the ground directly at nadir could have a spatial resolution as high as thirty inches from an altitude of sixty-five thousand feet. But while the aircraft and its camera system may have been highly sophisticated, the tools of analysis were decidedly not. Photos were interpreted over light boxes of varying sizes, and the film was drawn across them by means of hand cranks. As for the viewing optics, they included everything from pocket stereoscopes to stereomicroscopes (National Photographic Interpretation Center 1991, 12). Not only were these optics tiring to use for long periods, they were also cumbersome. Analysts could only view small portions of the photos at any one time and had to constantly move the optics from one feature to another.

During the month of August two U-2 overflights of Cuba were conducted—on the fifth and twenty-ninth. The photos from the 5 August mission revealed greater activity than expected; personnel and material were being delivered at an accelerated rate. For the first time construction activity was noted, and although the exact nature of the construction could not be determined from the photos, it appeared that some type of sophisticated electronics equipment was being installed, possibly surface-to-air missile related (McCone Memorandum of 21 August 1962, cited in McAuliffe 1992, 31). At a meeting on 10 August to review the progress of Operation Mongoose, CIA director John McCone mentioned the possibility of the Soviets installing MRBMs on Cuba. He reiterated this possibility to the president and pressed for more U-2 overflights, "for he interpreted the SAMs as harbingers of offensive surface-to-surface missiles" (May and Zelikow 1997, 45).

The U-2 photography of 29 August confirmed many of the earlier suspicions. Eight surface-to-air missile sites (SA-2s) were identified under construction; it was estimated that several of these sites could be operational within a matter of a week or two. Also identified on the photography were missile boats, tanks, self-propelled guns, and additional military personnel. But perhaps most important, a new type of missile site was identified near Banes; because it differed in configuration from the SA-2 sites, it was identified as a possible tactical SSM site under construction (Brugioni 1991, 126). In time the Banes installation would be confirmed as a cruise missile site. Although analysts concluded these weapons were clearly defensive in nature, White House officials took the opportunity to once again warn the Soviets against deploying offensive weapons in Cuba.

The next overflight, for the purpose of photographing the central and eastern portions of the island, took place on 5 September. Unfortunately, eastern Cuba was covered by clouds, but photography of central Cuba revealed the existence of three new SA-2 sites. As planning for additional September flights was under way, two incidents that would strongly influence the frequency and routes of the proposed overflights occurred. On 30 August a U-2 inadvertently violated Soviet airspace over Sakhalin Island; while the Soviets did not attack the aircraft, they did make a formal protest of the intrusion. President Kennedy issued an apology for the incident and assured the Kremlin it would not happen again. Then, on 8 September, a U-2 piloted by a Nationalist Chinese was downed over mainland China. Several of Kennedy's advisers, including both Secretary of State Dean Rusk and National Security Adviser McGeorge Bundy, began to question the wisdom of continuing U-2 flights over Cuba. All agreed that were a U-2 downed, the "Soviets would exploit the propaganda value to the utmost" (Brugioni 1991, 136).

The concerns raised by Rusk and Bundy were legitimate. With several SA-2 sites on the verge of becoming operational, the risk of a U-2 being downed was increasing with each mission. There were also concerns for the wear and tear these missions were having on the aircraft themselves. These were not sturdy aircraft, and they were built for long flights at low speeds. Missions over Cuban territory, to the contrary, were typically short and at relatively high speeds. With so few U-2s available, each and every overflight had to be justified.

Originally, two overflights of the island of Cuba were planned for the month of September, but in the aftermath of the discussions concerning the U-2's increased vulnerability, it was decided that four short missions, only two of which would actually overfly Cuban territory, would be conducted. As it turned out, however, the weather was so poor during this period that no usable photography was acquired between 5 and 26 September. This was extremely unfortunate, for the first MRBMs arrived on 8 September aboard the Soviet freighter *Omsk*; more arrived a week later on the *Poltava*. The missiles were unloaded at night and secretly transported to the launch sites, but their presence could not be entirely hidden from Cuban citizens (Lebow and Stein 1994, 85).

During this period the CIA would issue a Special National Intelligence Estimate (No. 85-3-62) under the title "The Military Buildup in Cuba." In what may have been their most significant statement the authors concluded, "The USSR could derive considerable military advantage from the establishment of Soviet medium and intermediate range ballistic missiles in Cuba, or from the establishment of a Soviet submarine base there. As between the two, the establishment of a submarine base would be more likely" (SNIE 85-3-62, cited in McAuliffe 1992, 93). McCone, on a honeymoon trip to Paris, was unhappy with the estimate. He continued to hold to the view that "the deployment of SA-2s was to hinder the U-2s from detecting the arrival of surface-to-surface missiles" (Brugioni 1991, 148).

It was not until 26 September that the first of the four planned reconnaissance flights could be conducted. The flight was successful, covering Guantanamo Bay and the Banes area at the eastern end of Cuba, and three new SA-2 sites were subsequently identified on the photography. The second flight, covering the Isle of Pines, was completed on 29 September; the resulting photography revealed another SA-2 site and a cruise missile site at Siguanea. Because of poor weather the third flight in the series had to wait until 5 October. When the photography from this flight was analyzed another SA-2 site was discovered. When four new SA-2 sites were found on photography from the fourth flight, completed on 7 October, the evidence proved overwhelmingly that an islandwide SA-2 defense network was being installed.

At the same time the U-2s were monitoring events in Cuba, carrier-based naval aircraft were photographing Soviet merchant ships as they approached Cuba. Many of the ships rode high in the water, yet they had large cargo hatches and carried a heavy boom adjacent to the largest hatch. Photointerpreters at NPIC could find no evidence of missiles so concluded the ships were simply carrying large quantities of military equipment; most such ships were destined for the port of Mariel near Havana. On 28 September navy reconnaissance aircraft brought back photos of a large-hatched vessel, the *Kasimov*, which was carrying several long (nearly sixty feet) containers. It was determined that these were fuselage crates for IL-28 Beagle Bombers (Brugioni 1991, 181). Although there was growing unease over the situation, the Kennedy administration continued to believe that the types of weapons being shipped to Cuba were for defense purposes only.

On 12 October the operational control over the U-2 flights was transferred from the CIA to the Joint Chiefs of Staff and SAC. They would henceforth be flown by pilots of SAC's 4080th Strategic Reconnaissance Wing—a change that reflected the White House's continuing concern over the SA-2 threat. It was concluded there "would be less embarrassment if a downed U-2 were found to have a military pilot" (Gribkov and Smith 1994, 117). This view was, of course, just the opposite of President Eisenhower's. He had insisted that U-2s overflying Soviet territory appear to be piloted by civilians, and he required SAC pilots to become contract employees of the CIA.

The transfer of the U-2s to SAC command had no impact on the handling of the photography. Film canisters were flown directly to the Naval Photographic Intelligence Center in Suitland, Maryland, for processing.

Duplicate photos were then delivered to NPIC, SAC, and DIA for analysis. Though early in the crisis there was an attempt to restrict the number of individuals having access to the photography for security reasons, the increased volume of photos to be analyzed soon made this impossible.

The first SAC U-2 mission was undertaken on 14 October, when a pair of aircraft took off with Majors Anderson and Heyser at the controls. The mission had two objectives. The first was to discover whether there was any missile-related construction under way in the area immediately to the west of Havana. A number of agent reports had mentioned the existence of suspicious activity here although an analysis of earlier photography revealed nothing; nevertheless, CIA analysts had designated the area around San Cristobal as the location of a "possible MRBM site." The second objective was to ascertain the operational status of the SA-2 sites at the most advanced stage of construction. Since these, too, were located west of Havana, this region was accorded highest priority for photographic coverage. The concerns about this region proved only too real; photos revealed for the very first time the presence of MRBMs on Cuba.

The south-to-north route of mission 3101 took the U-2s over the western end of Cuba about forty nautical miles west of Havana at its closest point. While the mission itself was operationally routine, what the mission uncovered was anything but expected. The resulting photos revealed the existence of an MRBM site and two associated military encampments near the Sierra del Rosario mountains in west-central Cuba. One site contained a variety of vehicles including fourteen canvas-covered missile trailers, approximately eighty feet in length, of a configuration associated with the transport of SS-3 and SS-4 ballistic missiles. The second site held eight more such trailers, but in addition there were four other pieces of equipment that were used for missile erection on the field (Lundahl Memorandum of 16 October 1962, cited in McAuliffe 1992, 155). No missile trailers were visible in the third area.

Photointerpreters at NPIC were greatly aided in their work by having access to classified materials on Soviet missile systems provided by Col. Oleg Penkovsky, a senior GRU official who served as a defector-in-place from April 1961 to October 1962. Before being arrested and later executed by the KGB, he had become one of the most important Soviet spies to serve the West during the cold war. It was from a diagram of an SS-4 site in the Soviet Union supplied by Penkovsky that NPIC photointerpreters were ultimately able to identify the SS-4 deployments in Cuba. In addition, detailed descriptions of SS-4 installations accompanying the diagram made it possible for photointerpreters to calculate how much longer it would take to make the sites operational (Schecter and Deriabin 1992, 334).

Both the SS-3 and the SS-4 were single-stage, road-mobile ballistic weapons that could be deployed with a minimum of construction activity, since they required only a hard surface to be fired. The SS-3 was capable of carrying a 3,000-pound warhead nearly seven hundred nautical miles, which meant it could strike targets in the southeastern United States, including the cities of Savannah and New Orleans. The SS-4, on the other hand, could carry the same warhead eleven hundred nautical miles and could, therefore, strike a number of cities throughout much of the continental United States, including Washington, D.C. In addition, the SS-4 could reach "a significant number of military targets, including eighteen SAC bomber and tanker bases, an ICBM base, and three major naval bases" (CIA Memorandum of 16 October 1962, cited in McAuliffe 1992, 143).

The photographic evidence was presented to President Kennedy over breakfast on the morning of 16 October. He reacted to the news calmly, though it was clear he was deeply angered by the fact that Khrushchev had been lying to him. As recently as 11 September TASS had reiterated that Moscow had no intention of deploying ballistic missiles beyond the borders of the Soviet Union, yet missiles must have already arrived in Cuba at the time of the TASS statement. Thus, for Kennedy it was never a question of whether the missiles would be removed since he had made a prior public commitment to keep "offensive weapons" out of Cuba. The only issue was how to get the missiles out. Fortunately, intelligence analysts had discovered the missiles before they had become operational, so Kennedy had at least a few days in which to ponder his options.

The president's first act was to appoint a group of advisors to assist him in making decisions during the missile crisis. Originally code-named Elite, the group "became known as the Executive Committee (EXCOM) of the National Security Council and would be formally established by National Security Action Memorandum 196 signed by the President on October 22, 1962" (Brugioni 1991, 239). From 16 October until the crisis was resolved on 28 October, EXCOM remained in almost continuous session.

Even after that it would continue to meet on an almost daily basis for another six weeks (Andrew 1995, 289).

During the first few meetings of EXCOM a range of possible options was discussed, though as Kennedy made clear, there was no question about the ultimate objective—the missiles would have to be removed; anything short of this was unacceptable. The Joint Chiefs recommended a surprise air strike to be directed not only at the missiles themselves but also against airfields, MiG aircraft, SA-2 sites, and any other weapons systems that posed a threat to the United States. The air strike might have to be followed with an invasion of the island, although on this point the military appeared uncertain. Initially, there was considerable support for an air strike among EXCOM members, but as the deliberations moved along this option began to lose some of its appeal, at least as a first response. For one thing, a surprise air strike would involve heavy casualties, Cuban as well as Soviet. George Ball would liken the proposed option to another Pearl Harbor, which, he concluded "is not conduct that one expects of the United States" (May and Zelikow 1997, 143). Most bothersome to committee members was the military's admission that an air strike would destroy at best only about 90 percent of the missiles on the ground, leaving the possibility that one or more surviving missiles could be launched against the United States. The political consequences of a Soviet missile striking an American city, not to mention the potential loss of life, presented too great a risk; there had to be another way to get the missiles out.

By 18 October EXCOM members had begun to settle on a somewhat less provocative course of action: a limited blockade designed to prevent further offensive weapons from flowing into Cuba. The blockade would commence only after the president had made a public address during which he would display the evidence provided by reconnaissance aircraft. And while our allies would be appropriately briefed on the United States' intentions, they would have no input on the decision itself. The advantage of the blockade was that it could be tightened, or eased, depending upon the Soviet response, and most members expected an aggressive response (McCone Memorandum of 19 October 1962, cited in McAuliffe 1992, 194). It also conveyed a sense of resolve and Kennedy "wanted to forestall another challenge in Berlin" (Lebow and Stein 1994, 103).

In order to ensure that EXCOM had at its disposal the most up-to-date intelligence on the situation within Cuba, the number of U-2 overflights was increased dramatically. For just the three-day period of 17–19 October, seventeen missions were undertaken. So great was the photographic activity that a nationwide shortage of aerial film developed. Fortuitously for the U-2 pilots, Soviet forces in Cuba were under orders at this time not to fire on U.S. aircraft; in fact, "SAM commanders were not even allowed to use their radars to track the spy planes overhead" (Gribkov and Smith 1994, 51). This policy was meant to avoid providing the United States with any unnecessary indication of what was being constructed. But it may also have been the case that Soviet commanders in Cuba did not immediately "tell Moscow that the missile sites had been overflown and that the Americans probably knew about the missiles" (May and Zelikow 1997, 681).

By 19 October sufficient overflights had crisscrossed the island to provide a relatively complete picture of Soviet missile-related activities on Cuba, and it was an increasingly threatening one. It was now definite that there were two SS-4 ballistic missile sites near San Cristobal, and a nearby third site, at an early stage of development, was a possibility. At each of the first two sites eight missiles, as well as four field-type launchers, were visible; there also appeared to be backup missiles for each launcher. These two sites were now declared operational; that is, they were capable of launching missiles eighteen hours after a decision was made to do so. In addition to the San Cristobal complex, two new SS-4 sites were identified in the Sangua La Grande area east of Havana. Each site contained four launch pads, and since associated buildings and equipment were identical to San Cristobal, it could be logically concluded that sixteen missiles would also be deployed here.

While nearly everyone with access to the Cuban materials (now code-named Psalm) expected additional MRBM sites to be found, the discovery on mission 3107 photography of two fixed IRBM (SS-5) sites in the Guanajay area near Havana was totally unexpected. Although photo-interpreters could not actually identify any SS-5 missiles on the ground, the pattern exhibited by the construction activities was unmistakable. The SS-5, with its capability of carrying a 3- to 5-megaton warhead nearly twenty-two hundred nautical miles, was simply too heavy to be deployed on a mobile launcher; instead, it required a fairly substantial system of concrete service roads and launch pads to handle it. From the air an SS-5 site in Cuba looked little different from an SS-5 site in the Soviet Union.

Since the SS-5 was capable of striking targets throughout most of the continental United States and portions of Canada as well, its presence served only to ratchet up the seriousness of the Soviet threat to a more dangerous level. In aggregate there were twenty-four launchers under construction, each of which would presumably have a refire capability; when operational these missiles would represent a nuclear warhead potential equal to one-half of the Soviet Union's total ICBM capacity. More important, not only could these missiles strike their targets within minutes of launch, but they were not covered by the U.S. early warning system that faced north toward the Soviet Union. Thus, at one stroke Khrushchev had, at small financial cost, dramatically altered the strategic nuclear balance (Pope 1982, 23).

In addition to these missile systems, photointerpreters had now identified a total of twenty-six SA-2 sites, sixteen of which were estimated to be operationally ready. Each site comprised six launchers arrayed around its command and control system; each launcher was supplied with an extra missile, so it too had a refire capability. There were also three coastal missile sites that had been identified on Cuba. These sites contained ground-to-ground cruise missiles having a range of thirty-five to forty nautical miles (Joint Evaluation of 19 October 1962, cited in McAuliffe 1992, 207). And, finally, at San Julian Airfield on the westernmost tip of Cuba, photointerpreters found twenty-two crates, each about sixty feet long, which appeared to be the IL-28 bombers spotted earlier on the deck of the Soviet freighter, *Kasimov* (May and Zelikow 1997, 173). Technicians were just beginning to assemble these aircraft.

The magnitude of the total Soviet missile force being deployed on Cuba was unlike anything the Soviets had done in other client states; the evidence suggested Cuba was being developed into a strategic base for the Soviet Union, and based on the evidence provided by the U-2 photos, the Soviets were in for the long haul. Khrushchev must have believed the missiles would act as a deterrent to attacking the island. It was a huge gamble on his part, and as both the defensive and the offensive missile systems came closer to becoming operational, the risks were increasing for Kennedy as well.

While the EXCOM had been deliberating these issues, Kennedy himself had been out campaigning for midterm elections; for the moment, at least, he did not want the public to know a crisis was brewing. By the morning of the twentieth, however, the situation had become too serious for him to remain away from Washington. That afternoon Kennedy met with his EXCOM, and together they received a briefing from Ray Cline and Art Lundahl, who displayed the latest U-2 photography. Lundahl reported that nearly the entire island of Cuba had been photographed in the past several days and the full extent of the Soviet missile force had now been documented. There were six MRBM bases with a total of twenty-four launch pads and three IRBM bases with a total of twelve launchers. The IRBM sites were still at an early stage of construction so would in all probability not be operational for at least another four weeks. However, at least half of the MRBM launchers appeared to be operational and the rest would be so within a week. It was reiterated that to this point "we have not seen nuclear warheads for any of these missiles," but it was added that "we do not rely on ever seeing them in our photography" (Cline Briefing, cited in McAuliffe 1992, 223).

At the conclusion of the briefing, and after thanking Lundahl for NPIC's contribution to the intelligence effort, Kennedy declared that he would announce a limited quarantine of Cuba in a televised address once America's chief allies had been briefed on the situation (Andrew 1995, 292). The next day senior emissaries, carrying a personal letter from Kennedy, briefing notes, and an advanced copy of the president's address to the American public, were on their way to brief the heads of government of Britain, France, West Germany, and Canada. At McCone's suggestion copies of U-2 photography were also sent along with a senior intelligence official to explain them. Harold MacMillan, Konrad Adenauer, Charles de Gaulle, and John Diefenbaker of Canada all pledged their support for Kennedy's proposed plan of action, although Diefenbaker's would be the least enthusiastic. His government found U.S. policies toward Cuba "annoying" (Thompson 1992, 264), a view that continues to this day. Nevertheless, Kennedy was extremely pleased with the response: "No previous president had made such dramatic use of peacetime intelligence for purposes of Allied diplomacy" (Andrew 1995, 293).

Even before Kennedy had delivered his address on the evening of 22 October, American military forces were already moving to their assigned locations. The quarantine would be supported by elements of the U.S. Second Fleet, specifically Task Forces 135 and 136. The former consisted of two aircraft carriers, the USS *Enterprise* and the USS *Independence*, and fifteen destroyers; the latter was comprised of the aircraft carrier *Essex*, the cruisers *Newport News* and *Canberra*, and nineteen destroyers. The task of intercepting Warsaw Pact merchant ships would be the responsibility of antisubmarine warfare forces supported by navy patrol craft and SAC bombers, which would maintain surveillance over major shipping lanes between Europe and the Caribbean; they were aided in this task by the navies of Canada and Britain (Brugioni 1991, 345). Yet it was a big ocean and there was no guarantee the quarantine would work.

One concern in the back of Kennedy's mind was that if the Soviets became convinced that an invasion was imminent, they might just launch a preemptive strike against U.S. forces now heavily concentrated in Florida. Visiting Florida, he had been dismayed to see U.S. aircraft aligned wing-to-wing along airport runways and ordered them to be dispersed to make them less vulnerable to attack. When nothing was done, he secretly authorized that aerial photographs of the air bases be taken by reconnaissance aircraft based outside of Florida. The resulting photographs displayed clearly and much "to the discomfort of the military, that our aircraft were still highly concentrated" (Sorensen 1965, 708). LeMay, however, remained unconcerned, concluding it was better for the aircraft to remain on "good concrete airfields." In any case, the airfields were generally deemed beyond the range of the Cuban-based MiG-21s while the Soviet IL-28 jet bombers sent to Cuba had yet to be removed from their packing crates. The issue was dropped.

The afternoon of 22 October was a busy one for the president. First, he met with his National Security Council to go over the various policy options one more time; he then met with his Cabinet. Since most of his Cabinet members were not members of his EXCOM, the briefing they received was sobering indeed. At five that afternoon Kennedy met with congressional leaders and provided them with a complete briefing, including a display of U-2 photo enlargements and comments by Lundahl and Ray Cline. Kennedy concluded the meeting by laying out his plans for the quarantine. Concern was expressed that Kennedy was not being sufficiently firm, and at least two senators expressed the view that an air strike

trust
but
verify

would be a more appropriate response (Thompson 1992, 262). At the same time this meeting was taking place, Dean Rusk was presenting a copy of Kennedy's upcoming address to Soviet ambassador Anatoly Dobrynin, along with U-2 photographs of the missile sites in Cuba. The Soviet ambassador appeared genuinely surprised and claimed that Moscow had given him no clue as to what was taking place in Cuba (Dobrynin 1995, 79).

At seven that evening President Kennedy made a thirty-minute televised address to the nation. Viewers sat transfixed to their television screens as Kennedy described how Khrushchev had deceived the United States by deploying MRBM and IRBM missiles just a few miles from the U.S. mainland on the island of Cuba. He went on to discuss his plans for the blockade, warning Americans the crisis might take months to resolve. At the conclusion he made clear that Soviet missiles would be withdrawn or destroyed. At no time during his address, however, did he make specific mention of the U-2s, only that the surveillance of Cuba would continue (Andrew 1995, 294).

Simultaneous with the president's address, the Pentagon placed the U.S. military establishment around the globe on Defcon 3, an increased state of alert (Brugioni 1991, 371). SAC bombers carrying nuclear weapons went airborne, ICBMs were readied for firing, and nuclear submarines went to their assigned positions. Since there was a very great fear that the Soviet Union would institute a blockade of West Berlin, military bases in Europe went on increased alert. Finally, military bases in the southeastern part of the United States were scenes of frantic activity as ninety thousand marines and other airborne forces were being readied as an invasion force along with appropriate support personnel from the U.S. Navy and Air Force (Kennedy 1969, 55).

The next day, 23 October, the EXCOM approved the quarantine order, "Interdiction of the Delivery of Offensive Weapons to Cuba," and sent it along for the president's signature; the quarantine would go into force the following morning. That evening, in one of the cold war's great ironies, the British government released to the BBC some of the U-2 photographs of Cuba that had been part of the briefing package. In the four years the U-2 had overflown the Soviet Union, Eisenhower had, at some cost to his own credibility, never made U-2 photographs public. Kennedy likewise had not displayed U-2 photos during his address to the American public so as not to reveal the quality of our overhead reconnaissance. "Thus it was," notes Andrew (1995), "that the most highly classified U.S. imagery intelligence ever to be released was seen first by British rather than American viewers" (296). The following day Kennedy had copies of the photos delivered to all news media, including the United States Information Agency, which would ultimately distribute fifty thousand prints worldwide (Thompson 1992, 298).

The initial reaction to the U.S. quarantine was predictable. The American public overwhelmingly supported the action; a Gallup poll showed 84 percent in favor (Thompson 1992, 278). Castro went on Cuban television to denounce American aggression; he also placed his military forces on highest alert. Warsaw Pact forces were also placed on alert, but there were no threatening moves made on Berlin. There was, most significantly, no official response from Khrushchev. In his memoirs Soviet ambassador Dobrynin has reported that a "sense of total bewilderment . . . enveloped Khrushchev and his colleagues after their plot had taken such an unexpected turn" (Dobrynin 1995, 83).

The real danger was now represented by the eighteen Soviet merchant ships approaching the quarantine line, five of which had large cargo hatches. The president had issued instructions to military personnel to use all possible restraint to avoid the loss of life. However, Secretary of Defense McNamara had made it abundantly clear that "the United States would not hesitate to sink Soviet ships delivering offensive weapons to Cuba should they refuse to follow orders given by American warships" (Dobrynin 1995, 80). After a long day of waiting, reports began reaching the White House early on the twenty-fourth that sixteen of the eighteen Soviet ships, including the five with large cargo hatches, had stopped dead in the water before reaching the quarantine line; two of the five with the large hatches had already been singled out by the U.S. Navy for boarding. Within the next two days, however, all sixteen had turned around and were heading back to the Soviet Union. As Dean Rusk was to have remarked upon hearing that the vessels had stopped, "We're eyeball to eyeball and I think the other fellow just blinked" (Rusk 1990, 237).

On the afternoon of the twenty-fourth, on instructions from the president, UN ambassador Adlai Stevenson faced off against Soviet ambassador

Valerian Zorin on the floor of the Security Council in what is now considered one of the cold war's most historic confrontations. When Soviet ambassador Zorin refused to answer Stevenson's question— "Do you deny that the Soviet Union has placed or is placing medium and intermediate-range missiles and sites in Cuba?"—Stevenson remarked, "I am prepared to wait for my answer until hell freezes over, if that's your decision. And I am also prepared to present the evidence in this room" (Kennedy 1969, 76). At that point Stevenson revealed, for all Council members to see, a series of U-2 photo enlargements documenting the construction of missile sites on Cuba. It was another first for intelligence photos; they had been used to score a major propaganda victory for the United States.

In the absence of any formal response from Khrushchev, U.S. reconnaissance aircraft continued to monitor Soviet activities on Cuba. Beginning on 23 October a series of low-level reconnaissance missions were conducted in addition to the daily U-2 overflights. The low-level missions became the responsibility of the air force's 363d Tactical Reconnaissance Wing out of Shaw Air Force Base in Sumter, South Carolina, assigned for the duration of the crisis to MacDill Air Force Base in Tampa. Pilots of the 363d flew unarmed RF-101 Voodoo fighters, which were capable of sweeping in over targets at airspeeds in excess of one thousand miles per hour. Missions were also flown by the navy's F8U pilots of Patrol Squadron 56 from Norfolk but deployed to Guantanamo Naval Base on Cuba (Infield 1970, 183).

The low-level missions had two objectives: first, they were to acquire the detailed intelligence on each and every target that would be attacked if air strikes were ordered. Of greatest importance were the nuclear weapons storage bunkers, which analysts were still trying to identify. In addition, however, these missions were also meant to ease some of the burden on the U-2s. By the twenty-third the U-2 pilots were beginning to succumb to exhaustion and the stress of photographing targets defended by SA-2 systems whose radars were now locking onto their aircraft. For Kennedy, the intelligence provided by these flights had become indispensable, and he could ill afford any interruption in its flow. A report based upon the analysis of photography acquired on 25 October noted that there was no evidence the Soviets were dismantling the missile sites. In fact, five of the six sites were now considered to be operational and the sixth would probably become so in two or three more days. Furthermore, the Soviets were now camouflaging everything—missiles, launchers, trucks, tanks, and even buildings. Analysts freely admitted that without the aid of earlier photos they would no longer be able to locate the missiles.

But his was not the only significant discovery made on the 25 October photography. At a vehicle park near Remedios analysts identified what they concluded were launchers for FROG (free rocket over ground) missiles in the company of thirty or so T-54 tanks and a host of other armored vehicles. The FROG was an unguided tactical nuclear weapon with a range of twenty to thirty miles. Their presence on the island represented just one more reason why an invasion would be a very costly affair.

In spite of the growing Soviet military presence on the island, by the morning of the twenty-sixth even Kennedy had to admit that an invasion might be the only way to get rid of the missiles. U.S. military forces were already on full alert, but SAC forces now went to Defcon 2, the final readiness level before initiating a full-scale nuclear attack on the Soviet Union, and the only time during the cold war SAC would go to such a level. When the EXCOM met that morning the hawks on the committee pushed vigorously for an air strike, but no decision was made. The majority of the committee members, including Kennedy himself, needed no reminding that an air strike not only would result in heavy casualties but probably would not destroy all the missiles as well. While Kennedy could not afford another Bay of Pigs disaster, neither did he want to start a nuclear war.

Finally, on the evening of the twenty-sixth, Kennedy received his first direct response from Khrushchev. The message, which was long and at times convoluted, seemed to suggest a bargain: the withdrawal of Soviet missiles in exchange for a pledge by the White House not to invade Cuba. The sense of optimism generated by this message was further strengthened when John Scali, an ABC news reporter, contacted the White House to describe a similar proposal made to him by an official of the Soviet Embassy (Kennedy 1969, 90). However, Khrushchev appeared to up the ante for a resolution of the crisis the next morning when a news story reported that Soviet missiles would be withdrawn from Cuba only if U.S. missiles were removed from Turkey. Shortly after the news story appeared Kennedy received a second, more urgent letter from Khrushchev in which he "defended the missiles in Cuba as a justifiable response to the Jupiters in Turkey" (Lebow and Stein 1994, 46). Sensing that Khrushchev was wavering, Kennedy chose to ignore his second letter and respond to the first. In this message he "welcomed Khrushchev's desire to seek a prompt solution, but he insisted that first all work on missile sites in Cuba should be stopped and all offensive weapons in Cuba should be rendered inoperable under international control" (Dobrynin 1995, 86). If this were done, the United States would end the quarantine and give the necessary assurances that Cuba would not be invaded by the United States or any other country in the Western Hemisphere.

Suddenly, on the afternoon of the twenty-seventh, the crisis escalated when a U-2 aircraft was downed over Cuba by an SA-2 missile; the pilot, Maj. Rudolf Anderson, was killed. The possibility of this happening had become a major concern, especially after pilots returning from low-level missions began reporting they were being fired upon by Cuban antiaircraft artillery. It was assumed, therefore, that the U-2 had been downed by Cuban artillery, but, as it turned out, the U-2 was brought down by a Soviet antiaircraft unit though authorization to fire on the unarmed U-2s had never been given. Apparently, once the Cubans had begun firing on U.S. aircraft, Soviet commanders had erroneously concluded all restraints had been lifted.

From the beginning of the crisis it had been agreed that if a U-2 were fired upon by an SA-2, the site from which the missile was launched would be destroyed. However, before EXCOM could even formulate a response to this incident, word was received that a U-2 operating out of Alaska had accidentally intruded into Soviet airspace, causing both Soviet and American F-102A interceptors to be scrambled. Because the F-102As were on alert, they were armed with nuclear-tipped air-to-air missiles, which their pilots were authorized to use if it became necessary. Fortunately, no missiles were fired and the U-2 made it back safely to international airspace. When Kennedy was informed of the incident, he is said to have remarked calmly, "There is always some son of a bitch who never gets the word" (Thompson 1992, 328).

Although Kennedy was now advised by EXCOM to destroy the SAM site responsible for downing the U-2, at the last minute, as fighter pilots from Homestead Air Force Base were preparing for the attack, the president sent word that the mission was to be postponed (Kennedy 1969, 98). He decided to first transmit his answer to Khrushchev's letter and to see how Khrushchev responded before initiating any form of direct military action. Well aware of the potential consequences of his actions, Kennedy did not want to be pushed into escalating the crisis, especially by the military.

That same evening, however, the president dispatched his brother, Robert, to meet with Ambassador Dobrynin, at which time Khrushchev's second letter was, in essence, answered. The United States, Kennedy reported, wanted the missile sites out of Cuba and would bomb them out if necessary, but if "the missiles in Turkey represented the only obstacle to a settlement" (Dobrynin 1995, 87), President Kennedy was prepared to remove them in a matter of a few months. Regrettably, nothing public could be said about this part of the bargain. If Moscow were to make any mention of the Jupiters, they would not be withdrawn. An answer would have to be forthcoming by the next day. In the meantime SAC bombers would remain airborne, members of the 5th Marine Expeditionary Brigade would begin boarding the ships for transport to their staging areas, and the fourteen thousand air force reservists recently called up by President Kennedy would move to their active-duty stations (May and Zelikow 1997, 629).

By the next morning (28 October), exactly two weeks to the day since the first MRBM site on Cuba had been positively identified, the crisis was over; Khrushchev had decided to accept Kennedy's proposals without delay. The concessions were crucial because they "enabled him to withdraw with honor" (Lebow and Stein 1994, 140). To head off any possible attack on Cuba, Ambassador Dobrynin was instructed to notify Robert Kennedy that Khrushchev's response would be broadcast on Moscow radio "and the answer will be highly positive" (Dobrynin 1995, 84). In accepting Kennedy's terms, the English language broadcast made no mention of the missiles in Turkey, but it stated that instructions had been sent to the appropriate authorities in Cuba to halt all construction and begin dismantling the sites in preparation for returning the offensive missiles to the Soviet Union. The White House was jubilant, though Kennedy "asked his advisers to be reserved in their public comments and cautioned that no one should be under the illusion that the problem of Soviet weapons in Cuba was solved" (May and Zelikow 1997, 636).

Khrushchev's response had arrived just in time. A report, based upon low-level photography of 27 October, announced that all twenty-four

MRBM launches appeared to be operational. Furthermore, camouflage and concealment measures being undertaken at these sites were becoming more effective. As for the IRBM sites, construction was continuing though it was evident they would not be operational for some time; no missiles, transporters, or erectors could be identified. And since no new missile sites had been detected, intelligence analysts were confident their inventory of missile activities in Cuba was complete (Supplement 9, cited in McAuliffe 1992, 350). Nevertheless, had Kennedy felt forced to order an attack on the missile sites after the twenty-seventh, almost certainly some of those MRBMs would have been launched against targets in the United States.

In theory, all that remained now was to see that the missiles were, in fact, removed from Cuba. To negotiate with the Soviets on carrying out this commitment, Kennedy established the Special Coordinating Committee on the Cuban crisis. The quarantine would not be lifted until there was ample evidence that the missile sites were being dismantled. In addition, aircraft overflights would remain the primary method of inspection until on-site or some other type of verification procedure could be instituted (Brugioni 1991, 503).

The Kennedy administration was prepared to allow the United Nations to verify that the missile sites were being dismantled, but this would require on-site inspection since the UN had no photoreconnaissance capabilities. The Soviets, however, made it clear that UN personnel would not be allowed to inspect returning ships while Castro was even more adamant that no UN team was going to inspect missile sites on Cuban soil (Brugioni 1991, 503). Under these circumstances Kennedy felt he had no choice but to keep the quarantine intact and resume reconnaissance overflights; SAC aircraft would also remain on alert.

Since the downing of the U-2 on the twenty-seventh only low-level reconnaissance missions were being conducted. These missions, flown by navy, marine, and air force pilots, met no opposition as they flew repeatedly over the missile sites. As late as 31 October evidence seemed to suggest that construction and concealment activities were continuing at many sites. On the other hand, the photos revealed that a number of MRBM launchers had been moved, and to some analysts this represented the first indication that the dismantling process had begun. Subsequent photos, taken over the next several days, would reveal this was in fact the case; the missiles, launching equipment, and camouflage netting had been removed and the launch sites themselves were being bulldozed.

During this critical period, Soviet authorities inquired whether the United States would suspend reconnaissance overflights in order to calm Castro, who had become irate over recent Soviet actions. Not only did Kennedy reject this request out of hand, he actually authorized an increase in the number of missions in order that the intelligence community could compile a complete photographic record "of the dismantling of the sites, the loading of the equipment, the movement of the equipment along the roads, and its arrival at port and loaded aboard ships" (Brugioni 1991, 519). The Soviets cooperated by providing U.S. officials with the names of the vessels that would carry the missiles back to the Soviet Union. Reconnaissance aircraft photographed the missiles, which were to be stored on deck for counting purposes, as the ships put to sea; U.S. Navy warships escorted the Soviet ships back to home ports in the Baltic and Black Seas.

Tension between the United States and the Soviet Union did not end with the removal of the missiles and the destruction of the launch sites; there still remained the issue of the IL-28 bombers, which Kennedy had publicly stated were among the offensive weapons systems that had to be removed from Cuba. Photography acquired on 2 November revealed that at San Julian Airfield IL-28s were being uncrated and assembled; at least two appeared to be operational. Several crates were also detected at Holguin Airfield on the eastern side of the island. There were now about forty IL-28s on Cuba, and "the Soviets were continuing to assemble them and prepare them for action" (Gribkov and Smith 1994, 150).

Meanwhile, in a 4 November letter to Kennedy, Khrushchev rejected the United States' claim that the IL-28s represented offensive weapons, but by this time he had little leverage left to exert. On 11 November, without notifying Castro, Khrushchev informed Kennedy that the bombers would be removed "at such time when the Soviets had mended relations with Cuba" (Chang and Kornbluh 1992, 234). Kennedy reminded Khrushchev that without a specific time frame for the withdrawal of the bombers, the quarantine would be continued; Kennedy also notified European leaders that renewed action might be required to get the bombers out of Cuba. Khrushchev relented, and on 19 November he informed Kennedy that the bombers would be dismantled and returned to the Soviet Union within thirty days. With Kennedy's public announcement of Khrushchev's decision on 20 November, the quarantine was lifted and the crisis ended.

This did not signal the end of reconnaissance overflights, however. Amid warnings from Castro that he would fire upon any reconnaissance aircraft overflying Cuba, the low-level missions were ended on 14 November. At the same time, U-2 overflights that had been suspended after the downing of a U-2 on 27 October were resumed. On 4 December President Kennedy would sign National Security Council Action Memorandum 208, "A Guideline for the Planning of Cuban Overflights," authorizing the continued monitoring of activities in Cuba by U-2 aircraft (Brugioni 1991, 535). The Kremlin objected vigorously to this humiliating violation of Cuban airspace, but Kennedy insisted that Castro's continued unwillingness to authorize on-site inspection made such overflights necessary. The U-2 overflights would continue until September 1974, when they were ended in favor of SR-71s. President Carter would finally order an end to all overflights of Cuba in November 1978 "as a gesture of good will to President Fidel Castro" (Halloran 1979, 18).

Neither, also, did the lifting of the quarantine resolve the crisis in a diplomatic sense; there was still the issue of President Kennedy's pledge not to invade Cuba. While Kennedy initially seemed disposed to formalize his pledge in writing, under pressure from the State Department he subsequently changed his mind. The State Department seems to have convinced Kennedy that such a pledge "would inhibit future U.S. policy toward Cuba" (Chang and Kornbluh 1992, 236). Entreaties by Khrushchev for the two sides to formalize their commitments in written documents were largely ignored, and in the end there was no formal conclusion to the missile crisis; "the U.S. and Soviet Union simply agreed to disagree" (Chang and Kornbluh 1992, 237).

If the resolution of the crisis did not meet Khrushchev's expectations, it was not without its frustrations for Kennedy as well. Because intelligence analysts could only confirm that thirty-six of the known forty-two missiles had been shipped back to the Soviet Union, critics of the Kennedy administration claimed the remaining missiles had been hidden on the island (CIA Memorandum of 29 November 1962, cited in McAuliffe 1992, 358). When it became clear the media were not about to drop the issue,

Kennedy authorized his secretary of defense, Robert McNamara, to make a televised presentation describing America's reconnaissance capabilities and the means by which they had been employed to monitor the removal of the missiles from Cuba. While this presentation appeared to resolve the issue as far as the public was concerned, it left the intelligence community upset that "too much had been revealed about photointerpretation methods and the quality and quantity of intelligence information that the U.S. was deriving from photographic sources" (Brugioni 1991, 563).

In time the public lost interest in Cuba, but not so the intelligence community, which made the missile crisis the subject of several reviews and conferences, including one held in Moscow in January 1989. A consistent conclusion drawn from these postcrisis analyses was the crucial role played by photographic intelligence during the crisis. However, it is also clear there were critical intelligence failures. In his book *Missiles of October,* Thompson (1992) declares the CIA had evidence of Soviet missiles in Cuba as early as March 1962 (213), although it is clear the first missiles were not shipped until July. Nevertheless, it appears that the Soviets found U.S. intelligence slow in detecting the presence of missiles in Cuba. Although aware of the Soviet military buildup, the United States did not understand its significance, "nor the mission of the troops on the island until nearly all the men had come ashore" (Gribkov and Smith 1994, 36). Much of this could be traced to the intelligence community's failure to order sufficient U-2 overflights during the critical month of September. In fact, for the period 5 September to 14 October there were only four U-2 missions, two of which were peripheral (Killiam Memorandum of 4 February 1963, cited in McAuliffe 1992, 364).

There was also the issue of nuclear warheads for the missiles. U.S. intelligence analysts admitted that during the crisis they could find no photographic evidence for the existence of nuclear warheads in Cuba. Soviet officials have reported, however, that the warheads for the MRBMs arrived at Mariel on 4 October on board the freighter *Indigirka* and were moved to storage bunkers at Bejucal, about thirteen miles south of Havana. In addition to these warheads the freighter also carried eighty cruise missile warheads, six atomic bombs for the IL-28 aircraft, and a dozen atomic charges for the Luna rockets. With the exception of the atomic bombs, which were stored close to the IL-28 aircraft, most of the other warheads were also stored at Bejucal. Another freighter, the *Alexandrovsk*, carried the twenty-four warheads to the port of La Isabela, but they were never unloaded (Gribkov and Smith 1994, 45–46). Curiously, while Soviet officials have stated that the warheads were never mated to the missiles, Brugioni has claimed that a postcrisis review of the photography "made it obvious that the Soviets had fueled and mated the warheads and had practiced moving the missiles to erectors" (1991, 548).

And then there was the question of how many Soviet troops had been sent to Cuba, an issue that would come back to haunt the administration of President Carter. U.S. estimates, as late as 1992, placed the number of Soviet troops at no more than ten thousand. In fact, the Soviets had transported forty thousand military personnel to Cuba complete with weapons and equipment (Gribkov and Smith 1994, 169). So successful were they in camouflaging the magnitude of this transfer that the United States exerted little pressure on the Soviet Union to remove these troops, choosing instead to place the emphasis on the removal of the weapons. At the conclusion of the crisis, however, and at Castro's insistence, Khrushchev left behind a twenty-eight-hundred-man motorized rifle brigade that would go undetected until 1979, when its discovery would create such a firestorm for President Carter that he would be unable to win Senate ratification for the SALT II agreement. Under pressure from Washington, Brezhnev agreed to rename the brigade a training unit rather than a combat unit, but it remained in place until 1990, when finally Gorbachev ordered it home (Gribkov and Smith 1994, 163).

In spite of these failures, photo intelligence proved indispensable to the successful resolution of this crisis. Its most critical contribution was the time it gave President Kennedy to make a reasoned response to a dangerous situation. As Robert Kennedy was later to remark, "If we had had to make a decision in twenty-four hours, I believe the course that we ultimately would have taken would have been quite different and filled with far greater risks. The fact that we were able to talk, debate, argue, disagree, and then debate some more was essential in choosing our ultimate course" (Kennedy 1969, 111). This time was provided not only because American photointerpreters detected the missiles in Cuba more quickly than Khrushchev had anticipated but also because they were able to closely monitor construction activities at the sites, thereby providing the president and EXCOM with continuous information on the operational status of the missiles. And when the president finally made his decision, it was only after NPIC had provided him with a complete inventory of Soviet military hardware on the island: "Every major weapons system introduced into Cuba by the Soviets was detected, identified, and reported (with respect to numbers, location and operational characteristics) before any one of these systems attained an operational capability" (McCone Memorandum of 28 February 1963, cited in McAuliffe 1992, 375).

Unlike President Eisenhower, who steadfastly refused to make U-2 photographs public, Kennedy effectively employed them in a variety of venues. To be absolutely certain he had international support for his quarantine of Cuba, Kennedy had U.S. intelligence officials privately brief allied leaders by means of U-2 photos and later had members of the UN Security Council briefed in much the same manner. In the aftermath of the missile crisis Secretary of Defense McNamara appeared on television to inform the American public of how the crisis was resolved, and again U-2 photos were used in the presentation. Noting that in each instance an intelligence analyst had to explain to the audience what the photos revealed, Sherman Kent (1972) remarked, "Never have so many taken so much on the say-so of so few" (42).

For Kennedy there was never any doubt about the importance of photo intelligence to the successful resolution of the crisis, and he was generous in his praise of those who were part of the photoreconnaissance process. He personally presented the 363d Tactical Reconnaissance Wing the air force's Outstanding Unit Award, and to each of the wing's sixteen pilots who had flown missions over Cuba he presented the Distinguished Flying Cross. Major Rudolph was posthumously awarded the Distinguished Service Medal (Infield 1970, 189–90). Kennedy also commended NPIC for its outstanding service during the crisis and singled out for special praise its director, Art Lundahl. Finally, the CIA and its director, John McCone, received its fair share of credit. In fact, the prestige of the agency, which had been so badly damaged by the Bay of Pigs debacle, was now largely restored, and it would go on to play the leading role within the intelligence community.

Yet for all the photographic evidence, postcrisis analyses, and joint Soviet-American conferences on the topic, there remain a surprising number of questions for which satisfactory answers have never been completely given. For example, why did the Soviets make so little effort to camouflage their construction activities? They were certainly aware of the quality of U-2 photography since they had acquired considerable quantities of it when Powers's aircraft had been downed two years earlier. And why didn't the Soviets make their SA-2 sites operational before commencing construction of the strategic missile sites? The SA-2 threat alone may have kept U-2s from detecting the missile sites. Khrushchev, however, appears to have missed this point. In his memoirs he seems only to be thinking of an air attack when he responds, "There's a limit to the number of missile installations you can put on an island as small as Cuba. Then, after you've launched all your missiles you're completely unprotected" (Khrushchev 1971, 549).

Finally, there is the broader issue of the missile crisis's impact on the cold war, for which there is also some difference of opinion. On the one hand, the peaceful resolution of the crisis appeared to bring some measure of calm to U.S.-Soviet relations, at least over the short term; officials on both sides made clear their support for arms control negotiations. There was, in fact, a measurable reduction in tension over the issue of Germany. A "hot line" was established to improve communications between Washington and Moscow, and in August 1963 the two countries signed the Limited Test Ban Treaty (LTBT), which restricted nuclear testing to underground explosions. While various seismic and air-sampling devices would help monitor compliance, photographic reconnaissance satellites would monitor test preparations: "The use of space-based systems of verification had been established and would pave the way for more far-reaching accords" (Burrows 1986, 151).

Over the longer term, however, the impact of the missile crisis could be interpreted far more negatively. For Soviet military leaders the resolution of the crisis was a humiliating experience; both their pride and their prestige were severely damaged: "Khrushchev's failure to insist on a public pledge by Kennedy cost him dearly . . . because no one knew about the secret deal" (Dobrynin 1995, 91). Thus, within two years of the crisis, Khrushchev would be removed from his position as party secretary and replaced by Leonid Brezhnev. The crisis also served as a catalyst for a debate on Krushchev's military policies. By the time Brezhnev assumed his duties, the decision had already been made to phase out the SS-7s and SS-8s and proceed with the deployment of the third-generation SS-9 and SS-11 ICBMs and the Yankee-class SLBM (Burr 1994, 11). This decade-long effort would not end until the Soviets had attained strategic parity with the United States.

As an ironic postscript to the missile crisis, a mini-replay of it, with a similar outcome, would take place in late summer of 1970. NPIC analysts examining a recent batch of U-2 photographs of Cuba detected new construction activities at the port of Cienfuegos. When subsequent photographs of the port revealed Soviet ships unloading what were determined to be "vessels of the type used for servicing nuclear submarines" (Andrew 1995, 374), President Nixon immediately dispatched Kissinger to warn Soviet officials that the construction must be halted. Although the Soviets responded they had had no intention of establishing such a base, construction activities did, in fact, cease. And so, once again, timely information acquired by means of U-2 overflights enabled an American president to checkmate his Russian counterpart and prevent him from expanding Soviet military capabilities in the Caribbean.

With its ten engines, the Convair RB-36D had a greater range than any previous aircraft; however, it proved too slow to penetrate the air defenses of the Soviet Union. U.S. Air Force Collection (negative no. A-39684 AC), courtesy of the National Air and Space Museum, Smithsonian Institution

The Boeing RB-47 was designed as a medium-range aircraft, but by means of in-flight refueling it could be employed on long-range missions. It also proved inadequate for missions into the interior of the Soviet Union. U.S. Air Force Collection (negative no. +47421 AC), courtesy of the National Air and Space Museum, Smithsonian Institution

Lockheed's most famous aircraft, the U-2. Modified versions of the aircraft, which was developed in 1955 and used for nearly five years to photograph critical Soviet military installations, continue to fly operational missions to this day. Courtesy of National Air and Space Museum (negative no. 88-18022), Smithsonian Institution

CANVAS COVERED MISSILE TRAILERS IN HOLD REVETMENT

NET COVERED LAUNCHERS

CANVAS COVERED FRUIT SET SURROUNDED BY VERTICAL NETTING

BULLDOZER BURYING TANK IN REVETMENT WALL

CANVAS COVERED MISSILE TRAILERS

VEHICLE REPAIR RAMP

Low-level photograph of an SA-2 site at Bahia Honda, Cuba. The Star of David pattern unique to Soviet SAM sites made them extremely easy to identify on aerial photographs. Courtesy of the John F. Kennedy Library

Crates containing IL-28 bombers awaiting assembly at Cuba's San Julian Airfield. This was one of a number of photos used by the Kennedy administration during the Cuban missile crisis to brief members of Congress and, later, the American public. Courtesy of the John F. Kennedy Library

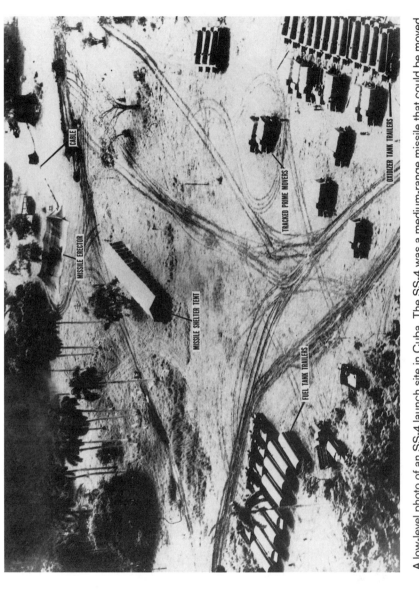

A low-level photo of an SS-4 launch site in Cuba. The SS-4 was a medium-range missile that could be moved about and fired from literally any hard surface. Courtesy of the John F. Kennedy Library

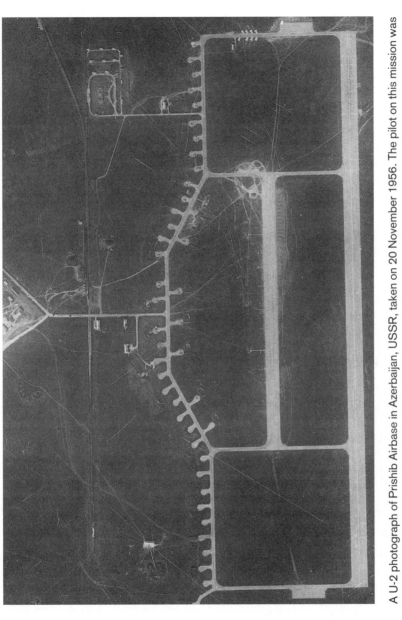

A U-2 photograph of Prishib Airbase in Azerbaijan, USSR, taken on 20 November 1956. The pilot on this mission was Francis Gary Powers, who in May 1960 would be shot down by Soviet air defenses. Courtesy of the Central Intelligence Agency

A KH-4 photo of a Soviet IRBM (SS-5) launch site. The SS-5s were among the missiles being deployed to Cuba at the time of the missile crisis in October 1962. Courtesy of National Archives

A KH-4 photo of the Severodvinsk Shipyard on the White Sea near Arkhangelsk. Regular coverage of major shipyards by reconnaissance satellites enabled analysts to accurately assess the pace and nature of Soviet shipbuilding activities. Courtesy of National Archives.

Satellite photos of factories such as this one, which produced rocket motors, led analysts to develop models for estimating annual production of various critical commodities. Though the results were not always accurate, the models nevertheless helped analysts better understand Soviet production techniques. Courtesy of National Archives

# 4

## Project Corona

The Corona satellites, which would replace the U-2 as the chief means of acquiring strategic intelligence on countries behind the Iron Curtain, were the result of a joint CIA–U.S. Air Force effort formally authorized by President Eisenhower in February 1958 (McDonald 1995, 691). The director of the Corona Project was Richard Bissell, who in his capacity as special assistant to the DCI for planning and development had been responsible for the successful development of the U-2; Bissell's air force counterpart was his former deputy, now brigadier general, Osmond Ritland. The two were charged with assembling a team for developing an interim satellite reconnaissance system that could meet the intelligence community's broad area search requirements until a more advanced system could be made operational. Like the U-2 program that preceded it, Project Corona was a great success. For a system originally designed as interim, Corona satellites would become the mainstay of the U.S. photoreconnaissance program for nearly twelve years, taking over eight hundred thousand images from space and establishing a number of historic firsts.

The management team assembled by Bissell and Ritland did not have to design a system entirely from scratch; a considerable amount of research had already been undertaken by the air force as part of Weapon System 117L (WS-117L), the Advanced Reconnaissance System. The WS-117L program, authorized in July 1956, had as its objective the development of a family of separate satellite reconnaissance systems capable of acquiring data in the photographic (visible), infrared, and microwave regions of the electromagnetic spectrum. The impetus for WS-117L was the air force's successful development of a propulsion system capable of launching an ICBM or boosting a reconnaissance satellite in orbit. Once this capability had been achieved, the air force's Ballistic Missile Division was assigned the satellite project that became WS-117L (Ruffner 1995, 4).

Initially, the Eisenhower administration viewed the WS-117L program as a low-priority, long-term effort, but with the successful Soviet launch of *Sputnik* all that changed and a new sense of urgency gripped Washington. Already the U-2s had been overflying the Soviet Union for more than a year, and it was not certain how much longer the program could be maintained. There was also a growing problem of security; a program as large as WS-117L could not be kept entirely secret, and stories about American spy satellites were beginning to appear in the press. Eisenhower was especially worried about such stories because of their potential impact on U.S.-Soviet relations. While the U-2 overflights of Soviet territory remained a secret to the American public, they were no secret to the Soviet leadership. Media reports, many of them vastly exaggerated, regarding American spy satellites would serve only to exacerbate already strained relations. In response to this situation it was decided that "the photographic subsystem of WS-117L offering the best prospect for early success would be separated from WS-117L, designated Project Corona, and placed under a joint CIA–U.S. Air Force management team" (Ruffner 1995, 5). Corona would now become the blackest of the black programs.

The new Corona program faced a bewildering array of problems, not the least of which was money. Bissell had wrongly assumed that the Thor booster rockets the air force was providing to the WS-117L program would be provided to Project Corona under the same arrangements; in fact, the boosters would now have to be purchased from the air force. Because there were insufficient funds, however, Bissell had to ask President Eisenhower for more money to purchase not only these boosters but also the second-stage boosters (the Agena) from Lockheed, the project's prime contractor.

One of the earliest decisions made by the Corona management team also turned out to be one of the most critical: the choice of a data retrieval system. Because the data readout techniques available at that time provided such poor image resolution, it was decided to employ a simpler but risky film-recovery system proposed originally by RAND engineers. The proposed system, if successful, promised high-resolution imagery, but it required that the film capsule, or satellite recovery vehicle (SRV), as it was called, physically separate from the Corona satellite and be carried by parachute to a designated recovery area, where it would be "caught" by a circling aircraft. For the SRV to come down in the designated recovery area a series of retro-rockets had to fire at precise intervals, and even then split-second timing was required for a successful snatch. Not surprisingly, there were initially many failures, but in time the technique was perfected and all subsequent photoreconnaissance satellite systems came to depend upon it (Ruffner 1995, 7).

No sooner was the decision made on a data retrieval system than Fairchild announced it was having design problems with the camera it had proposed to develop for the Corona satellites. At this point an unsolicited proposal came forward from Itek Corporation, which had recently purchased Boston University laboratories. Itek proposed to develop a twenty-four-inch panoramic camera for the satellites based upon a twelve-inch model it had developed for the WS-461L reconnaissance balloon program. The camera would photograph a strip of the earth's surface 10 by 120 miles at a spatial resolution of under twenty-five feet. Like most aspects of the Corona program, it would experience its share of failures as well. Many problems were related to the low temperatures of space, which, among other things, made the acetate-based film being used brittle and prone to breaking. Kodak resolved this problem by developing a new, much tougher polyester-based film. Modified versions of the Itek camera system would be used in all Corona satellites (Anselmo 1994, 6–7).

By mid-1958 the final project proposal had been forwarded to President Eisenhower for his authorization. Lockheed was selected as the prime contractor, with Itek, Fairchild, and General Electric as the project's chief subcontractors. The project was now moving along well, though it was clear that the original schedule calling for a first test in mid-1958 was hopelessly unrealistic. Bissell's final proposal called for a first test no later than mid-1959.

While the White House had made a big issue of separating the Corona program from WS-117L, much of the subtlety of this had been lost on the American public, which perceived them all as military reconnaissance projects. A greater effort would have to be made to separate the two programs, especially once the tests began since they could not be hidden from public view. Thus the satellite film-recovery system known as Corona was officially canceled and WS-117L was redesignated Sentry (and later Samos). Meanwhile, Corona was resurrected as a covert program, complete with its own cover, and renamed Discoverer (Day, Logsdon, and Latell 1998, 113). A press release described the satellite program as having a biomedical purpose—to explore environmental conditions in space—a cover story that had a definite ring of authenticity to it because it was public knowledge the United States was launching satellites into orbit as part of the International Geophysical Year (IGY) then under way.

It was in part the orbital path required of reconnaissance satellites that made it so difficult to keep these programs hidden from the public. Since the former Soviet Union was such a vast country and located so far to the north, it was necessary to place reconnaissance satellites in a near-polar orbit to obtain photographic coverage of the entire country. A missile, therefore, had to be launched either to the north or to the south, and within the continental United States there were few locations where such a launch would not take place over populated areas. One of the few places where this was not a problem was Vandenberg Air Force Base in California. A missile launched from Vandenberg went out over the Pacific, and debris from any failure would drop into the sea. Still, this region was heavily populated and no launch would ever take place unnoticed.

By January 1959 the project's designers decided that the Discoverer (Corona) system should undergo its first test. The necessary launch facilities at Vandenberg had been completed, the remote control and tracking system was in place, and the Thor-Agena combination appeared ready. On 21 January the countdown for the first test began, but the launch had to be aborted before the countdown was completed. The problem fortunately was resolved quickly, and it was thereupon determined that a schedule of one test per month of the Discoverer system should be maintained. Notes Ruffner (1995), "Beginning in February and extending through June 1960 an even dozen launches were attempted, with eight of the vehicles carrying cameras, and all of them were failures; no film capsules were recovered from orbit" (14). The causes of the failures were varied, ranging from launch malfunctions to camera problems, and the short intervals between launches did not always provide engineers sufficient time to determine the cause of the problem and how to resolve it before the next launch. Adding to the pressure was the fact that many launches were being publicized in advance by the media.

The string of failures could not have come at a more inauspicious moment for Eisenhower. In May, Francis Gary Powers's U-2 had been downed over Soviet territory, forcing the president to bring that critical intelligence-gathering program to an end. The entire handling of the incident had become an embarrassment to the Eisenhower administration and led to the collapse of the Paris Summit and along with it any hope Eisenhower may have had of negotiating a nuclear test-ban treaty. At a time of increased tension with the Soviet Union, then, the United States suddenly found itself with no means of monitoring activities on Soviet territory and with little hope it would be able to do so in the immediate future.

There were other, equally troubling concerns. Though the United States had yet to successfully test its satellite reconnaissance system, the Soviets were already reacting angrily to it. As early as 1952 "Soviet journals had sharply criticized suggestions by [Wernher] von Braun and [James] Forrestal to the effect that observation of strategic targets from space was quite feasible and most desirable" (Burrows 1986, 139). In spite of the precedent set by their launch of *Sputnik* in 1957, the Soviets began calling for a ban on all military uses of space, including photoreconnaissance. Ironically, their demands became more shrill with every failure of the Discoverer system; and when it became clear their demands were being ignored, the Soviets resorted to threats. If Soviet air defenses could down a U-2, claimed Khrushchev, they could certainly do the same to U.S. reconnaissance satellites, which were mentioned by name and mission.

At this point Khrushchev's threats were merely bluster since the Soviet Union possessed no antisatellite (ASAT) capability. However, if America's national security were to become increasingly dependent upon reconnaissance satellites, then the threat was not to be ignored. After all, the U.S. Army had been examining the feasibility of antisatellite weapons at its Redstone Arsenal facilities even prior to the launch of *Sputnik* (McDougall 1985, 49). Within a year all three branches of the armed services were exploring such weapons, but when the air force requested that it be authorized to develop an antisatellite interceptor on an urgent basis, Eisenhower refused; he did not want an antisatellite system. Furthermore, he ordered that any discussion of antisatellite weapons be heavily classified. Eisenhower concluded that given the closed nature of Soviet society, reconnaissance satellites would be of far greater significance to the United States than to the Soviet Union, so the Soviets should be given no excuse to initiate antisatellite warfare (McDougall 1985, 52).

It was one thing for the United States not to develop an antisatellite capability, but how would it protect its own vulnerable satellite systems? Because there were no technological means available for protecting U.S. satellites, Eisenhower chose to employ "politico-legal" means of doing so. His space policy was, therefore, strategic rather than tactical in nature. He intended to establish the basic legal principles that would guide space activities well into the future, and in this sense Eisenhower was very successful, using the United Nations and its ad hoc Committee on Peaceful Uses of Outer Space (COPUOS) to promote a very laissez-faire attitude toward space that was clearly in America's best interests. His successor, however, would not be so sanguine about legal protections. In 1963 President Kennedy would establish two antisatellite installations in the Pacific— one on Johnston Island and the other on Kwajalein; they would remain in operation until the ABM Treaty was signed in 1972.

On the tactical level Eisenhower did not enjoy the same success, largely because he failed to appreciate the powerful symbolic role that space played during the cold war. The United States was not involved in any space race, Eisenhower constantly reiterated, and would not engage in space "stunts." Thus appearing to downplay the importance of space, he presented the Soviets with diplomatic advantages that they eagerly seized upon to feed the crisis atmosphere in the aftermath of *Sputnik* (Peebles 1997, 11).

While pursuing his international initiatives, Eisenhower also had domestic political concerns with which to contend. During his term in office he had become especially exasperated with the air force because of its constant bickering with the CIA over budget appropriations, control of the photoreconnaissance systems, and annual estimates of Soviet military capabilities. The air force had also displayed a willingness to lobby Congress directly when the president refused to support its budget requests. This had happened during the period of the so-called bomber gap, when the air force had successfully pressured Congress for more B-52s than Eisenhower had considered necessary, and was repeated near the end of Eisenhower's second term, when Congress, after intense lobbying by the air force, provided more funds for the Samos Project than Eisenhower had requested.

Finally, in the aftermath of the Powers incident, which caused him so much personal embarrassment, Eisenhower authorized a study of the entire intelligence community. At the conclusion of its work, the Joint Study Group, as its members were collectively known, presented Eisenhower and his National Security Council with a number of recommendations, two of which were adopted just days before Eisenhower left office. One was creation of the Defense Intelligence Agency, the function of which was to coordinate the intelligence requirements of the entire military community; the other was creation of the National Photographic Interpretation Center, which was to serve the imagery requirements of the entire intelligence community but would be administered by the CIA.

As President Eisenhower labored to leave America's photoreconnaissance program on a firm footing, testing of the Discoverer system continued. August would represent the turning point in the test series, and for the first time Eisenhower would begin to see his patience in the program rewarded. During the second week of August, *Discoverer 13* was launched. The test did not include a camera system, but it did carry an American flag. Everything about the flight went well, except that the empty film capsule came down outside the recovery zone. Nevertheless, the splashdown was sufficiently close to the zone that the capsule was recovered before it sank, making it the first object ever to be orbited and recovered from space. "This American space 'first,'" Ruffner notes, "beat the Russians by just nine days" (1995, 22).

The success of *Discoverer 13* was a prelude to the program's greatest achievement, which was to occur just one week later. On 18 August *Discoverer 14* (the ninth test to include camera and film) successfully carried an Itek camera with twenty pounds of film into space. On its seventeenth pass the SRV was ejected and became the first midair recovery when it was hooked by a C-119 piloted by air force captain Harold E. Mitchell on his third pass over the descending chute. Ironically, it was Mitchell who had failed to catch *Discoverer 13*'s recovery vehicle, requiring it to be fished out of the Pacific by the navy (Ruffner 1995, 24). The film from *Discoverer 14* was quickly developed and rushed for analysis to PIC (soon to be NPIC), where interpreters found the photographs lacked the high quality and spatial resolution of U-2 (Talent) photos but compensated for this by providing coverage of areas of the Soviet Union never reached by U-2 aircraft. By any measure *Discoverer 14* was a highly successful test, but as its designers clearly recognized, similar successes on future missions could not as yet be assured.

The real success of *Discoverer 14* was, of course, the intelligence it provided. Mission 9009 made eight north-south passes over the Soviet Union, acquiring three thousand feet of photography, 25 percent of which was cloud-free. The quality of the cloud-free portion was very good, with a spatial resolution of twenty-five to thirty feet. According to the OAK Report of Mission 9009, coverage included "the Kapustin Yar Missile Test Range (KYMTR), the western portion of the presumed 1,050 nautical miles impact area of KYMTR, twenty newly identified hexadic SA-2 surface-to-air missile sites and six possible SA-2 sites under construction, the Sarova Nuclear Weapons Research and Development Center, several new airfields, and numerous urban complexes" (Ruffner 1995, 120). Although the areal coverage was obviously limited, no evidence was found to support the claim of a "missile gap."

In early August at the request of the president, Allen Dulles, the DCI, had established a new organization to coordinate overhead reconnaissance requirements for the Soviet Union and other denied areas. Composed of representatives from the U.S. Intelligence Board, the Committee on Overhead Reconnaissance would replace the previous committees that had handled U-2 overflights. As its first task COMOR had to establish security procedures for handling the new satellite reconnaissance materials. It was determined that these materials would be tightly held and bear the designation Talent-Keyhole (TKH).

While there would be several more Discoverer launches during President Eisenhower's remaining months in office, there would be only one more success. *Discoverer 18*, launched on 7 December, remained in orbit for three days before the recovery vehicle was snatched in midair following its ejection on *Discoverer's* forty-eighth pass. This was the first successful mission employing a slightly modified version of the original C camera. Referred to as C Prime or C' (there would later be a C Triple Prime or C'''), the camera produced photos of high quality. Among the targets for which coverage was obtained were the missile test centers at Tyuratam and Sary Shagan. It would not be until early 1962 that launches would become consistently successful. In fact, between the launch of *Discoverer 18* and the last Discoverer mission, *Discoverer 38*, there were twenty launches, two of which were radiometric missions in support of the Corona cover story. Of the eighteen launches for reconnaissance purposes, only seven were considered complete successes! Nevertheless, those seven provided photo coverage of nearly twenty million square miles of the earth's surface, the bulk of it behind the Iron Curtain.

In addition to the Corona system, two related reconnaissance systems were developed at this time. Argon was a system for acquiring precise geodetic data for use by the U.S. Army Map Service in pinpointing strategic targets within the Soviet Union. Between February 1961 and August 1964 twelve Argon missions were attempted, six of which were successful. These missions were all flown independently, but after August Argon missions tended to be piggybacked on Corona satellites in order not to tie up the launch facilities at Vandenberg (McDonald 1995, 694). A second system, Lanyard, was developed with a camera designed for the Samos system. With a sixty-six-inch focal length this camera system was expected to provide high-resolution photographs of the intelligence community's highest priority targets. Three missions were attempted, but only one was even partially successful (Ruffner 1995, 31). Although the photos acquired by the Lanyard system achieved a spatial resolution of under ten feet, these results were deemed unsatisfactory and the program was terminated.

While the specifics of reconnaissance satellite missions were always kept highly secret, there was a certain openness about launch activities that dated from the Eisenhower administration. By the time Kennedy became president, this policy was under review; there was a growing concern that too much openness surrounding these missions might just encourage the Soviets to again protest these overflights as a violation of international law. As early as January 1961 Kennedy ordered that information on upcoming launches be significantly reduced, but to his great irritation the air force continued to seek publicity for its space activities. Finally, on 23 March 1962, at Kennedy's insistence, the Defense Department issued a directive that banned advance announcements of all military space launches from Vandenberg and Cape Canaveral. In addition, this directive, which became known as the "blackout" directive, prohibited the use of project names such as Discoverer and Samos and replaced them with numbers (McDougall 1995, 65). Though there was considerable opposition to this directive, it remained in force until 1978, when President Carter officially mentioned reconnaissance satellites for the first time.

On the final Discoverer mission (9031) the Corona satellite carried a new camera system called the Mural, or M, camera. In fact, the system simply comprised two C''' cameras, one of which pointed forward, the other aft; in this configuration the system provided photointerpreters with a stereoscopic capability that enabled them to measure objects vertically as well as horizontally. As a result of the "blackout" directive the M camera system was designated KH-4, KH for Keyhole, the name given to all satellite reconnaissance missions, and 4 because it utilized a fourth-generation camera system. Retroactively, the C camera system became KH-1, the C' became KH-2, and the C'' became KH-3; Argon would be designated KH-5 and Lanyard KH-6. This terminology continued to be employed until 1985, when a new terminology for imaging systems was introduced.

Before the Corona program ended in 1972 there would be two more modifications of the KH-4 camera system, designated KH-4A and KH-4B. The KH-4A camera (also known as the J-1) was almost identical to the KH-4, but it could handle a larger film load and contained a second recovery vehicle or bucket. When the first bucket was filled it could be ejected from the satellite independently; the second bucket could either be filled immediately or be delayed for a few days (Ruffner 1995, 32). A total of thirty-six thousand feet of black-and-white photography was acquired for each mission! The KH-4B camera (also known as the J-3) provided high-resolution photos for detailed analysis of intelligence targets. "A secondary purpose," McDonald (1995) notes, "was to provide photogrammetric control data with the required geometric accuracy to assist cartographers in constructing accurate terrain maps from imagery collected by Corona" (696). The KH-4B camera yielded a spatial resolution at nadir of five to seven feet (Ruffner 1995, 37).

With the launch of the KH-4 system, the intelligence community could begin to depend on receiving photography of the Soviet Union on a regular basis. By this time most missions were successful, and since there were approximately twelve to fifteen launches per year, photography was received every three to four weeks. Even with an estimated 50 percent cloud cover for any specific mission, the yield of usable photography was immense. When the two-bucket system was introduced the amount of photography was more than doubled. In a matter of just four years there had been an increase in film capacity from twenty pounds on KH-1 to one hundred sixty pounds for the two SRVs on the KH-4A and KH-4B systems (Ruffner 1995, 32). The increasing frequency of photo coverage was nearly as important to intelligence analysts as the improvement in its spatial resolution.

From the beginning Corona missions provided a wealth of intelligence information, and the analysis of every newly arrived frame of satellite imagery became an event in itself. The most immediate impact of Corona-derived intelligence was to destroy the myth of a missile gap. Although Kennedy had made effective use of the missile gap issue as a candidate during the 1960 presidential campaign, once he became president and had access to TKH materials, he quickly recognized that no such gap existed. Kennedy responded to critics that while he had clearly overstated the significance of this issue during the campaign, he had done so in good faith; the evidence to the contrary had simply never been presented to him in the briefings he was given by CIA and Pentagon officials. He readily conceded that "Eisenhower was right in downgrading the 'missile gap' dangers in 1960" (Sorensen 1965, 612).

While the evidence provided by U-2 photography plus *Discoverer 14* and *Discoverer 18* flights suggested no missile gap existed, missions 9017 (July 1961) and 9023 (August 1961) confirmed it. Keeping in mind that NIE 11-8-59 had predicted a Soviet ICBM force of 140–200 ICBMs on launcher by mid-1961 (to which the air force had added a footnote that these numbers could increase to 385 on launcher by mid-1962 and 640 on launcher by mid-1963), NIE 11-8/1-61, prepared on the basis of missions 9017 and 9023, estimated the number of ICBM launchers at ten to twenty-five! The NIE went on to predict that this number would not change much in the immediate future. After closely examining the launch facilities identified on the imagery, intelligence analysts concluded that while several first-generation SS-6s were operational at launch sites such as the Tyuratam Missile Test Center, these missiles were too cumbersome and awkward to handle in the field to be deployed on a large scale. Deployment would have to await the development of a smaller, more easily handled missile, but this could not possibly happen before the latter half of 1962.

In deriving their estimates, intelligence analysts were taking into account the time required for testing a new missile and constructing the appropriate launch complexes. Based upon these factors they predicted that the Soviets would possess approximately 75–125 operational ICBMs by mid-1963. At this point the pace of Soviet ICBM deployment would depend in large part upon U.S. actions, although it was assumed that the Soviets had every reason to deploy a force of several hundred missiles as quickly as possible. Several of Kennedy's advisors argued that the United States should cut back on its own deployments, especially of the Minuteman and Polaris missiles. Kennedy was not convinced, but the arguments influenced Kennedy's defense secretary, Robert McNamara, who in time would begin to slow the deployment of U.S. missile systems.

What the imagery from the two Corona missions revealed was the existence of five ICBM complexes under construction, only three of which had previously been suspected on the basis of Talent and SIGINT (signals intelligence) information (there were other suspected sites not covered by these missions). The three previously suspected sites were located at Plesetsk (northwest of Moscow), Yur'ya (northeast of Moscow), and Verkhnyaya Salda (in the Urals); the two new complexes were both located several hundred miles to the east of Moscow—Yoshkar Ola and Kostroma. All five were located in remote, densely wooded areas where observation from the ground would be difficult. However, the launch sites were all very vulnerable from the air, so SA-2 surface-to-air missile sites were being constructed around them. At this point in time missiles were not "hardened" inside underground concrete silos but were "soft," either being housed in unprotected support buildings or standing on launch pads.

While the five complexes appearing on the imagery differed in terms of their stages of construction, they nevertheless bore a close resemblance to launch installations at test centers. Deployed ICBM complexes were very large, with multiple launch pads and extensive support facilities for the handling, erecting, and fueling of the missiles; they were also rail served. Later, when stereo imagery became available, analysts could actually see the excavations for missile silos and the trenches for the underground cables as the Soviets moved to harden their launch sites. Since each type of missile had its own particular configuration of roads, support buildings, and launch facilities, the detection and identification of missile complexes became relatively easy. What never became easy was determining whether the silos actually contained missiles or whether the support buildings held additional missiles for use in a second salvo. This difference between missiles and launchers would often lead to vast discrepancies in the estimates of Soviet ICBMs derived by the CIA and DIA. It was also the reason the 1972 SALT I agreement limited ICBM silos and SLBM tubes rather than actual missiles, since the former could be verified while the latter could not.

The Corona missions may have confirmed there was as yet no ICBM gap, but they also revealed that the Soviets were in the midst of a large-scale deployment of medium-range (seven hundred and eleven hundred nautical miles) ballistic missiles. In a belt stretching from the Baltic to the Black Sea, that is, within easy range of NATO countries, approximately fifty sites with a total of two hundred launch pads were confirmed. Support buildings within the complexes were determined to house perhaps as many as two additional missiles per launcher. Since these facilities were so vulnerable to air attack, they were each defended by SA-2 surface-to-air missile batteries (Ruffner 1995, 145).

The estimate of operational MRBM launchers was even higher. Since many areas in the west were cloud-covered on both missions, it was estimated on the basis of other information that another 25 sites were located there, bringing the total number of launchers in the west to about 300; of this number 200–250 were thought to be operational. Another 50 launchers—targeted primarily on China, though some were also aimed at American bases in Japan, South Korea, and the Philippines—were suspected to exist in a swath extending from the Caucasus to the Pacific. In addition to these missile sites, a third configuration of support buildings and roadways had been identified that led intelligence analysts to conclude the Soviets were about to deploy a new ballistic missile, this one with an estimated range of two thousand nautical miles. Depending on the speed with which this new intermediate range missile (IRBM) could be deployed, the Soviets might have as many as 350–450 operational launchers by 1963 (Ruffner 1995, 146). The magnitude of this deployment clearly caught intelligence analysts by surprise, though U-2 photography had certainly provided some indication of what the Soviets were up to; it also should have served as a warning of what they might expect concerning the deployment of ICBMs.

NIE 11-8/1-61 made clear that long-range estimates on the future pace of Soviet ICBM deployment would be heavily influenced by the international political climate and U.S. defense policies, both of which were rapidly changing even as the estimate was being prepared. During August without warning the Berlin Wall went up; two weeks later, before the West had fully recovered from that surprise, Khrushchev pulled another by unilaterally breaking a moratorium on nuclear testing with a new series of tests. The following summer Khrushchev began a major buildup of Soviet forces in Cuba, culminating in the October missile crisis. Faced by what Kennedy could only interpret as a calculated test of his toughness and his willingness to use the military force at his command, he responded by dramatically increasing defense spending and strengthening U.S. military forces abroad. By 1963 at the time of his death, Kennedy's military buildup had cost "$17 billion in additional appropriations" (Sorensen 1965, 612).

The Cuban missile crisis would have a major impact upon Soviet defense policy. Humiliated by having to dismantle its missile sites and return them to the Soviet Union under the scrutiny of U.S. military forces, a succession of Soviet leaders vowed "never again to be in a position in which on military calculations alone they could be outfaced by America" (Ranelagh 1986, 488). To make this a certainty, the Soviet Union embarked on a massive program to surpass the United States in military strength: "This meant first, a permanent increase of ground forces to something over four million men. . . . It also meant the creation of a world class navy—and especially a submarine fleet—capable of operating in all the oceans of the planet. It meant, finally, nuclear and ballistic parity with the United States" (Malia 1994, 371). So began an arms race that would last for a quarter of a century and end only when it became clear to a new generation of Soviet leaders that their country did not have the economic capacity to sustain such a contest.

Ironically, the arms race began amidst a climate of improving relations between the United States and the Soviet Union, which by 1967 had developed into a decade-long period of détente. In the aftermath of a crisis that brought the world closer to a nuclear conflict than at any time during the cold war, both Khrushchev and Kennedy concluded that a reduction in tensions between their two nations was in order, though for reasons quite different. Khrushchev emerged from the crisis politically weakened at home and under attack abroad by the Chinese, who "thought him foolish for putting missiles into Cuba and cowardly for removing them" (LaFeber 1991, 227). He saw improved relations with the United States as a potential weapon against the Chinese. Kennedy, on the other hand, whose political influence was strengthened by the missile crisis, unwittingly played into Khrushchev's hands by turning his attention to Vietnam, where he now hoped to restrain Chinese expansionism much as he had just done with the Soviet Union in Cuba. The agreement negotiated by Kennedy and Khrushchev in the summer of 1963 to prohibit above-ground testing of nuclear weapons served to strengthen relations between the United States and the Soviet Union while angering and isolating the Chinese.

Within months of the test-ban treaty's signing both Kennedy and Khrushchev were gone—Kennedy, the victim of an assassin's bullet, and Khrushchev, the victim of a Kremlin coup. Their successors, as it turned out, were just as eager for improved relations as their predecessors. President Johnson chose to continue Kennedy's Vietnam policy, which quickly led to even deeper U.S. involvement. Meanwhile, at home he declared a "war on poverty" but remained loathe to raise taxes to pay for either of these campaigns. As the Vietnam War dragged on, Johnson hoped the Soviets would help him by convincing Ho Chi Minh to sue for peace. Unfortunately for Johnson, the Soviets had more to gain by keeping the United States mired in this conflict. Already the war had damaged the image of the United States in the Third World, where the Soviets were working to increase their influence. Perhaps of even greater importance to the Soviets was the fact that the United States was beginning to deal with them as an equal, reflecting the Soviets' improved military situation.

In July 1963 the United States launched its first "close-look" satellite, the KH-7, code-named Gambit. In order to acquire "close-look" photographs, KH-7 satellites were placed in highly elliptical orbits, enabling them to sweep in over the earth at altitudes of less than eighty miles. The resulting photographs often had spatial resolutions as high as eighteen inches (Richelson 1997, 301). Typically a KH-4 satellite would be used to provide broad-area coverage while the KH-7 would follow-on to acquire high-resolution coverage of targets identified on the KH-4 photography. By 1964 missions were averaging about one per month, and though there were regular gaps in coverage of sometimes up to three weeks, there were nevertheless more than enough photos to keep analysts busy.

And just what were analysts discovering? NIE 11-8-64 noted that the pace of ICBM research and development had increased significantly, though the authors of the report reaffirmed their belief that Soviet leaders had no intention "of matching the United States in numbers of intercontinental delivery vehicles" (Steury 1996, 192). The NIE estimated that the Soviets had approximately two hundred operational ICBM launchers, most of which were second-generation SS-7s. The report concluded that the deployment of SS-7s appeared to have ended and the Soviets were probably preparing for the deployment of new third-generation missiles. As a result of this apparent pause in deployment, the estimate for mid-1970 was in essence revised *downward*, to an ICBM force of four to seven hundred.

The critical year turned out to be 1965. For several years intelligence analysts had forecast Soviet missile deployments fairly accurately, but from the mid-1960s on they would begin to consistently underestimate them. For several months satellite photos had been indicating a significant shift in the Soviet missile program. Analysts found evidence of early warning radars under construction, of excavations for the first missile silos, and of the deployment of what appeared to be a new missile, the SS-8. They also found evidence that the pace of missile deployment was accelerating. With each satellite mission analysts detected new ICBM silos under construction; the pressure for more satellite missions intensified

From the size of the silos and the configuration of roads and support facilities it became clear that even newer missile systems were being deployed, and for the first time some of them appeared to be liquid-fueled, which shortened the time to make them launch ready. The NIE for 1965 was, therefore, a difficult one since it had to estimate the pace of deployment for three new missile systems, the SS-8, the SS-9, and the SS-11. The SS-8, it quickly became evident, was little more than a modified SS-7, but a difference of opinion arose over the SS-9 and SS-11. Analysts at DIA concluded that the SS-9 would become the chief threat to the United States because it was the heavier missile and could handle multiple reentry vehicles (MRVs). The CIA, on the other hand, decided the smaller but more accurate SS-11 would be deployed more quickly. In opting for the SS-11, CIA analysts were making the determination that Soviet leaders intended their ICBMs to be deterrent rather than first-strike weapons. The SS-9s were clearly developed for use against hard targets such as U.S. Minuteman silos, a requirement for any first-strike capability, while the SS-11s were built for survivability and reliability, qualities more appropriate for a retaliatory strike against undefended cities. Ultimately, the CIA analysts were proved correct; by September 1968 there were an estimated 520 SS-11s on launcher, compared to 156 SS-9s (NIE 11-8-68).

The year 1966 proved an especially bountiful one for the imagery community as three new systems came on line. In January the first SR-71s were delivered to the air force. Like its precursor, the A-12, the SR-71 could fly at speeds of Mach 3+ at altitudes of eighty thousand feet. It was estimated that the aircraft could photograph a thirty-mile strip extending from the East Coast to the West Coast in just over an hour. As it would turn out, the SR-71 would never be used to overfly Soviet territory, the role for which it had been originally designed. It would, however, fly hundreds of combat reconnaissance missions during the Vietnam War and conduct a highly secret mapping program of the Chinese mainland. Still, less than three dozen SR-71s were ever built, and by the 1970s wear and tear on these aircraft was beginning to take its toll. Finally, in 1992 the SR-71 was officially decommissioned though not before it had set a host of altitude and speed records. In recent years several have been returned to service, but the bulk remain in their hangars at Beal Air Force Base in California, the home of the 9th Strategic Reconnaissance Wing, which over the years was responsible for flying both the SR-71 and the U-2.

In addition to the SR-71, two new satellite reconnaissance systems were orbited in 1966: the KH-4B and the KH-8. The KH-4B provided higher resolution than its predecessor, the KH-4A; at nadir resolution was about five feet (Richelson 1997, 302). The KH-8 was a superb photographic system, as any analyst who worked with it will attest; a high-resolution strip camera with two film buckets, it produced long photos of narrow width. When the spacecraft was placed in a highly elliptical orbit (at perigee it could be as low as seventy miles), the resulting photography could have spatial resolutions in the three- to twelve-inch range. The KH-8 was thus used to monitor special events such as the testing of a new missile. Once these systems became operational, there was no further need for the KH-4A and KH-7 programs, and in 1967 they were terminated.

With these new satellite systems, analysts were able to document the rapid deployment of Soviet missiles. NIE 11-8-67 estimated the Soviet ICBM force at nearly 700 operational launchers deployed in twenty-five large complexes, a tripling of the Soviet ICBM force in just two years. By the end of 1968 the number of ICBMs on launcher was expected to reach 1,000, approximately the same number as the United States would have at that point. These figures not only exceeded the CIA's projection of 330–395 (NIE 11-8-64), but even that of the air force, 600–900 by mid-1970 (NIE 11-8-64). In fact, by mid-1970 the Soviets had nearly 1,300 ICBMs on launcher.

The intelligence community had assumed that the Soviets would deploy sufficient missiles to enable them to attain parity with the United States. Perhaps they would deploy a few more for prestige purposes so that they could, in fact, claim to have numerical superiority. Analysts, however, were guilty of what has been called "mirror imaging," that is, they assumed Soviet leaders would act much like their American counterparts and make similar decisions in similar situations. They also failed to realize the extent of the sacrifices Soviet leaders were prepared to endure to match or exceed U.S. missile deployments. As a result intelligence analysts were forced to continually revise their projections upward to keep pace with Soviet deployments. They would continue to do so until 1972, when by the signing of the SALT I Treaty the number of Soviet ICBMs would be capped at twenty-four hundred.

The missile gap that developed after 1965 was exacerbated by America's own defense policies and, especially, McNamara's decision to restrain the deployment of American missiles. Until now America's nuclear doctrine had been one of "massive retaliation" reflecting this country's overwhelming strategic superiority, and the major postwar crises in Korea, Berlin, and Cuba had been contained precisely "because the cost of pushing them beyond a certain point always appeared exorbitant to Moscow" (Kissinger 1982, 259). McNamara now believed, however, that the rapid development of Soviet nuclear forces no longer made this strategy credible; instead, he argued for a doctrine of "mutually assured destruction" (MAD) whereby both nations would have a roughly equal number of warheads in their possession. That way, if one nation were the victim of a surprise nuclear attack by the other, enough of its warheads should survive the attack that it could inflict "unacceptable damage" on the aggressor. With the elimination of the threat of surprise attack, "there would disappear as well the danger of hair-trigger decisions that might escalate a crisis into conflagration" (Kissinger 1982, 1008). In keeping with this strategy McNamara had encouraged President Johnson to slow the deployment of several missile systems as well as the deployment of an antiballistic missile (ABM) system, but by 1967 even McNamara had to acknowledge that the deployment of Soviet missiles had been more rapid than anticipated, and as a result a real missile gap was beginning to emerge (Ranelagh 1986, 489).

The alleged "failure" of the intelligence community to accurately predict the pace of Soviet ICBM deployment has to be put into perspective. Imagery analysts were able to provide the White House with an extremely accurate inventory of operational ICBM complexes as well as those under construction. Since it took months to construct these complexes, policymakers were given plenty of warning before they became operational. They could also monitor missile test centers for the development of new missiles. Analysts were immeasurably aided after 1966 by the high-resolution KH-8 satellite system. If it were placed in a highly elliptical orbit the KH-8 satellite could be brought in as low as sixty-nine miles over its intended target, producing "photographs with a resolution of between three and four inches" (Burrows 1986, 235). For an experienced imagery analyst this was almost like being there.

The problem, then, was one of projecting these activities into the future in quantitative terms, and it is the failure to do this accurately that damaged the credibility of the CIA, especially with the Nixon White House. Yet these projections required anticipating the decisions of Soviet leaders made in almost total secrecy. As Prados (1982) has pointed out, however, these projections were neither that important to policymakers nor that inaccurate. He suggests that much of the CIA's underestimate after 1966 can be accounted for by one faulty, though reasonable, assumption— "that the Soviets would dismantle the old SS-7s and SS-8s as modern silo-based missiles were emplaced." This single error would account for two hundred of the CIA's underestimated ICBM totals (198).

In the course of monitoring the Soviet missile buildup, intelligence analysts from the CIA and DIA found themselves embroiled in a number of disputes involving significant budgetary and policy implications. Given the organization of the intelligence community, these disputes were probably inevitable. Eisenhower had been the first to recognize the potential conflict of interest in having the Pentagon play too dominant a role in the intelligence-gathering process, but it was left to Presidents Kennedy and Johnson to institutionalize a larger role for the CIA. Kennedy's motivation arose from feeling he had been ill-served by the military during the Bay of Pigs fiasco. In a letter to John McCone dated 16 January 1962, he greatly expanded the responsibilities of the DCI by making him the "coordinator" for the intelligence community and the "principal intelligence officer for the President" (Leary 1984, 85). Kennedy also increased the CIA's role in the production of strategic intelligence, which heretofore had been the responsibility of the Pentagon. Ironically, though, he may have weakened the CIA's role within the National Reconnaissance Office (NRO), which he had established in September 1961.

Complete control over the overhead reconnaissance program had always been a goal of the air force. From the NRO's inception the air force been given total responsibility for the management of the reconnaissance systems themselves, but now they were pushing for greater control over the collection, processing, and analysis of the satellite data. The CIA fought back, reminding President Johnson that air force dominance of the NRO would not only mean that the acquisition of tactical intelligence would receive higher priority than strategic intelligence, but that the air force "would gain an enormous advantage in pressing its claims over those of the other military services" (Leary 1984, 87). President Johnson became convinced, and in 1965 he authorized a restructuring of the NRO that achieved the needed balance between the interests of the air force and CIA. He did this by establishing the three-person Executive Committee within the NRO, comprised of the deputy secretary of defense, the DCI, and the president's scientific advisor. The EXCOM reported to the secretary of defense, but its chair was the DCI, whose authority on the committee was enhanced by his right to appeal directly to the president any decision made by the Secretary of Defense with which he did not agree (Day, Logsdon, and Latell 1998, 154).

The expanded role for the CIA almost certainly assured the White House of greater objectivity in the assessments it received, but it also embroiled the CIA in frequent conflicts with the Pentagon over the nature of the threat posed by various Soviet activities. This frequently occurred when assessments were derived from satellite imagery. Typically, DIA imagery analysts interpreted Soviet actions more threateningly than did CIA analysts. Two such disputes occurred over the "Tallinn system" and the SS-9.

The dispute over the Tallinn system was ostensibly little more than a difference of opinion on the function of a new missile complex being constructed near the city of Tallinn on the Baltic Sea. Literally from its discovery in 1963, analysts at the CIA concluded it was an SA-5 missile complex for use against aircraft; DIA analysts, on the other hand, came to believe it was an antiballistic missile system, or at the least, a missile system that had the potential to be upgraded to one. The stakes in this dispute, however, would become very high, as its resolution would influence not only the U.S. decision to deploy an ABM system of its own, but what its negotiating position should be in the upcoming SALT talks. As so often happened in such disputes, imagery analysts often found themselves caught squarely in the middle.

The issue of ballistic missile defense (BMD) had been around for a number of years. As early as 1957 the army had been working on the development of an ABM, the Nike-Zeus, which it successfully tested in 1959; Eisenhower remained unconvinced of its effectiveness, however, and refused to authorize its deployment. In 1958 a U-2 aircraft overflying the missile test center at Sary Shagan photographed what appeared to be ABM radars under construction. Then, in 1961, one of the first Corona satellites provided evidence of a complex under construction near Leningrad that comprised features similar to those found at the Sary Shagan missile test center. Because of the location of this complex, "squarely across the planned flight corridors of American ICBMs en route to points in European Russia" (Prados 1982, 153), a number of analysts concluded it represented an element of the nationwide ABM system frequently referred to by Soviet officials. In fact, the Leningrad system never became operational, but while it was under construction it helped reinforce the growing concern that a Soviet ABM system could destabilize the nuclear balance by undermining the doctrine of "mutually assured destruction."

At about the same time the Tallinn complex was detected, imagery analysts also identified construction activities at several SA-1 sites near Moscow, which seemed to indicate these sites were being modified to handle a new missile. A few months later military attachés attending the November parade in Moscow commemorating the Bolshevik Revolution reported sighting a new high-altitude defensive missile, the SA-5, code-named Griffon. The combination of these events appeared to confirm Soviet claims that they were deploying an ABM system. Accordingly, the NIE that year projected a rapid increase in the size of Soviet ABM forces to an estimated two thousand long-range interceptors plus six to eight thousand shorter-range missiles like the SA-5 (Prados 1982, 157).

The NIE's conclusions, especially about the Tallinn complex, were not supported by a number of analysts at the CIA. For one thing, each missile complex at Tallinn was composed of three batteries of six individual launchers surrounding a single, extremely vulnerable, engagement radar. Furthermore, this radar appeared to be mechanically operated and capable of tracking only one incoming object at a time. If these determinations were correct, the system would be incapable of tracking a ballistic missile; the system had to be for antiaircraft purposes. This conclusion was reinforced when a new missile with a confirmed ABM function (the Galosh) was observed in the November 1964 Moscow parade. The CIA thereupon termed the Tallinn complex, as well as a host of other similar sites, Probable Long-Range SAM Complexes (PLRSCs). In total there would be thirty-four such complexes.

By 1966 the positions in this dispute were clarified when under intense pressure from the Joint Chiefs the DIA concluded that Tallinn was an ABM system. There was certainly evidence around to support such a contention. Soviet leaders, for example, continued to make statements to the effect they had created a reliable ABM defense. Satellite photography found no shortage of installations under construction to support Soviet claims. Three ballistic early warning radars (designation Hen House) were identified as well as new Galosh ABM facilities around Moscow; there was also evidence that construction at the Tallinn complex itself was proceeding more rapidly. DIA analysts simply viewed Tallinn as an integral part of an accelerating Soviet ABM program.

As a result of this debate President Johnson found himself under great pressure from the Joint Chiefs of Staff to deploy some type of ABM system. They were even able to go around the president and successfully lobby Congress to appropriate "$160 million for advanced preparations to support ABM deployment" (Prados 1991, 190), although McNamara would impound these funds. The Joint Chiefs took the position that the existence of a Soviet ABM system required the United States to deploy one of its own, especially in light of the ongoing Soviet ICBM buildup. The Pentagon provided members of the National Security Council with mountains of "scientific data" in an attempt to convince them that Tallinn was more than just an antiaircraft system; at a minimum, it was suggested, the SA-5 system could be upgraded to become an ABM system. In the short term the Pentagon's campaign was successful as it generated sufficient political support to force Johnson to authorize deployment of an ABM system. The system authorized by President Johnson, however, was clearly a limited one; he even went so far as to claim it was not directed against the Soviet Union but rather "against the Peoples Republic of China or to negate any accidental missile launch" (Prados 1991, 192).

In spite of the Pentagon's lobbying success, it was the CIA's interpretation of the Tallinn system that proved correct. Additional intelligence, much of it provided by the new high-resolution KH-8 satellites, confirmed that Tallinn was not an ABM system but an antiaircraft system, although analysts could never determine exactly against which aircraft it was directed. But the issue of Tallinn would not disappear. In 1968 as the United States was preparing for the SALT I talks, the Pentagon raised again the issue of whether the SA-5 system could be upgraded to give it an ABM capability; if it could, then the SA-5 should be included in the negotiations of the ABM portions of the proposed treaty. Clark Clifford, McNamara's replacement as Secretary of Defense, appeared to put the matter to rest when he publicly accepted the CIA's interpretation of Tallinn and added that financial and technological considerations made upgrading the SA-5 system highly unrealistic. In fact, the issue died away only with the signing of the ABM treaty, at which point the SA-5's NATO designation, Griffon, was "quietly changed to Gammon in order to rid the missile of identification with the earlier Tallinn dispute" (Prados 1982, 169).

A similar intelligence dispute with equally significant policy implications involved the SS-9. The dispute began in 1964 when photography from the new KH-4A system revealed that the Soviet Union was testing

a massive new missile, the SS-9, that was capable of carrying a 10,000-
to 15,000-pound payload a distance of seven thousand nautical miles
(McDonald 1995, 703). Within the intelligence community a debate arose
over the mission of such a huge missile. One theory that gained considerable support was that the SS-9 had to deliver a warhead with sufficient
destructive power to compensate for its lack of accuracy. A few analysts
saw the SS-9 as a first-strike missile that could be used "to attack U.S.
launch control centers, each of which controlled ten of SAC's Minuteman
missiles" (Prados 1982, 204). Others saw it as a counterforce weapon, to
be employed against an aggressor's cities if the Soviet Union were the victim of a surprise attack. In general, analysts at the CIA supported the counterforce theory.

Deployment of the SS-9 began in 1965, and for imagery analysts the
task of monitoring construction was made easier by the fact that the silos
were so large. Before the end of the year analysts had detected a total of
"sixty-six SS-9 silos under construction" (Prados 1982, 205). Since at this
point the United States was already involved in the development of a missile system capable of handling multiple independently targetable reentry
vehicles (MIRVs), it was assumed that the Soviets were also working on
such a capability. While no evidence could be found to suggest the Soviets had developed MIRV technology, there was general agreement within
the intelligence community that once they did possess it, the SS-9 would
be the likely carrier for a MIRV warhead.

It was the CIA's contention at this time that the Soviet Union was far
behind the United States in MIRV technology. On the other hand, Pentagon officials began to claim that the SS-9 was intended to be MIRVed
and pressured analysts at DIA to support their position. In addition they
now pressed the Johnson administration to support "a larger American
MIRV program but also improved missile defenses" (Ranelagh 1986, 492).
These requests, however, were not well received by Secretary of Defense
McNamara, who tended to accept the CIA's interpretation. For one thing,
the costs of the Vietnam War were escalating rapidly as American involvement deepened there and McNamara did not want to add to them the billions of dollars that a runaway arms race would require. For another,
McNamara did not want anything to interfere with his policy of "mutually assured destruction"; he did not, in other words, wish to see the

United States get too far out in front of the Soviet Union in terms of missile development. Ultimately, the pressure from the Pentagon became too great, and he found himself with little choice but to recommend that President Johnson authorize the MIRVing of the Polaris A-3 and the Minuteman III missiles.

By October 1967 imagery analysts had confirmed 114 operational SS-9s on launcher. CIA officials found themselves under such great pressure to acquire information on the SS-9 that they directed U.S. reconnaissance satellites to pass over the Soviet Union 117 times during the first six months of 1968, "including forty-one consecutive days in January and February when the CIA thought an SS-9 test at Tyuratam was imminent (Prados 1982, 208). Still they found no evidence that the SS-9 was MIRVed. In fact, they concluded that even if the Soviets decided to MIRV the SS-9, it would require two to three years of testing, which would not go undetected.

In August 1968 the Soviets began testing a modified SS-9 carrying three individual warheads or MRVs; in total there would be about twenty such tests conducted over the next two years. The CIA would claim that in none of these tests were the reentry vehicles shown to be independently targetable; the Soviets, the CIA concluded, had yet to develop a MIRV capability. Not to be denied in this debate, the air force now suggested that the SS-9 could become the "functional equivalent" of a MIRV if the Soviets could only "delay the separation of each reentry vehicle from the launching platform for seconds or fractions of a second, they could alter slightly the ballistic paths of each successive one" (Prados 1982, 208). While the system was still not technically a MIRV, it would have much the same effect. The military did not stop here, however; it was further suggested that the impact pattern of the warheads, its "footprint," resembled the configuration of silos in a Minuteman missile complex (Prados 1982, 209). The Pentagon claimed the SS-9 was, therefore, a first-strike weapon aimed at America's Minuteman sites and an ABM system to protect these sites was an immediate necessity.

When Richard Nixon took over the Oval Office in January 1969 he found himself facing a real missile crisis, not the mythical one that had contributed to his political defeat by Kennedy in 1960. He became quickly convinced that the United States needed an ABM system to shield itself from the Soviet missile threat, but he also realized he would have to first gain congressional support for the idea. In March Secretary of Defense Laird initiated the campaign by announcing that "the Soviet Union had embarked on an arms buildup that would enable it to wipe out U.S. defenses in a single strike" (Andrew 1995, 355). While his comments clearly applied only to America's land-based missiles, he chose not to clarify the issue since the basis of his claim was the SS-9. At the same time the CIA found itself under great pressure from the White House to change its estimate; after all, its failure to accurately forecast Soviet missile deployments had in part contributed to this crisis. Could CIA analysts once again be underestimating Soviet strategic capabilities?

After several months of reexamining the available intelligence, a new NIE (11-8-69) that appeared to have the support of the intelligence community was produced. The update reiterated the CIA estimate that the SS-9 was not a MIRVed system and claimed that a highly accurate MIRV system could not be made operational before the mid-1970s, or 1972 at the earliest. In what turned out to be its most controversial statement, it added that the Soviets would not achieve a first-strike capability during the period covered by the NIE. Laird was furious because it contradicted statements he had made to the Senate Foreign Relations Committee. He demanded that the DCI, Richard Helms, withdraw the statement on first-strike capability, which Helms did reluctantly and to the great frustration of intelligence analysts, who felt they were now under pressure to make their estimates conform to White House policy. However, George Denney Jr., the State Department's acting director of the Bureau of Intelligence and Research, inserted a footnote to the final document that he did not see how the Soviet Union "would be able within the period of this estimate to achieve a capability to launch a surprise attack against the United States with assurance that the USSR would not itself receive damage it would regard as unacceptable" (Steury 1996, 261).

In spite of Helms's action, the Nixon White House continued to believe the CIA was understating the Soviet military threat and undermining the administration's case for deploying an ABM system. President Nixon publicly rejected the CIA's estimate of the SS-9: "He had not told them that a tailored Estimate was an element in his strategy to bring the Russians to the negotiating table and ultimately frighten people sufficiently about the prospects of a nuclear strike to enhance the magnitude of his achievement for peace and give the impression that he had secured major concessions from the Russians after twenty years of cold war" (Ranelagh 1986, 541). Accordingly, Nixon went ahead and authorized the deployment of the Safeguard ABM system, and although it won Senate approval, it required the vote of Nixon's vice president, Spiro Agnew, to do so.

The CIA would continue to stick by its estimate of the SS-9, and in time the agency would be proved correct. The SS-9 was never MIRVed; the Soviet Union would not conduct its first test of a MIRV system, the SS-18, until August 1973. When, in fact, the Soviets began to deploy a MIRV system, it was not until December 1974 (very close to the mid-1970s date projected by NIE 11-8-69), and it was not the SS-18, but with its successor, the smaller SS-19. Furthermore, the accuracy of the SS-9 was never improved, so concern over its three warheads being the "functional equivalent" of a MIRV dissipated. On the other hand, there were costs to being correct and not supporting the White House. The CIA lost prestige with both the Pentagon and the White House. Nixon, who believed the CIA was there to serve the president, was angered by the independent stance it adopted and would not give Helms the access to the Oval Office that the DCI had enjoyed with previous presidents (Ranelagh 1986, 498–99).

By the time Richard Nixon became president, the Corona program was already in the process of being phased out to make way for newer generation systems. From 1970 to the final Corona launch on 25 May 1972, there were only eight missions, all KH-4Bs; four would take place in 1970 and two each in 1971 and 1972. During this period three new systems would become operational—the third-generation KH-7 and KH-8 systems in 1966 and the fourth-generation KH-9, known as the Big Bird, in 1971. All three of these systems would have improved capabilities over the various systems comprising the Corona program.

For an interim system, Corona reconnaissance satellites compiled an impressive list of intelligence achievements. Because they provided photographic coverage of literally the entire Soviet Union, imagery analysts were able to amass a fairly complete inventory of all Soviet ICBM, IRBM, MRBM, and SAM complexes. Repetitive coverage of missile test centers and production facilities enabled analysts to determine what was being developed, when it was being deployed, and how long it would take to become operational. A similar inventory was prepared for other strategic weapons, such as long-range aircraft and nuclear (and nonnuclear) submarines. These types of data were used to generate target maps for SAC's bomber pilots, complete with access and egress routes free of SA-3 and SA-5 missile batteries. They were also required for the strategic analyses that formed the critically important national intelligence estimates. Finally, Corona-derived data put to rest the myth of the "missile gap" and helped resolve the debates over the SS-9 and the Tallinn system.

It was the Corona satellites that provided the conclusive evidence during the late 1960s of the rapid Soviet deployment of newer and bigger ICBMs along with the ABM systems to defend them. While Corona satellites may have paved the way for arms control, though, they were inadequate for the tasks before them. Effective arms control monitoring required photography of a higher resolution than provided by Corona's cameras. The primary mission of reconnaissance satellites was not arms control monitoring anyway but rather to provide early indication and warning (I&W) of a surprise Soviet attack against either the United States or NATO forces in Europe. Corona's cameras could produce moderately high resolution photos, but four to five days were still required to get the film from the Pacific Ocean to Eastman Kodak for processing and then to NPIC for analysis; and in between missions there were often gaps of two to three weeks when no new photography was acquired. This situation made I&W impossible.

What was needed, then, was a high-resolution system capable of providing photography or imagery on a near-real-time basis. In fact, the CIA was already developing such a system. Unfortunately, the money to develop the new system had to be drawn from the budgets of the KH-8 and KH-9 programs, "thereby cutting into actual coverage of the U.S.S.R. at a time when several ballistic missile systems were being tested and deployed" (Burrows 1986, 243).

# → 5

# Imagery and Arms Control

In 1969, after a close presidential race in which he had charged the previous administration with endangering America's national security by doing little to challenge the buildup in Soviet military forces, Richard Nixon entered the White House. Essentially, Nixon wanted to create a more stable and predictable strategic environment without compromising America's military strength, but after eight years in Vietnam, "the American economy was feeling the strain of paying for a major military effort out of peacetime fiscal measures." Furthermore, "Congress and the country were clearly not receptive to costly new strategic force programs" (Ranelagh 1986, 505–6). In such circumstances Nixon's only alternative was to try slowing the deployment of strategic weapons on both sides until the United States had extricated itself from Vietnam, but this necessitated the cooperation of the Soviet leadership.

To the surprise of the Nixon administration, Soviet leaders appeared eager to improve relations with the United States and made clear their willingness to discuss a wide range of issues; Vietnam, however, was not one of them, since the Soviets saw U.S. involvement there as the only credible impediment to Chinese expansion into Southeast Asia. The strategic arms race was placing a heavy burden on the Soviet economy, although Moscow was not about to express this openly. From 1967 to 1977, for example, the Soviets were spending about 12 percent of their GNP on

124

but
verify

defense, a figure about twice that of the United States (Payne 1980, 69). The Soviet leadership's highest priority was for an agreement that would limit or eliminate ABMs, which were seen as both expensive and destabilizing; there was little interest in limiting offensive weapons for which the Soviets already enjoyed a numerical advantage. The Nixon administration insisted that the two had to be linked, and a compromise by which in return for an ABM treaty the Soviets agreed to accept short-term constraints on new ICBM deployments was finally reached. The United States, however, "had to accept a higher limit on Soviet offensive missiles than its own" (Payne 1980, 75).

The 1972 Interim Agreement freezing the deployment of additional ICBMs for a period of five years and the ABM Treaty prohibiting the construction of nationwide ABM systems were historical achievements. "Not even Eisenhower, by far the Cold War president most committed to putting a cap on the arms race, had been able to get anything as remotely concrete as Nixon had achieved" (Ambrose 1989, 442). Tragically, the Nixon administration, and in particular Henry Kissinger, oversold both Congress and the American people on what these agreements would, and would not, accomplish. When the Soviets continued to make qualitative improvements in their strategic missile forces, including the MIRVing of some missiles, Kissinger attempted to hold back this information for fear that the ensuing political fallout might make the continuation of SALT II discussions impossible. Inevitably, the information leaked out, and when it did, the CIA was accused of being unable to effectively monitor Soviet compliance with the agreements; the Soviets were simply accused of violating them. The reality was far more complex.

That the two agreements were signed at all was largely the result of improvements in the capabilities of the reconnaissance satellites on both sides; neither government at this point had sufficient trust in the other to employ something as intrusive as on-site inspection as the chief means of monitoring compliance. The Soviets, especially, feared that on-site inspections would reveal far more about their strategic strengths and weaknesses than about those of the United States (Ranelagh 1986, 506). For the United States, monitoring would be the responsibility of a new generation satellite reconnaissance system, the KH-9, code-named Hexagon but unofficially dubbed Big Bird. The KH-9, first launched on 15

June 1971, weighed thirty thousand pounds, making it considerably larger than any previous photoreconnaissance satellite. The spacecraft was originally designed for the air force's Manned Orbiting Laboratory (MOL), which, as the name implied, was supposed to have astronauts on board to operate its various sensor systems. The CIA, however, was able to have the MOL program killed on the grounds of its vulnerability to attack by Soviet antiballistic missiles (Burrows 1986, 236); it then received White House authorization to use the MOL spacecraft design for the KH-9 system.

Like the MOL, the KH-9 system was designed to include a wide array of sensors—photographic, SIGINT, and even individual ferret subsatellites. The primary sensors were a pair of panoramic cameras with sixty-inch lenses that could be employed individually or in tandem to produce overlapping photos for stereoscopic viewing. The KH-9 cameras photographed a swath of terrain 80 by 360 miles, twice that of the KH-4B, at a spatial resolution of two feet or less (Richelson 1997, 330). The satellite also carried four film buckets, compared to the KH-4B's two, allowing it to remain aloft for longer periods. When it was first launched, for example, the system had a lifetime of about 50 days, but by the early 1980s this figure had increased to 275 (Burrows 1986, 241). All systems to that point had their limitations, but the most significant of which was the time it took to get the finished photographs to the analysts: "What was needed was a single satellite that could produce uniformly high-quality area-surveillance and close-look imagery and get it down as the event being watched was happening" (Burrows 1986, 235). Such a system, however, was still a few years away.

As for the Soviets, they did not acquire their first intelligence photography from space until August 1962, nearly two full years after the first Corona photos. Their earliest photoreconnaissance satellites were called Zenit (Zenith), but like the United States they attempted to obscure their photoreconnaissance program by publicly designating all satellites as Kosmos. The first successful Zenit mission was Kosmos-7, 28 July to 8 August 1962. Several generations of Zenit satellites with a variety of camera systems would follow (Day, Logsdon, and Latell 1998, 164).

Zenit satellites were typically launched from Plesetsk and remained in orbit from eight to twelve days; only gradually did the orbital lifetimes of these satellites increase. One result was that the Soviets had to launch many more photoreconnaissance satellites than the United States; during the early 1970s the Soviets averaged thirty to thirty-five launches annually while the United States was averaging six to ten (Jasani 1987, 58–59). The major reason for the short lifetimes of these satellites was their lack of capability to eject individual film rolls; instead, the entire Soviet satellite had to be brought down within Soviet territory. One compensation, at least, was that camera systems could be reused. Whatever the differences between the U.S. and Soviet systems, the fact remained they were both capable of acquiring reasonably high resolution photography.

It would be these systems, then, because they would provide the chief means for verifying compliance, that would establish the parameters for any arms control agreement, although political considerations would ultimately shape the final document. To determine what restraints would be both militarily significant and verifiable, Henry Kissinger appointed a panel, known as the NSSM-28 Panel, composed of representatives from the NSC, Pentagon, CIA, State Department, and the Arms Control and Disarmament Agency (ACDA). As if the panel's discussions were not sufficiently complex, they took place amid the controversies surrounding the strategic weapons estimates, the SS-9, and the Tallinn system. In spite of these uncertainties, the panel brought forth a number of potentially verifiable restraints, which it then presented to the NSC.

At one of the NSC meetings with the NSSM-28, panel representatives from the CIA testified that all of the proposed options appeared to be verifiable without much difficulty, concluding that "Russian cheating would either be so minor as to have no impact on the strategic balance or else would have to be on such a scale that it could not escape detection" (Prados 1982, 229). The military, however, was not convinced by the CIA's presentation and, in fact, criticized the quality of its analysis; the White House, already annoyed with the agency over the SS-9 dispute, concurred with the Pentagon. In response, Kissinger decided to establish a new Verification Panel entirely within the NSC and with himself as chair. In time this panel would allow Kissinger to personally dominate the SALT negotiating process and bypass the military, the CIA, and even ACDA.

One of the major criticisms leveled at the CIA's analysis was that its standards for verifying Soviet compliance on the proposed restraints were insufficiently rigorous. The Pentagon, in particular, wanted to be absolutely certain that any restraints agreed upon could be effectively monitored with the photoreconnaissance satellite systems presently operational; for the summer of 1969, when these discussions were being held, this meant the KH-7 and the KH-8. More rigorous standards only further narrowed the options; verification would be confined solely to quantitative activities, that is, to things that could be clearly identified and counted. There would be no restraints placed upon qualitative activities such as the MIRV-ing of new missile systems, improving missile accuracy, or increasing throw-weight. At least for the present such activities would be impossible to monitor with any degree of confidence.

The Interim Agreement on Offensive Weapons, signed on 26 May 1972, pledged the United States and the Soviet Union to freeze the numbers of their strategic offensive missile forces, both land-based and sea-based, at the levels of mid-1972 for a period of five years, during which time a follow-on, long-term agreement would be negotiated. The missile ceiling for the United States was determined to be 1,710, for the Soviet Union, 2,400; included among the Soviet total were 308 "heavy" missiles (SS-9s and SS-18s) whose number was also frozen. In deference to the fact that intelligence analysts had no way of accurately counting individual missiles, the numbers in the agreement referred to launchers (silos or SLBM tubes).

In fact, at the time the agreement was signed, CIA and DIA imagery analysts were in dispute over the issue of nondeployed missiles. Not only was there a difference of opinion over whether there were extra missiles stored in readying buildings for use in a second salvo, as DIA analysts claimed, but some CIA analysts even questioned whether the Soviets had sufficient missiles for all of their silos. The issue would become even more contentious in the mid-1980s, when Pentagon officials would actually announce that a "warhead gap" had developed. Their claim that the Soviets had overtaken the United States in total number of warheads was based upon the dubious assumption that "the Soviets have reloads available for their full range of strategic, theater and tactical weapons" (Scott 1984, 43). Unfortunately, imagery alone was not capable of settling this dispute.

There was agreement, however, that silos were relatively easy to monitor since ICBM complexes were large structures that required months to construct. As for nuclear submarines, they too were very large and hence difficult to hide. There were also only two shipyards in the Soviet Union that built such craft (Severodvinsk on the Kola Peninsula and Nikolayevsk on the Black Sea), and they remained under constant surveillance. Furthermore, both sides had agreed not to conceal the construction of silos or nuclear submarines from the other nation's reconnaissance satellites or national technical means of verification (NTM), as they were referred to in the agreement. But even if, for example, the Soviets were able to clandestinely construct a nuclear submarine at one of their shipyards, it would sooner or later have to set out for sea trials, where it would inevitably be detected (Aspin 1979, 39).

In spite of the historic nature of the Interim Agreement, it came under heavy criticism. The major complaint was that the agreement too greatly favored the Soviets, who already held a numerical advantage in launchers but were far behind the United States technologically; now, it was argued, the Soviets were in a position to catch up to the United States in qualitative terms while still adhering to the conditions of the agreement (Ranelagh 1986, 507). Kissinger responded to his critics by claiming that the agreement did not weaken America's strategic arsenal. On the contrary, he explained, while the Soviet Union enjoyed a numerical advantage in launchers, the United States possessed a much greater advantage in the number of warheads—an advantage that would only grow in the future since the United States was already MIRVing its missiles. The Soviets, on the other hand, had yet to even test a MIRV system (Kissinger 1982, 256). Furthermore, America's "ICBMs were more precise and reliable than their Soviet counterparts, their submarines and launchers were qualitatively superior to those of the Soviet Union, and, the United States had advanced military bases near the Soviet Union" (Calvo-Goller and Calvo 1987, 38).

And this was not all. The Soviet Union in the early 1970s was building new launchers at a rate of about two hundred annually. To remain within the limits established by the Interim Agreement, nearly that number of older missiles would have to be dismantled; the United States, meanwhile, had no new ICBM system under development. As for ceilings on SLBMs, the Soviets would agree to one that allowed them to construct the number of submarine missile launchers they had already been planning, though at the time of the signing this was kept quiet (Dobrynin 1995, 216). The U.S. ceiling, Kissinger would explain, was meaningless since the Joint Chiefs did not want to build any new Poseidon SLBMs anyway;

they preferred to wait "for the more powerful Trident submarine and missile that would not be ready until at least 1978, or after the expiration of the Interim Agreement" (Kissinger 1982, 257).

The second component of SALT I was the ABM Treaty, which received far less immediate criticism because both sides had concluded that, at least for the moment, full-scale missile defense was simply too expensive and too technologically complex. Moreover, it was also becoming clear that ABM systems were inherently destabilizing because if one side expanded its ABM system, the other side would almost certainly respond by increasing the number of its offensive weapons and escalating the arms race. The United States, therefore, argued for a total ban on ABM systems, but under pressure from their military, Soviet leaders rejected this option on the grounds they already had a system under construction around Moscow. The result was a compromise: an ABM Treaty that limited each side to two separate ABM system deployment areas with a maximum of one hundred launchers per deployment area. One of these would be deployed to defend the nation's capital, the other to protect an ICBM site. However, by a protocol signed on 3 July 1974, the number of systems permitted under the ABM Treaty was reduced to one with a maximum of one hundred launchers (Calvo-Goller and Calvo 1987, 26).

The United States constructed its antiballistic missile system near Grand Forks, North Dakota, near one of its Minuteman ICBM complexes; by the late 1970s, however, the system was mothballed and has remained so ever since. The Soviets, on the other hand, elected to deploy their system around Moscow. Initially, the Moscow ABM system consisted of sixty-four long-range Galosh missiles at four complexes sitting atop reloadable above-ground launchers; they were designed to engage incoming ballistic missiles outside the atmosphere. Later, modified Galosh interceptors were placed in hardened silos and augmented by the addition of a shorter-range high-acceleration missile, the Gazelle, which was designed to engage incoming missiles once they had reentered the earth's atmosphere. Together the two systems totaled the one hundred launchers permitted by the ABM Treaty (Department of Defense 1989, 52).

At the heart of the ABM Treaty was the acceptance by both nations of the doctrine of "mutually assured destruction." By agreeing not to employ ABM systems, "each side was leaving its population and territory hostage to a strategic nuclear attack" (Ambrose 1989, 548). In such a circumstance, then, it was only natural for each side to develop its offensive capabilities. For the Soviets this meant both MIRVing and increasing the accuracy of its strategic missile forces; for the Nixon administration it meant gaining "Congressional approval of a number of new strategic programs including a B-1 bomber, the MX missile, the cruise missile, and the Trident submarine-missile system" (Ambrose 1989, 548). The ABM Treaty would, therefore, do much to encourage an arms race that the Interim Agreement was in little position to slow. In addition, SALT I would encourage innovations in missile systems that imagery analysts would find more difficult to monitor.

To manage the monitoring of the SALT agreement the intelligence community established the Steering Group on Monitoring Strategic Arms Limitations to be chaired by the DCI, who at this time was Richard Helms. The bulk of the staff work would be performed by the CIA's Office of Strategic Research (OSR). The process would work as follows: OSR would provide the Steering Group with regular reports and would immediately notify it if imagery analysts detected any Soviet activity that might be construed as noncompliance; the Steering Group would bring the matter in turn to the NSC's Verification Panel, which would determine whether the matter should be brought before the Standing Consultative Commission in Geneva, the body created under the SALT agreement "to resolve disputes which might arise from the treaty's implementation" (Dutton et al. 1990, 54). By dint of his position as chair of the Verification Panel, Kissinger had complete control over the process, but just to be certain, "Kissinger informed Helms to establish a formal procedure by which any potential Soviet violation would be referred immediately to the NSC; he wanted no written reports" (Prados 1982, 232). Kissinger knew that the reports of the Steering Group would be political dynamite "since they would inevitably confirm continuing Soviet weapons development and not the strict limitation Americans thought SALT I had established" (Ranelagh 1986, 508).

The critical role in the verification process was played by the CIA's imagery analysts; to them fell the task of ascertaining that no act of noncompliance on the part of the Soviets went undetected. Verification was, in fact, the single most important part of the SALT process, for the almost total absence of trust in Soviet behavior was "generally asserted as the foundation of U.S. compliance policy." For the United States verification was based "on the premise of distrust, that is, the assumption that states like the Soviet Union sign treaties while maintaining the option, if not the conscious intent, of secretly violating the agreements if an opportunity presents itself in the form of either complacency or irresolution in the other side" (Krass 1985, 160–61).

To monitor compliance with SALT I, imagery analysts would have to carefully examine each new batch of KH-8 and KH-9 photographs as they arrived. The priority was to monitor the construction of missile silos, ABM radars, and ABM launcher sites. They would also have to be on the look-out for any indication that the Soviets were building new submarines or missile installations. The construction on new roads or rail spurs was often the first evidence of a new missile complex (Greenwood 1973, 17). The task of imagery analysts was made somewhat easier by the Soviet system of central planning, which dictated that every facility, military or civilian, be constructed on the basis of a detailed set of norms. As a result, every SA-2 site, for example, looked identical whether located around Moscow, Warsaw, or Havana. Once an imagery analyst was taught what to look for, such facilities could be readily identified on satellite photos.

For the first few months SALT I appeared to be working as anticipated, and Kissinger was able to pursue negotiations on SALT II, which were intended to accomplish not only quantitative reductions on old weapons but qualitative restraints on new ones. Prospects for a SALT II agreement were sufficiently promising that Nixon had no difficulty winning election for a second term. In early 1973, however, imagery analysts made an unsettling discovery—the Soviets were making new excavations adjacent to launch control facilities at each of eight existing SS-11 complexes, and all of the excavations had been started after the signing of the Interim Agreement (NIE 11-4-73). What was even more peculiar about the excavations was the manner in which the Soviets were removing the earth. Rather than digging a large hole and later filling in around the new structure constructed there, the Soviets were more or less tunneling straight down, making it "more difficult to calculate the volume of the hole." When the issue of these "silos" was raised with Soviet officials they responded that the silos were "for launch-control centers that would become clear as construction continued" (Prados 1982, 234). The CIA accepted this interpretation because it appeared consistent with the

Soviet's ongoing program of hardening their ICBM complexes to increase their survivability. The activity was not considered a violation, and in time it did become clear that the silos were for the launch-control centers.

One of the critical strategic issues not directly addressed by the Interim Agreement was throw-weight, which determines the size of a warhead a missile can carry; ICBMs with a large throw-weight are referred to as "heavy" missiles. The issue of throw-weight was of concern because it was the one area where the Soviet Union enjoyed a considerable advantage over the United States; if the Soviets chose, therefore, to MIRV all their heavy missiles it would pose an unacceptable threat to America's strategic missile forces. However, Nixon and Kissinger were so unsure that Soviet compliance could be monitored, they chose to "confine verification to quantitative matters" (Ranelagh 1986, 507). This meant that instead of restricting throw-weight, U.S. negotiators would attempt to limit the number of heavy missile launchers deployed by the Soviets. And this is just what they did. The Interim Agreement not only froze the number of heavy missile launchers (for the SS-9s and SS-18s) at 308, the number under construction or already operational, but also prohibited the Soviets from converting their "light" missiles (SS-11s) into "heavies" and from replacing their old "heavies" (SS-7s and SS-8s) with new "heavies."

Even before the Interim Agreement was signed, however, the Soviets had begun an ambitious program to modernize their strategic forces, which included the testing of four new ICBMs—the SS-16, SS-17, SS-18, and SS-19. The SS-16 was a small, solid-propellant missile possessing twice the throw-weight of the SS-13 it was expected to replace. The SS-17, a medium, liquid-propellant missile, possessed twice the throw-weight of the missile it was to replace—the SS-11; it was being tested as a MIRV system. The SS-18, a very large liquid-propellant missile, had a throw-weight greater than the SS-9 it would replace; it was being tested as both a MIRV and a single-warhead system. Finally, the SS-19, a liquid-propellant missile with a throw-weight greater even than the SS-17: "It was technically a medium-sized missile measured against the monster SS-18. But by any other calculation it approached in effectiveness the 'heavy' missile limited in number to 308 by SALT I" (Kissinger 1982, 1011). Intelligence analysts predicted that all four of these systems would be deployed beginning in 1975.

Unfortunately for the United States, the only restraint to the deployment of these systems was the nonbinding Unilateral Statement added to the Interim Agreement by Henry Kissinger. The United States had tried to write into the Interim Agreement a definition of "heavies" that would include any missile larger than the SS-11 (Talbott 1984, 214). The Soviets, however, wanted no part of such a definition and let it be known, off the record at least, that they already had missiles larger than the SS-11 under development. Unable to reach agreement with the Soviets on any acceptable definition, Kissinger had added the Unilateral Statement, which the Soviets proceeded to ignore. In later years, amid complaints that the Soviets were violating the SALT I agreement, Kissinger would be accused of not making the nonbinding aspect of this definition clear to members of Congress.

At issue were two ICBMs, which the United States unilaterally designated as "heavies"—the six-warhead SS-19 and the four-warhead SS-17 (by contrast, the U.S. MIRVed Minuteman III carried only three warheads). The Soviets chose to designate these missiles as "light," which led critics of the agreement to talk about the "SS-19 loophole," suggesting it resulted from "Soviet deceit and treachery" (Talbott 1984, 214). Because no definition of "heavy" missiles had ever been agreed upon, the Soviets were guilty neither of treachery nor of violating the stipulations of the Interim Agreement.

As a sidelight to this dispute, imagery analysts discovered that the new silos being constructed to hold the SS-17s and SS-19s appeared to be larger than allowed by the Interim Agreement. Under the terms of the agreement any new missile silos constructed by either party could be no more than 15 percent larger in diameter or 15 percent greater in depth than present silos. The United States interpreted this to mean that silos could be enlarged in only one dimension, either diameter or depth; the Soviets, on the other hand, interpreted this to mean 15 percent in both diameter and depth: "Fifteen percent in both dimensions created silos 50 percent greater in volume and new missiles were 40–50 percent larger than the SS-11" (Prados 1982, 236). Again the alleged violation was dismissed as a difference in treaty interpretation.

Within the intelligence community, however, concern over Soviet behavior continued to grow. Imagery of Plesetsk, where the Soviets were testing the solid-propellant SS-X-16, revealed that tent material was being employed to hide certain activities associated with the missile tests. One view was that the Soviets were developing a mobile version of the SS-X-16. If that proved to be the case and such a missile were deployed, it would constitute a violation of one of the unilateral declarations made to the Interim Agreement by the United States. Though this declaration, too, was nonbinding, the United States hoped the Soviet Union would abide by the declaration's intent. Unfortunately, many in Washington did not fully understand the nonbinding nature of unilateral declarations (an ambiguity Kissinger did nothing to dispel). The Soviet penchant for ignoring these declarations, then, only served to strengthen the perception that the Soviets were using the Interim Agreement to gain some strategic advantage over the United States.

For his part, Kissinger did everything possible to limit the public's access to information on Soviet activities under the Interim Agreement for fear it would jeopardize the success of the ongoing SALT II negotiations. His use of "holds" on classified intelligence reports, meaning they could not be distributed, was his primary means of doing so. Alleged violations were often raised with the Soviets by back-channel means of communication to keep them from being made public. Unfortunately for Kissinger, knowledge of his actions began to leak out, and it had the effect of making people imagine the worst about Soviet behavior. The intelligence community, and especially its imagery analysts, were caught squarely in the middle of Kissinger's deception. Though they had a very clear picture of the extent of the Soviet arms buildup, under Kissinger's orders they could say nothing about it. Their silence added to the suspicion that there was a coverup going on and that U.S. reconnaissance satellites were not up to the task of monitoring Soviet compliance with the SALT I Treaty.

In fact, imagery analysts had concluded that the large-scale deployment of ICBMs had largely come to an end; by mid-1974 there were just over sixteen hundred launchers deployed, about fourteen hundred of which were operational. From this point on the Soviets would be emphasizing the replacement of older systems with newer, more powerful missiles. In addition, the silos being constructed to house these new systems were being made several times harder than the ones they replaced, thus making them much more difficult to destroy. Evidence was also plentiful that the Soviets were modernizing their fleet of nuclear submarines. They had launched a new D-class submarine with twelve launch tubes that would be carrying the new SS-N-8 missile; they also appeared to be developing a stretch version of this submarine large enough to contain sixteen to eighteen launch tubes. Then there was the Backfire strategic bomber, which was being added to Soviet Long Range Aviation and already causing a major dispute within the intelligence community over its mission. This was a modernization program unprecedented in scope and one NIE 11-8-73 concluded "involves more than can readily be explained as merely trying to keep up with the competition" (Steury 1996, 325).

In what would turn out to be his final foreign policy initiative, President Nixon would travel to Moscow in June 1974 in the vain hope that a SALT II agreement could be reached. From the U.S. perspective it was not an auspicious moment for arms talks. Nixon was negotiating from a position greatly weakened by impeachment charges, which would lead to his resignation within two months of the Moscow Summit. As Soviet ambassador Anatoly Dobrynin has described it, Nixon "let Kissinger conduct the major portion of the talks and discussions, although he would tersely state the American position at crucial moments. But most of the time he appeared brooding, absorbed in his thoughts" (Dobrynin 1995, 313). Little progress was made, though Nixon took the occasion to invite Brezhnev to meet with him again later in the year in an effort to reach an accord. Brezhnev accepted.

On 8 August 1974 Richard Nixon resigned as president of the United States and was replaced by his vice president, Gerald Ford. The new president promptly notified Brezhnev that he intended to continue Nixon's policy of improving relations between the two countries and as one indication of this he would be keeping Henry Kissinger on as his secretary of state and national security advisor. The centerpiece of the U.S.-Soviet relationship was obviously the SALT negotiations, which had been slowed by Watergate and Nixon's subsequent resignation, but there were now added pressures for reaching an agreement. For one thing, the Interim Agreement was about to expire, and for another, Ford was already thinking ahead to his 1976 presidential campaign and his need for a foreign policy achievement of some kind. He quickly, therefore, agreed to meet with Brezhnev in the Soviet Far Eastern city of Vladivostok to negotiate the outlines for a SALT II agreement.

The summit took place in December, barely four months after Ford had become president. The meetings lasted two days with, once again, Henry Kissinger playing the leading role, since he was far more familiar with the issues than Ford. At the end it was agreed to limit the number of strategic weapons for a period of ten years. The Vladivostok Accord, as it became known, set aggregate limits of 2,400 for intercontinental bombers and single-warhead launchers and 1,320 for MIRVed launchers. Symbolically, the accord was important because it provided some badly needed continuity to the SALT process, but as it turned out, it did nothing to calm its critics. The greatest uproar was caused by the aggregate limits because they were based upon the principle of strategic nuclear equality. The notion of military parity was one most Americans were simply not prepared to accept, but just as important, the accord left unsettled exactly what delivery systems should be counted toward the aggregates. In question were SLBMs, cruise missiles, U.S. F-111 fighter-bombers based in Europe, and the Soviet Backfire bomber, which now became the focus of a major dispute within the intelligence community when it was charged that Kissinger had allowed the Soviets to exclude it from their aggregate.

The Tu-26, or Backfire, bomber was first spotted on satellite imagery in 1969 at an airframe plant in Kazan; at the time it was described as a "supersonic medium bomber" (Prados 1982, 258). Over the next two years, as several prototypes were identified, more was learned about the aircraft. While more than twice as fast as either the Bear or the Bison bombers, it was smaller and judged to have a considerably more restricted unrefueled combat radius. Although this radius could not be determined precisely, NIE 11-8-72 concluded that the Backfire was best suited for operations in peripheral theaters such as Europe and Asia. In a concession to the air force, however, a statement was added to the effect that the aircraft "might" have an intercontinental attack capability.

Once the Vladivostok Accord had been signed what had begun as a minor squabble over the estimated unrefueled range of the Backfire bomber quickly evolved into a major disagreement between the air force (supported by DIA) and the CIA. "Both the CIA and DIA scrutinized satellite imagery to analyze the Tu-26's shape, fuel capacity, altitude, in-air refueling capacity (or lack of it), weapons carrying capacity, and other factors" (Burrows 1986, 231). The DIA came to believe that with aerial re-fueling the Backfire had sufficient range to reach the contiguous United States. Analysts at the CIA, on the other hand, basically supported the Soviet claim that the Backfire could not reach American territory. They insisted the aircraft displayed no evidence that it had an aerial refueling capability, and besides, they claimed, Soviet Long Range Aviation possessed no aerial tankers. Accordingly, CIA analysts concluded the aircraft was best suited for operations against targets on the Eurasian periphery. However, since the outcome of this dispute could have a significant impact on the SALT negotiations in Geneva, the DCI agreed to have several aerospace companies independently review the CIA's and DIA's data and make their own estimates of the Backfire's unrefueled range. Not surprisingly, the data provided by DIA yielded the higher range—forty-five hundred to six thousand nautical miles; the CIA's data produced a range of thirty-five hundred to five thousand nautical miles. A range of fifty-two hundred nautical miles was finally agreed upon by the intelligence community (Prados 1982, 260).

Although the CIA never retreated from its estimate that the Backfire possessed only marginal capabilities for operations against the contiguous United States, the air force's interpretation prevailed. Negotiators in Geneva now pressed the Soviets to accept the inclusion of the Backfire in their aggregates. The Soviets, clearly annoyed by this change in negotiating position, responded by reopening several other issues, including the status of the United States' F-111, whose exclusion from the Vladivostok Accord had been linked to the exclusion of the Backfire. The Backfire issue would help stall the SALT II negotiations until well in 1979, and even then it would take Brezhnev's personal intervention to resolve the impasse. Interestingly, among the concessions Brezhnev made to save the treaty was one that supported the CIA's estimate of the Backfire bomber. In a written declaration, which critics of SALT would claim had no legal value, the Soviets agreed not to upgrade the Backfire in any way to give it intercontinental range including providing it with an in-flight refueling capability (Calvo-Goller and Calvo 1987, 80).

The Backfire bomber was just one of a number of issues confronting imagery analysts in the mid-1970s. SALT II negotiations, at least, were stalled, but SALT I was in force and there were mounting allegations that

138

the Soviets were deliberately pushing the limits of the treaty, if not out-right violating it. To many, it appeared more that the Soviets were testing the effectiveness of America's monitoring capabilities. In most instances in which the Soviets were confronted with potential violations detected by intelligence analysts, they either ceased the offending activity or were able to explain it away to the satisfaction of U.S. officials. For example, when analysts suspected that a new SA-5 radar was being tested as an ABM radar, a violation under the ABM Treaty, U.S. representatives raised the issue at the SCC. Though the Soviets vigorously denied the claim, they nevertheless stopped the tests.

A more serious violation appeared in the making when in late 1975 imagery analysts detected four *Delta*-class nuclear submarines heading out for sea trials. If the Soviets were not to violate the launcher cap established by the Interim Agreement, then an equivalent number of launchers (SS-7s and SS-8s) would have to be destroyed. The Soviets, in fact, did not complete the destruction of the launchers in time and were, therefore, in technical violation of the agreement. When the issue was formally raised with them, the "Soviets admitted the violation and the launchers were dismantled" (Prados 1982, 242). Supporters of the SALT process believed that compliance problems like these "simply reflected the inability of any agreement to cover any contingency. Critics believed the problems reflected concerted Soviet efforts to secure unfair advantage" (Krepon 1986, 41).

In addition to these activities, imagery analysts were also monitoring those activities allowed under the Interim Agreement, which included the deployment of new systems to replace older ones. In July 1976 they counted 40 SS-17s, more than 50 SS-18s, and 140 SS-19s. All three of these systems were not only MIRVed but also possessed greater throw-weight, were more accurate, and were less vulnerable to attack, because of harder silos, than the systems they were replacing. As Burrows (1986) has pointed out, "Such precise inventories would produce national intelligence estimates that were a far cry from those of the fifties and sixties that could only refer to 'from 100 to several hundred bombers' and so forth" (242). Yet, ironically, these more precise figures appeared to do little to calm the growing criticism of the CIA's handling of the national estimates and of its monitoring of Soviet activities under SALT.

Among the CIA's sharpest critics was the director of DIA, Maj. Gen. Daniel Graham, who complained publicly that his agency's estimates were never given the same weight as the CIA's in the preparation of NIEs, though DIA analysts were often more accurate in their judgments. Higher DIA estimates were dismissed, he claimed, because they were seen less as realistic appraisals of Soviet strength than as another means of lobbying for higher defense appropriations. Graham's complaints appeared to hit their mark, and William E. Colby, the DCI, responded by appointing a joint CIA-DIA working group in which for the first time analysts from both agencies would work together as equals (Ranelagh 1986, 622).

The CIA's autonomy in the NIE process came under further attack in 1975, when George Anderson Jr., chairman of the President's Foreign Intelligence Advisory Board (PFIAB), suggested to President Ford the idea of introducing "competitive analysis" into the preparation of the Estimate of Soviet intentions and capabilities. This would be accomplished by having two estimates done—one by the CIA's Soviet experts and another by a group of experts from outside the intelligence community. The PFIAB would then decide which of the two provided the more realistic assessment. Ford chose to ignore Anderson's suggestion in 1975, but the following year he decided there was some merit to it.

The United States' bicentennial, 1976, was also a presidential election year, and Gerald Ford was facing an uphill battle in his bid to win the political office he had inherited with the resignation of Richard Nixon. Finding himself under attack both from Democrats and from conservatives within his own party for not doing enough to counter the growing Soviet threat, he agreed to have the current year's NIE prepared by means of competitive analysis—the so-called A-Team/B-Team Experiment. The A-Team was composed of Soviet experts from the CIA who would derive their estimates following established procedures. The B-Team, however, would be selected by the NSC and would comprise Soviet experts from outside the intelligence community who had publicly criticized the CIA for systematically underestimating Soviet strategic capabilities. They would be given access to the same data as the A-Team, and when they had completed their estimate they would have an opportunity to debate their conclusions with members of the A-Team. An independent panel would then hear the estimates of both teams and draw up its own recommendations.

In fact, the B-Team chose not to follow the agreed-upon approach, instead developing its own, based largely upon "the role played by ideology, strategic doctrine, and national character in determining Soviet nuclear policy" (Steury 1996, 335). In its report the B-Team made a number of criticisms of the way estimates were derived. For one thing, B-Team members felt analysts depended too heavily upon "hard" data, such as those provided by satellite imagery, while ignoring "soft" data concerning Soviet strategic concepts. Analysts were also charged with "mirror imaging," that is, assuming Soviet leaders would act much like Americans in similar situations. Thus, it was claimed, estimates consistently ignored the possibility that the Soviets might not only be prepared to fight a nuclear war but expect to win it. Finally, and not surprisingly, given the composition of the group, the B-Team was much harsher in its analysis of Soviet behavior. The report concluded that Soviet military activities made clear their determination to achieve strategic superiority over the United States. But even if they did not achieve such superiority, the Soviets would be "less deterred than we from initiating the use of nuclear weapons" (B-Team Report, 6, in Steury 1996, 371).

In the end what divided the two teams was Soviet intentions; Team B essentially endorsed a worst-case scenario, while Team A was moderately optimistic about the prospects for future arms control agreements. Both teams made their presentations before the PFIAB, and later Team B would declare that its arguments had a major impact on that year's estimate of Soviet intentions and capabilities. George Bush, the new DCI, would go out of his way to deny this, but there is evidence that subsequent NIEs were more concerned with Soviet intentions. While neither Gerald Ford nor his successor, Jimmy Carter, was much influenced by the Team B report, Ronald Reagan would be (Andrew 1995, 423). The "evil empire" approach Reagan adopted toward the Soviet Union during his first term was entirely consistent with the assessments of Soviet behavior expressed in the B-Team's report.

The same concerns that led to the A-Team/B-Team Experiment were also responsible for another flap that appeared to catch the CIA by surprise. The issue concerned Soviet civil defense efforts, which, in fact, imagery analysts had been carefully monitoring since the late 1960s. The Soviet program involved the construction of vast underground complexes intended to shelter critical defense industries along with the necessary labor force to keep them operating in wartime; many of the complexes had been camouflaged, but since analysts had been observing their construction from the very beginning, even the concealment measures had been documented. Soviet leaders had probably initiated the civil defense program in response to the U.S. strategy of "mutually assured destruction," which included industrial cities in its targeting plans as well as military facilities. These civil defense efforts were far more ambitious than anything undertaken in the United States and appeared to increase in intensity during the mid- to late 1970s, when it was estimated that over a hundred thousand full-time workers were involved in the project. Shelters were allegedly available for 10 to 20 percent of the urban population; plans called for the remainder of the urban population to be evacuated within a forty-eight-hour period (Payne 1980, 86–87).

In the early 1970s the CIA had assigned a couple of analysts to keep track of the civil defense program on a part-time basis, but it was an issue for which there was no audience, that is, until air force general George Keegan seized upon it. Keegan had already become an outspoken critic of détente and of the SALT treaties, and he saw further proof in the civil defense program that the Soviets were developing the capability to initiate and win a nuclear war. He claimed that the civilian and industrial sheltering program could be viewed as a substitute for the nationwide ABM system the Soviets, and the United States, gave up under the ABM Treaty. Consequently, the treaty was nothing more than a diplomatic deception on the part of the Soviets (Steury 1996, 359).

For a brief period, Keegan's comments made the Soviet civil defense program a "hot" issue; everyone in Washington, it seemed, was interested in it. Whereas initially the CIA had two analysts working on the problem, now an entire office became involved. By the early 1980s, however, the Soviets appeared to bring the program to a halt and policymakers lost interest. Later visits by Westerners to these shelters suggest many were never completed or at least properly provisioned, but within the intelligence community, the issue has never entirely died. Deep within the interior of Russia, in the Ural Mountains, imagery analysts have monitored for many years the construction of a mammoth underground complex. Little information on the complex exists, other than what has been gathered by satellite imagery, and the Russians have refused to comment on its purpose. The best guess among those analysts following the issue is that the complex is intended as an underground nuclear command post (Gordon 1996, 1).

For over fifteen years imagery analysts would be largely dependent upon two systems—the high-resolution KH-8 and the KH-9, which had high resolution and BAS capabilities, respectively (Adam 1986, 47). The great advantage of these systems from the analysts' point of view was that possessing a film base, photography could be enlarged many times without the image becoming grainy; on the newest light tables, for example, eye pieces were capable of enlarging portions of photos up to five hundred times. With such an enlargement capability, objects on the photography could be measured with great accuracy, be they Backfire bombers, missile canisters, or ammunition storage depots. This led to the science of "crateology," which referred to the ability of imagery analysts to fairly accurately determine what type of weapons systems the Soviets were shipping to their clients by the dimensions of the packing crates.

But for all their advantages, these systems possessed major liabilities that, critics like General Keegan claimed, enabled the Soviets to pursue certain activities in violation of SALT without fear of detection. The greatest problem was frequency of coverage; even with two or more systems aloft at any one time there were substantial gaps in coverage, not including those days when targets were obscured by clouds. Burrows reports, for example, that in 1976 there were only 248 days of coverage (Burrows 1986, 242). Analysts could go days, if not weeks, without adequate photography of their targets; only the highest priority targets received frequent coverage. It must be remembered that each satellite contained a finite amount of film, and once it was used up, the satellite was useless. As a result there was often intense competition among agencies and analysts to obtain coverage of their targets.

To these gaps in coverage, the Soviets added practices of their own to prevent activities from being monitored. Although the use of direct camouflage had largely been prohibited by SALT I, this did not prevent the Soviets from employing false targets on occasion. In the late 1970s imagery analysts detected what appeared to be a new ballistic missile submarine in the Barents Sea near Murmansk. Shortly after a violent storm had struck the region analysts were amazed to find the submarine was bent in half; it had been made of rubber (Smith 1985, 32). More commonly, the

Soviets ceased trials of new weapons systems or covered construction activities when satellites passed overhead since orbits are highly predictable. The United States would do similar things. In 1985, for example, a force of U.S. naval vessels crossed the Atlantic without Soviet knowledge "by timing their speed of transit to avoid passing satellites" (Broad 1987, C3).

One significant result of these limitations was that imagery analysts tended to focus on missile deployments rather than missile production; clearly, this had an effect on the accuracy of missile projections embodied in NIEs. Because the construction of missile complexes took months to complete and make operational, gaps in photo coverage presented few problems. However, techniques for estimating missile production had to await systems capable of providing imagery on a much more frequent basis. For example, DIA estimates of deployed SS-20 missiles made during the 1980s were reasonably close to the number provided by the Soviets under the INF (Intermediate-Range Nuclear Forces) Treaty. Analysts had identified forty-nine SS-20 shelters, each of which was built to house 9 launchers for a total of 441; the Soviets claimed 405. Though such differences tended to have little military significance, their political significance could be considerable (Adam 1988, 30).

For all their limitations, however, air force officials found themselves supporting the continuation of the KH-8 and KH-9 programs, though it would be a losing battle. The programs were already being phased out, as the CIA was drawing heavily on the NRO's funds to develop a new system of its own not dependent on film, an electro-optical system—the KH-11. The feud between the air force and CIA that erupted over this issue was anything but new. It was simply one more skirmish in the ongoing conflict over control of imaging satellites that had begun back in the Eisenhower administration. Needless to say, it had not helped that the CIA had played a prominent role in killing the air force's MOL project only to then turn around and make it the base for its KH-9 system. Or that the CIA's new system had borrowed from the air force's SAMOS system that the agency had also opposed.

The new generation system, the KH-11, was launched in December 1976; it had been under development by TRW since 1972. Code-named Kennan/Crystal, the system was developed to provide high-resolution imagery on a near-real-time basis (Dutton et al. 1990, 102). Unlike its photographic predecessors, the KH-11 was an electro-optical system, much like NASA's Landsat, which consisted of arrays of tiny charge coupled devices (CCDs) or picture elements (pixels) capable of detecting even small amounts of electromagnetic radiation reflected from the earth's surface (Burrows 1986, 243). This radiation is focused onto the arrays by a powerful telescope and a series of highly polished mirrors where voltage readings are amplified, converted to a digital format, and downlinked to antennas located at Fort Belvoir, Virginia, via Satellite Data System (SDS) spacecraft or NASA's Tracking and Data Relay Satellites (TDRSS) (Covault 1991, 25–26). The data values of these pixels are converted into gray tones and assembled into black-and-white images of the earth's surface.

The lack of dependence upon film meant that the KH-11 had a much longer lifetime than its predecessors—the KH-8 and KH-9; the operational life of early KH-11s was about three years. However, KH-11/6, launched on 4 December 1984, remained in operation until October 1995. KH-11s were typically placed in elliptical sun-synchronous orbits approximating three hundred by one thousand kilometers. This enabled any individual satellite to repeat its ground track at four-day intervals. Properly synchronized, then, two KH-11s could provide coverage of a target every other day, weather permitting (Pike 1997b). This capability dramatically increased U.S. coverage. Whereas the film-return systems had enabled imagery analysts to monitor approximately twenty thousand targets (80 percent of which were in China or the Soviet bloc), the KH-11 increased this number to over forty thousand—half of which were now outside China and the Soviet bloc (Richelson 1991, 39).

Once the KH-11 became operational, the days of the KH-8 and KH-9 were numbered; they would, in fact, be "the last in the line of distinct close-look and area-surveillance platforms" (Burrows 1986, 227). Nevertheless, until the mid-1980s the KH-8 and KH-9 programs continued to operate. Normally, two KH-11s were maintained in orbit at all times with one KH-8 and one KH-9 launched each spring (Pike 1997b). At first, KH-11 imagery lacked the same high quality of film products, but over time the gap was closed. Ultimately, resolutions of two to four inches were reported (Dutton et al. 1990, 101). With three different systems operating simultaneously, including perhaps three KH-11s, imagery analysts never had it so good in terms of frequency and quality of target coverage.

One of the unexpected bonuses of the KH-11 system occurred during its first few months of operation. Analysts working with the imagery were amazed to discover the Soviets were building a space shuttle that looked uncannily like the American space shuttle. No previous mission had photographed the spacecraft. The *Buran*, as the Soviets named their shuttle (they actually built two), turned out to be a replica of the American version because it had been copied from designs that had appeared in scientific journals. Over the years the Soviets would spend $10 billion on developing their shuttle, but they never devised a mission for it. The Soviets, concerned the American shuttle might be used to deliver nuclear weapons, concluded that they, too, must have one. The Soviet space shuttle flew only once, on 15 November 1988. Today the two *Buran* spacecraft have been mothballed and stored at Tyuratam. A "ground-test" *Buran*, however, can be found in Gorky Park, where for thirty-five American dollars a visitor can enjoy a simulated flight into outer space (Hoffman 1996).

The *Buran* had been detected only by chance; the Soviets did not realize the KH-11 was a reconnaissance satellite. Whenever a KH-9 satellite had overflown the test center where the *Buran* was being built, activities had been suspended and the *Buran* covered by netting (Adam 1986, 55). There would not be many bonuses like this. A CIA employee, William Kampiles, who had only joined the agency in March (1977), resigned several months later in frustration over his duties. In leaving, Kampiles took with him a classified document describing in considerable technical detail the operation and capabilities of the KH-11 system, which he sold to the Soviets in Athens for the sum of three thousand dollars. However, in one of the cold war's great ironies, the KGB official initially meeting Kampiles when he stepped into the Soviet compound was Serge Ivanovich Bokhan, who was, in fact, spying for the CIA. Bokhan quickly got word to the CIA about the manual, and Kampiles was arrested immediately on his return to the United States (Earley 1997, 120).

Coincidentally, the first KH-11 imagery became available on 20 January 1977, which happened to be inauguration day for Jimmy Carter (Andrew 1995, 427). The new president was shown the imagery the next day, and he expressed amazement at its quality. He quickly recognized the importance of the KH-11 system to the SALT negotiations and emphasized his eagerness to press ahead with them. His first priority, though, would have to be the restoration of America's military role in the world, which had been seriously weakened by the Vietnam War. He also wanted to reestablish America's moral standing in the aftermath of Watergate and Nixon's resignation by emphasizing a policy of human rights. In combination, these policies would serve to strain U.S.-Soviet relations and slow progress toward an arms control agreement.

The first indication that the Carter administration intended to take a tougher stand with the Soviets was a change in the U.S. negotiating position in the SALT talks. Determined to show he could produce a better arms control agreement than his predecessors, Carter ordered the Vladivostok Accord substantially revised. He especially wanted to see reductions in the size of the aggregates of strategic bombers and MIRVs, as well as in the number of heavy missiles the Soviets were allowed. In the eyes of the Soviets, at least, Carter was "seeking substantial reductions in *existing* Soviet systems in exchange for marginal cuts in *future* American systems" (Dobrynin 1995, 389). These suggested revisions were rejected by Soviet leaders, and it would require two more years of negotiations before an agreement was signed.

It would not only be the United States' tougher bargaining stance on numerical limits that would slow negotiations; the problems of verification had become more complicated for both sides. Verification under SALT I involved the counting of fairly large, and in most cases immovable, objects—missile silos and nuclear submarines. Negotiations over SALT II, on the other hand, were concerned with smaller and more mobile weapons, such as cruise missiles and mobile missiles, which both sides had an interest in protecting through dispersal, camouflage, and other techniques designed to make them unverifiable. Furthermore, there would be greater emphasis placed upon restricting qualitative improvements to existing ICBM systems. When SALT II was finally signed it included the provision that no existing ICBM system could be altered in length or diameter by more than 5 percent. Since the smallest Soviet ICBM at that time was the SS-11, which had a diameter of about six feet, the KH-11 would be expected to detect modifications in this system as small as four inches (Burrows 1986, 248). Critics of SALT doubted "it would be possible to determine whether this threshold had been crossed" (Krepon 1999, 40).

As for the Soviets at this point, they remained somewhat behind the United States in the technological sophistication of their surveillance satellites. They were still dependent upon a variety of film-return systems, but at least by 1975 the lifetimes of their missions had increased to about fifty days with the launch of a fourth-generation, high-resolution system, which carried four independently releasable film capsules and swept over North America at an altitude of under one hundred miles (Adam 1986, 67). These lifetimes were still much shorter than the typical KH-9 mission (two hundred days), so the Soviets had to compensate by launching over thirty missions per year (Richelson 1985, 92). They would have to wait until 1982 before orbiting their first near-real-time electro-optical system, though. In the meantime, they were attaining high resolutions with their photographic systems. Their demand for greater specificity in the SALT II agreements indicates they had to be acquiring photography of at least one-foot resolution, if not higher (Adam 1986, 68). This was later confirmed when in the 1980s they began marketing some of this photography in the West.

It was at about this point that a new issue arose to further complicate the already strained relations between the two countries; it involved the SS-20 missile, which the Soviets began secretly deploying in late 1976. The missile had a range of about twenty-seven hundred nautical miles, carried three MIRVs, and was mobile, that is, it was moved about on a trucklike vehicle called a TEL (for trailer-erector-launcher) and did not require fixed sites to support launches; it could also be reloaded and refired. The SS-20 had clearly been designed to avoid the restrictions of both SALT I and the prospective SALT II. With a range of twenty-seven hundred nautical miles (three thousand miles), the missile fell just short of the three-thousand-nautical-mile (thirty-five-hundred-mile) range established by SALT I as the minimum range for a missile to be designated an ICBM. The SS-20 was, therefore, designated an IRBM, a missile category on which neither SALT I nor SALT II placed any restrictions. This deployment was seen by Western leaders as just one more example of the "Soviet penchant for playing as close as possible to the edge of what is permissible under existing or prospective arms-control agreements, stopping just short of violating the letter of these agreements" (Talbott 1984, 30).

By deploying the SS-20 within the western regions of its country the Soviet leadership intended to dramatically shift the strategic nuclear balance in Europe to its favor and just possibly "break-up NATO by driving a wedge between the United States and its allies" (Malia 1994, 380). The decision, however, turned out to be a disastrous one for the Soviets since the United States already had missiles of its own to deploy against the SS-20. By December 1979 the NATO Council had accepted a U.S. proposal to deploy 464 Tomahawk cruise missiles and over 100 Pershing missiles in Europe; the latter could strike Moscow within ten minutes of launch. The proposal was later approved by the various Western European governments, in spite of a vigorous campaign directed against it by the Soviets, who claimed, among other things, that the missiles violated the SALT I agreement. Once the deployment of these missiles began in 1983, "military tensions rose in Europe, and the overall strategic nuclear balance shifted in favor of the United States" (Dobrynin 1995, 430).

As the debate raged over the SS-20s, Carter received another blow to his prospects for getting a SALT II agreement. Throughout 1978 fundamentalist forces in Iran had been openly challenging the shah's government. The U.S. government, finding itself unable to provide the shah with any substantial aid, stood by helplessly as the shah was forced from power in early 1979 and replaced by the Ayatollah Khomeini, who was brought back from Paris after a fourteen-year exile. The shah's fall was a great blow to the United States, which had invested heavily in his government. Not only was Iran seen as a dependable ally of the United States, it was considered one of the few stabilizing influences in the Middle East. While these losses would inevitably have long-term consequences for U.S. policy in the region, there was a more immediate concern for the intelligence community—the necessity of shutting down two critical NSA listening posts at Behshahr and Kabkan. These two SIGINT stations were the chief means by which the United States monitored missile tests from Tyuratam, and they were irreplaceable. It was said the stations could "intercept telemetry signals from Soviet missiles at altitudes of only 100 km" (Adam 1986, 61).

The loss of these posts did nothing to calm Senate critics of SALT. Under these circumstances Carter felt it necessary to reassure the American public of U.S. capabilities to effectively monitor any SALT II agreement. For the first time a president spoke openly of U.S. surveillance satellites, which were referred to as our "national technical means" of verification. Carter also directly intervened in the SALT negotiations. He personally discussed with Soviet Foreign Minister, Andrei Gromyko, the problems caused by the Soviet encryption of the SS-18 missile tests (Andrew 1995, 443). As a result he received assurances from Brezhnev that telemetric transmissions from Soviet missile tests would not be encoded. For his part, Carter dropped his demand for substantial cuts in the aggregate totals. The way was now cleared for an agreement, and on 18 June, the SALT II Treaty was signed by Carter and Brezhnev, in what would be their only meeting, at a summit in Vienna.

The SALT II Treaty was based largely upon the Vladivostok Accords. It established a numerical ceiling on delivery systems—heavy bombers, launchers, and SSBNs—of 2,400, a total that was to be reduced to 2,250 by 1 January 1981. For MIRV systems (and air-launched cruise missiles), the aggregate number was not to exceed 1,320, for MIRVed missiles alone the limit was 1,200, and for land-based MIRVs the limit was 820, the number possessed by the Soviets at that time (Prados 1982, 394). "Each side," LaFeber (1991) notes, "retained its high card. For the United States the card was its small cruise missile, which could fly too low for Soviet detection; for the Russians it was their 300 huge land-based missiles" (296). Both sides were restricted to the development of one ICBM and that had to be a "light" missile. Some progress was also made on restricting some of the more controversial systems such as the cruise missile and the Backfire bomber, though clearly more needed to be done. SALT II represented a significant improvement over SALT I, but it was far from perfect.

The SALT II Treaty presented far greater challenges to imagery analysts, even though each side agreed to neither obstruct the other's national technical means of verification nor undertake deliberate concealment measures, such as constructing shelters over ICBM silos. Making certain that the Soviets did not exceed the agreed upon numbers of strategic systems was little different than SALT I, only now the number of strategic bombers had also to be monitored. Fortunately, the production lines for two of the existing strategic bombers, the Bear and Bison, had been shut down so analysts could concentrate on monitoring the one plant that produced the Backfire bomber. Otherwise, there were only about ten airfields in the Soviet Union that handled strategic bombers, and they were photographed on a regular basis. Since these aircraft were all very large, they were not easy to conceal and any significant increase in their numbers would be noted (Aspin 1979, 39).

The issue of mobile missiles, an especially difficult weapon for analysts to monitor, was handled through a special protocol that would remain in effect until 1982. The protocol essentially banned the testing and deployment of all mobile missiles during this period. For the Soviets this meant ending their testing and deployment of the SS-16, a mobile variant of the SS-20; any existing SS-16s would have to be dismantled. The SS-16 posed unique problems for imagery analysts. Since the SS-20 represented the first two stages of the three-stage SS-16, it would fall to imagery analysts to ascertain that the Soviets were not secretly concealing SS-16 third stages in order to quickly convert SS-20s to SS-16s in some future crisis (Aspin 1979, 40).

There were other verification problems. Analysts had to make certain that the Soviets did not upgrade the SS-20 into a strategic weapon system. There were similar issues surrounding the Backfire bomber. Then there was the problem of detecting any attempt by the Soviets to convert a single-warhead system into a MIRV. Imagery analysts were greatly helped in this regard by the SALT II provision that any type of missile that "has been tested in a MIRVed mode or has been fired from a launcher with a MIRVed warhead would be counted against the MIRV ceiling" (Aspin 1979, 41). Furthermore, launchers of MIRVed missiles were required to be distinguishable from non-MIRVed missiles by what the treaty termed "externally observable design features" (Calvo-Goller and Calvo 1987, 55).

For all the potential verification problems, the Carter White House became convinced that the capabilities of America's NTM were sufficient to detect any cheating by the Soviets on a scale that would threaten the nation's national security. The hope was that SALT II would be quickly ratified in order that work could begin on a SALT III agreement requiring major strategic arms reductions. There would be no ratification, however; a succession of crises would now arise to make impossible not only ratification of the SALT II agreement but also Carter's reelection.

The first crisis was largely of the Carter administration's own making and involved the discovery of the so-called Soviet brigade in Cuba. NSA may have inadvertently initiated the crisis when it notified White House officials that an intercept revealed the Soviets were rotating a detachment of troops through Cuba (Andrew 1995, 445). The existence of these troops was then confirmed both through satellite imagery and through specially acquired SR-71 photography (Prados 1991, 403). Since the Carter administration had assured Congress there was no significant Soviet presence on the island, these troops presented a problem. Carter asked for a suspension of the SALT debate until they were removed. Soviet troops, however, had been in Cuba since the missile crisis in 1962, and when, after some embarrassment on the part of the intelligence community, this was pointed out to Carter, he attempted an apology. The Soviets simply interpreted the episode as an attempt by SALT's opponents to delay ratification, but, in fact, SALT's opponents interpreted the crisis as a reason for killing the treaty. If image analysts, they claimed, could not detect the presence of Soviet troops in Cuba, how could they be expected to detect Soviet violations of SALT?

The delay caused by the Cuban crisis would prove costly to Senate ratification of the SALT II agreement. On 4 November 1979, the U.S. Embassy in Tehran was seized by Muslim extremists and the diplomatic personnel taken hostage; they would be held for the duration of Carter's presidency, nearly fourteen months. An even greater blow to the treaty occurred just over a month later, when on 28 December a force of fifty thousand Soviet troops invaded Afghanistan in order to secure its southern borders "threatened by the growing instability inside Afghanistan itself and the obvious ineptitude of the Amin government" (Dobrynin 1995, 441). Carter was outraged and declared his intention to make the Soviets pay dearly for their perfidy. As one of his first actions Carter asked the Senate to postpone debate on the SALT II agreement. Ratification was probably a dead issue anyway and Carter knew it. The Senate Armed Services Committee had already sent forward its recommendation, and it included not a single vote in favor of ratification.

Carter, like Kennedy during the Cuban missile crisis, felt the Soviets had deceived him. He accelerated his arms buildup, which had begun even before the invasion of Afghanistan, and with a nod to President Truman, he announced the Carter Doctrine, which declared that the United States would intervene militarily anywhere in the Middle East if it were determined American interests were threatened. Nevertheless, Carter's popularity continued to plummet, especially after an attempt to free the American hostages in Iran by force ended in failure. By the end of 1980 détente was dead, U.S.-Soviet relations had struck rock bottom, and Ronald Reagan had defeated Carter to become the next American president. The cold war had clearly returned.

In retrospect the SALT II agreement would have been impossible without the KH-11; the KH-9 system, in combination with the United States' SIGINT capabilities, could not have provided the security demanded by SALT's numerous critics. In the end, of course, even the KH-11 could not win SALT II's ratification in the face of the Soviet invasion of Afghanistan. Nevertheless, both sides agreed informally to abide by the provisions of SALT II, which indicated confidence in the technical means of verifying compliance. While few probably believed that intelligence analysts could detect every violation, the Carter administration considered America's verification methods to be "adequate," by which it meant that any significant violation would be detected before it could affect the strategic balance (Calvo-Goller and Calvo 1987, 231).

# 6

## The Second Cold War

Ronald Reagan arrived at the White House with a foreign policy that was simple and direct: halt Soviet expansion and begin the process of "rolling back" communism with the ultimate goal of winning the cold war. Reagan made clear his view of Soviet leaders at his first press conference when he described them as a group of individuals who "reserve unto themselves the right to commit any crime, to lie, to cheat" in order to further the cause of world revolution (Dobrynin 1995, 484). His first priority, he declared, was to regain military superiority over the Soviet Union. Accordingly, he increased defense spending by 10 percent, a figure twice what he had promised during his presidential campaign (Andrew 1995, 463), and ordered a massive increase in the number of strategic weapons systems, including the B-1 bomber, a new Stealth bomber, the MX missile, and the Trident nuclear submarine. The second cold war had begun.

Reagan's view on arms control was, at least initially, one of disdain: "Part of this was the ultra-conservative complaint that Nixon, Ford, Kissinger, and Carter had given away the store" (Beschloss and Talbott 1993, 113). So while administration officials did not explicitly declare their intention to stop adhering to existing agreements, they made clear the arms control process was to be put on hold until the United States had built up its military forces and redressed the perceived imbalance in strategic nuclear weapons. Imagery analysts were kept busy monitoring SALT agreements and compiling a list of possible violations, which Reagan frequently used to demonstrate how little the Soviets could be trusted. It would be characteristic of Reagan, especially during his first term, to sound "more belligerent than he in fact was" (Ranelagh 1986, 674), an approach that tended to keep Soviet leaders off guard because they never knew which Reagan they were dealing with at any moment in time.

A critical role in Reagan's strategy of global confrontation was to be played by the CIA, which during his campaign he had promised to "unleash" as soon as he reached the White House (Andrew 1995, 459). True to his word, the agency's work force and budget would grow dramatically over the next eight years, improving its technical data-gathering capabilities as well as its ability to conduct covert operations. Probably Reagan's most significant move in creating a more activist role for the CIA was in choosing William Casey to be his new DCI. A former OSS operative, a member along with Reagan of the Committee of the Present Danger, and most recently Reagan's campaign manager, Casey shared Reagan's view that the Soviet Union represented the greatest threat to Western values. Not only would Casey come to enjoy almost unlimited access to the Oval Office in his capacity as chief intelligence adviser, but he also would become the only DCI ever to hold cabinet rank.

The NIEs produced during Reagan's first term focused heavily upon two issues—growing Soviet military power and Soviet activities in the Third World. These two issues were now combined by Casey into a new analytical paradigm that interpreted overall Soviet foreign policy as an attempt by Kremlin leaders to use the country's growing military strength to achieve a dominant position in the Third World. Casey even took the unusual step of adding a Memorandum to Holders of NIE 11-4-78, a three-year-old document, pointing out the extent of Soviet activities in the Third World. This theme would help shape U.S. foreign policy during Reagan's tenure and provide the guiding principle for the CIA's covert activities under Casey.

But it was the Soviet Union's growing strategic capabilities that remained Reagan's dominant concern, and he missed no opportunity to repeat how the Soviets had moved ahead of the United States in the arms race. In fact, the Soviets were pushing ahead with the development and deployment of new generations of ICBMs, SLBMs, and strategic bombers.

Yet the NIEs of this period were not overly concerned about the Soviet Union's developing a first-strike capability. Rather, NIE 11-4-82 concluded that the Soviets would do everything possible to avoid a confrontation with the United States because it might lead to nuclear war, which would be catastrophic for both sides. Nevertheless, the authors added, nuclear war remained a possibility, and as long as it did, Soviet leaders intended to deploy a sufficiently large strategic force "to fight and win a nuclear war with the United States" (Steury 1996, 476).

From the viewpoint of imagery analysts, the early Reagan years were a time of abundance. With the KH-11 working in tandem with the KH-8s and KH-9s (Burrows 1986, 227), the amount of imagery flowing to analysts was prodigious. To handle this flood, the number of analysts was increased, promotions were speeded up, and photointerpreters, who were once viewed as little more than technicians, saw their status in the intelligence community rise as they became "all-source" analysts. In keeping with this newfound importance, the CIA's Imagery Analysis Service (IAS), located in Building 213, was upgraded to become the Office of Imagery Analysis and relocated to agency headquarters. Even the nature of the work began to change. The nearly daily coverage of high-priority targets allowed many analysts to move beyond the traditional "bean-counting" role, in which analysts were responsible for keeping track of the number of T-72 tanks or Backfire bombers in an area, to tasks requiring greater analytical skills: estimating the annual production of machine tools, crude oil, or diesel fuel; determining what types of weapons systems were contained within packing crates being loaded onto a Libyan freighter; or assessing the capabilities of certain ground forces units for engaging in chemical warfare.

The development of new analytical techniques did not eliminate the need for bean counting, however. In the early 1980s imagery analysts continued to monitor the deployment of both offensive and defensive strategic systems. Of primary importance were the fourth-generation ICBMs—the SS-17s, SS-18s, and SS-19s. They also noted the continuing deployment of the road-mobile SS-20 IRBM and watched as new *Delta*-class and *Typhoon*-class SSBNs completed their sea trials to become part of the world's largest ballistic missile submarine fleet. As for defensive systems, the mobile SA-10 surface-to-air missile was being deployed, while a new system, the SA-X-12, with the possible capability to intercept short-range ballistic missiles was being tested. Antiballistic missile radars were being constructed around the periphery of the country, and at the Sary Shagan Missile Test Center there were indications the Soviets were testing laser weapons both for antisatellite and for ballistic missile defense purposes. It was a busy time for both the Soviets and imagery analysts.

While strategic weapons systems had to be monitored carefully because of the threat they posed to the continental United States, conventional weapons systems could not be ignored. The possibility of an attack on Western Europe by the Red Army had been the primary reason NATO had been established, and it has remained a constant in all subsequent Western military planning. The operating principle was for NATO forces to blunt an attack by the numerically superior Warsaw Pact forces long enough for reinforcements to be brought in. The critical question, of course, was the role nuclear weapons would play. Both sides believed that if a nuclear war were to occur, it would probably result from a crisis originating in Europe. Under such circumstances, then, it was imperative that U.S. and NATO military planners have as much information as possible on the disposition, capabilities, and combat readiness of the troops facing them, not to mention any indication that an attack might be imminent.

To provide such information, imagery analysts were assigned specific areas of responsibility—Warsaw Pact ground forces, air forces, or naval forces. In fact, many intelligence agencies were organized in just this manner. Analysts in the ground forces branch, for example, would be responsible for creating and maintaining data bases on the numbers and capabilities of weapons systems by military district. These data bases would include information on each type of tank, infantry combat vehicle, armored personnel carrier, helicopter, multiple-rocket launcher, and self-propelled artillery. In addition, there would be information on ammunition and chemical weapons depots, POL (petroleum oil lubricants) storage areas, and nuclear warhead stockpiles. From monitoring the types of equipment (chemical decontamination equipment, for example), associated buildings ("shed-ology"), and field training exercises, analysts could determine combat readiness and a fairly detailed order-of-battle. Critical forward bases were examined on a daily basis for any activity that might signal preparations for a military action.

The Reagan administration's decision to challenge the Soviets' growing influence in the Third World led to a number of "low-intensity conflicts" in which U.S.-backed counterinsurgency forces, or "freedom fighters," as President Reagan preferred calling them, used guerrilla-warfare techniques to harass and hopefully overthrow Communist governments (LaFeber 1991, 308). Such conflicts were waged in Nicaragua, Angola, Afghanistan, and Kampuchea. In addition to arming and training guerrilla forces, the United States also provided intelligence, much of which was acquired by means of aircraft and satellite imagery. Analysts prepared maps and annotated imagery showing the location of military barracks, ammunition depots, airfields, and government border posts. Guerrilla leaders also received information on oil pipelines, POL storage areas, communications and power lines, transformer yards, and power stations. Not only was it expected that these facilities would become targets of guerrilla attacks, but CIA advisers would often provide the means and expertise to "do the job right."

Like President Kennedy before him, Reagan was not hesitant to use aerial and satellite photos to educate the public about Soviet military activities in the Third World. Declassified photos of Soviet military facilities appeared in a series of glossy publications produced by the State and Defense Departments on the Soviet threat to the Caribbean. Among the facilities shown were the San Antonio de los Banos Airfield, from which Soviet long-range reconnaissance aircraft monitored U.S. naval activities in the Atlantic and Caribbean, the Soviet intelligence collection facility at Lourdes near Havana whose purpose was to intercept U.S. military and space communications, the Corrinto port facility in Nicaragua where Soviet-bloc military equipment was delivered, and the Port Salinas Airfield in Grenada with its three-thousand-foot runway to accommodate a nonexistent Grenada air force (Department of State 1985). Ironically, Reagan's strategy of aggressively countering Soviet moves in the Third World netted few unqualified successes, but it did enable him to ride easily to reelection in 1984 on the crest of a "new patriotism," best exemplified by the cinematic hero Rambo in the film of the same name (LaFeber 1991, 311).

Even before Reagan's first term in office ended there were indications that the Soviet economy was experiencing serious difficulties. Growth rates in the most favored sectors were a fraction of what they had been in the 1950s and 1960s. In agriculture, growth rates were actually negative for some years, despite receiving unusually heavy investment during the Brezhnev years, and long lines and shortages of many food items attested to the failure of the collective farm system. Even in the energy sector problems were becoming evident, although they were not due to shortages of natural resources. At issue were the costs to the economy of exploiting the oil and gas resources found in the harsh environments of Siberia and the Far North. Under a market system it would probably have been found uneconomic to develop many of these sites.

Much of the analysis conducted on the Soviet economy was based upon data published by the Soviet government. Although these data were known to be heavily "padded" and unreliable, there were few alternatives and a considerable amount of effort was expended attempting to convert the ruble value of goods and services into dollar equivalents for purposes of comparison. It was the unreliability of this process that led analysts to develop techniques for estimating Soviet production of critical commodities from imagery as one way of improving upon Soviet data. For example, Soviet grain production figures were determined "in field" and included everything, even weeds. CIA-derived totals, on the other hand, began with "in field" estimates but proceeded to take into consideration subsequent losses resulting from inadequate harvesting, storage, and transportation techniques.

Imagery analysts had already become proficient in estimating the annual production of large items such as tanks, trucks, and aircraft, which after assembly were typically lined up in storage yards surrounding the plant, but techniques were also developed for estimating the production of less visible commodities like crude oil. Estimates were based upon surrogate structures—the number and areal extent of production wells, methods of recovery, the capacity of storage facilities and pipelines, as well as a solid knowledge of Soviet production practices. A CIA report of the Soviet oil industry, published in 1977, was heavily criticized for suggesting that problems in the industry would require the Soviet Union to begin importing oil by the early 1980s. The report failed only in not recognizing how much investment the Soviets were prepared to pour into the oil industry when world oil prices skyrocketed in the late 1970s. By the mid-

1980s, however, when world oil prices began to decline, so too did Soviet oil production.

Analysts also developed techniques for estimating the production of small but high-value items, such as machine tools, industrial robots, and electronic equipment and components. These techniques required of analysts, or "functional specialists" as they were often referred to, an intimate knowledge of the particular manufacturing process. In addition, exact measurements of factory buildings, storage areas, and packing crates all helped to determine plant capacity. The CIA even established a workshop at NPIC where analysts could have three-dimensional models of building complexes constructed from overhead imagery. These very detailed wooden or cardboard replicas, which in more recent years were replaced by computer-generated three-dimensional images (Finn 1997, A6), enabled analysts to better understand production processes. But these techniques also pushed imagery analysis to its limits; results were definitely mixed and often depended on the ingenuity of the individual analyst. Nevertheless, the estimates produced in this manner helped fill out the picture of a society in which the military was consuming a disproportionate share of the nation's manpower, capital, and resources; it was a condition that could not continue indefinitely.

During Reagan's first term there would be little progress in arms control. He did not even commence actual negotiations until the summer of 1982, at which time he renamed the process the Strategic Arms Reduction Talks, or START. This change reflected Reagan's belief that the arms-limitation approach employed in the SALT treaties had largely proved a failure. For the future the chosen alternative would be arms reduction (Arms Control Association 1989, 60). The Reagan administration's primary goal during this period, however, was to gain control over the negotiation process, and it was determined that the best way to accomplish this was to put Soviet leaders on the defensive.

This strategy became most obvious during 1983, a politically volatile year that has been termed "the most dangerous moment in U.S.-Soviet relations since the Cuban missile crisis" (Andrew 1995, 471). It began in March, when, in one of his more memorable speeches, Reagan denounced the Soviet Union as an "evil empire." He was, as Soviet ambassador Dobrynin has remarked, giving Soviet leaders "a dose of their own medicine" (Dobrynin 1995, 527). Reagan followed this speech a few days later by proposing his Strategic Defense Initiative (SDI), a space-based laser defense system capable, in theory at least, of destroying incoming Soviet missiles before they reached their targets. Yet Reagan would reserve his most vehement attack on the Soviet Union for its downing in September of an unarmed South Korean airliner (KAL 007), an incident he would describe "as an act of barbarism born of a society which wantonly disregards individual rights and the value of human life" (Andrew 1995, 474).

In spite of Reagan's rhetoric the arms control process continued on. From June 1982 to December 1983 there would be five rounds of negotiations. The objective of U.S. arms negotiators at this point was to reduce the advantages the Soviets enjoyed in the areas of "heavy" missiles and missile throw-weight. Accordingly, the United States made "warheads, throw-weight, and missiles, rather than launchers[,] . . . the primary units of account in the negotiations" (Arms Control Association 1989, 60). Soviet leaders, however, rejected this approach because it discriminated so obviously against their land-based missile forces. They preferred to push for the percentage reductions in all delivery systems that were employed in the SALT treaties. With such divergent negotiating philosophies progress was all but impossible, and when in November 1983 the United States began deploying its Pershing II missiles in West Germany, the Soviet government announced that it was suspending arms control talks with the United States until such time as the missiles were withdrawn. According to Ambassador Dobrynin, this "suited Reagan perfectly because Congress was voting him huge increases in military spending" (Dobrynin 1995, 543).

In keeping with the Reagan administration's strategy of putting the Soviet leadership on the defensive, officials began to publicly condemn the Soviets for violating the SALT treaties and therefore undermining the integrity of the negotiating process. Interestingly, between 1972 and 1980 thirteen compliance problems had come before the Standing Consultative Committee (SCC), five of which had been brought by the Soviet Union against the United States. All thirteen were considered serious issues, and all, apparently, were resolved by the SCC "to the satisfaction of both parties" (Bingham 1985, 36). Nevertheless, because of their apparent seriousness, Reagan was convinced by his advisers to go public with two potential violations detected in 1983. The first concerned the testing of a new missile, the SS-25, which appeared to be a violation of the SALT II agreement. The second apparent violation was a large phased-array radar (LPAR) for ballistic missile detection and tracking, identified by imagery analysts as under construction near the central Siberian city of Krasnoyarsk; the location and orientation of this radar appeared to violate the 1972 ABM Treaty. In tandem these two violations not only appeared to make the resumption of arms control talks impossible but also even threatened the continuation of existing agreements.

The SS-25 was first identified in February 1983 as it began its flight tests from the Plesetsk Missile Test Center. The missile was quickly determined to be a single-warhead, road-mobile ICBM. The SALT II agreement had limited each side to one new "light" ICBM, but the Soviets had previously notified the United States that the multiple-warhead SS-X-24 was to be their allowable new missile. Although the SALT II agreement also permitted modifications to be made to existing systems as long as they did not increase any dimension of the missile by more than 5 percent, the United States contended that the SS-25 could not be a permitted modification because its throw-weight exceeded the SS-13 by nearly 90 percent.

Soviet leaders claimed that the SS-25 did not exceed the 5 percent allowance if the calculations were made correctly. The United States, they claimed, was overestimating the weight of the SS-25 by including an instrumentation package employed only during testing while simultaneously underestimating the weight of the SS-13 by excluding the guidance and penetration aids packages for the final stage because they were carried on the booster rocket's third stage: "If the throw weight of the SS-13 were to include these additional devices and the throw-weight of the SS-25 were to exclude the testing package, the Soviet Union claimed the SS-25 would be within the permitted five percent variation" (Arms Control Association 1989, 149). While the language of the SALT II Treaty appeared to support the Soviet interpretation, it was still not certain the variation was less than 5 percent. Ultimately, the United States would not object to the violation on the grounds it could not be proved.

However, during the summer of 1984, imagery analysts noticed that the Soviets were beginning to construct new SS-20 bases. It soon became

evident that some of the new construction was for the purpose of relo-
cating SS-20s from former sites in order to replace them with SS-25s
(Department of Defense 1986, 36). This constituted a violation of SALT
I. The concern was that the SS-20 sites could be hidden within the SS-25
complexes since the housing structures for the two missile systems were
so similar. Furthermore, SS-25 complexes were off limits to on-site inspections under the INF Treaty because the SS-25 was considered a long-range
strategic missile. The only requirement for SS-25 commanders was to
open the roofs of launch garages within six hours if requested by U.S. officials to do so. Critics argued this would provide ample time to conceal
SS-20 missiles. Intelligence officials contended, however, that it would
still be necessary to periodically test fire SS-20 missiles and that they could
"distinguish SS-20 boosters from those of SS-25s by their exhaust plume
signatures" (Adam 1988, 31).

Only a few months after the SS-25 was first detected, imagery analysts
found the LPAR under construction near Krasnoyarsk. The discovery
proved somewhat an embarrassment to the intelligence community
because the radar had gone undetected during the first eighteen months
of its construction. However, the radar became an even greater embarrassment to Soviet leaders since the Reagan administration decided to go
public with the charge it violated the 1972 ABM agreement and then proceeded to make it "the centerpiece of its attack on Moscow for past treaty
violations" (Pincus 1987).

In signing the ABM Treaty both aides had recognized the need for ballistic missile early warning radars. However, they also recognized that
such radars could detect enemy ICBMs at considerable distances, so potentially, at least, they possessed a significant antiballistic capability (Department of Defense 1986, 45). Accordingly, any early warning radar constructed by either side would have to be located at the nation's periphery,
and it would have to face outward in order that it not be used to manage
a nationwide ballistic missile defense system. The Krasnoyarsk radar was
in violation of both these conditions—it was located about 450 miles from
the nearest international border, in this case with Mongolia, and it did not
face outward but northeast across 2,500 miles of Soviet territory.

The Soviets had apparently developed plans for a network of nine such
radars during the late 1960s. Approval to go ahead with their construc-

tion was given by the Politburo about the time the ABM Treaty was signed. Eight of the radars were constructed around the periphery of the country in compliance with the ABM Treaty; Krasnoyarsk would prove to be the exception. When the Soviets were initially asked about the apparent violation, they responded that the radar was to be used for tracking space vehicles, though in design the radar was identical to the other eight admitted by the Soviets to be ballistic missile early-warning radars. In fact, the radar was probably not built for battle-management purposes but as a cost-efficient early warning system. Ironically, its very location and orientation made it "of little value as part of a nationwide defense" (Arms Control Association 1989, 149). Whatever its intended function, the radar would remain a significant issue between the two countries until 1988, when the Soviets agreed to scrap the facility in return for a U.S. commitment to honor the ABM Treaty for another ten years (Associated Press 1988, 6).

If Reagan hoped his belligerent rhetoric would moderate Soviet behavior, he must have been disappointed; it appeared to have quite the opposite effect, as the Soviets adopted an even harder line. In response to the United States' deployment of Pershing II missiles in Europe, the Soviets announced they would deploy tactical missiles of intermediate range in the German Democratic Republic and Czechoslovakia, and they went ahead with plans to deploy the SS-25. The Soviets appeared to be adopting "Reagan's own distinctive thesis that Soviet-American relations could remain permanently bad as a deliberate choice of policy" (Dobrynin 1995, 544).

In fact, it would be Reagan who would now begin to moderate his "evil empire" rhetoric against the Soviet Union. Unquestionably the upcoming (1984) presidential election had something to do with it. While many voters favored Reagan's reassertion of American muscle around the globe, others had been turned off by his hard-line rhetoric. Reagan, though, also felt his policies had allowed the United States to regain the initiative in foreign policy, and it was now time to engage the Soviets in serious dialogue. As Andrew has pointed out, however, "the new tone of the president's rhetoric produced no instant thaw in East-West relations" (Andrew 1995, 477). For Soviet leaders it was simply too hard "to believe in Reagan's sincerity," especially after three years of almost continuous public attacks (Dobrynin 1995, 545).

In early February 1984 Yuri Andropov passed away, his poor health preventing him from making any dramatic changes in foreign policy. He was replaced as general secretary by seventy-two-year-old Konstantin Chernenko, who was himself suffering poor health. Neither by health nor by temperament was Chernenko the person to initiate reform. He was clearly a transitional figure and in Dobrynin's words "the most feeble and unimaginative Soviet leader of the [preceding] two decades" (Dobrynin 1995, 551). Moscow's policy appeared to be to let relations drift until after the presidential election. Not even a speech by Reagan in which he favored resuming arms control talks drew much of a response.

However, with Reagan's landslide victory, both sides now had reasons for resuming the negotiations. On 23 November 1984, the United States and the Soviet Union announced that talks would resume early in the next year and would include discussions on START, intermediate-range ballistic missiles in Europe, and space-based weapons. Before talks could formally get under way, on 10 March 1985, Konstantin Chernenko died; the following day Mikhail Gorbachev was elected general secretary. Since the Soviet press made "no great fuss over the new general secretary" (Kaiser 1991, 94), it was not immediately evident to most people that the era of "old thinking" had come to an end.

Efforts to improve relations would now be undermined by a series of scandals that rocked the CIA and led 1985 to be called "the year of the spy." During the course of the year Edward Lee Howard, a former CIA officer, was accused of selling secrets to KGB agents in Austria; Karl Koecher, a Czech translator or analyst, was convicted of selling lists and photographs of CIA employees to Moscow; Larry Wu-Tai Chin, another CIA translator, was caught and convicted of passing secrets to China; and Sharon Scranage, a CIA clerk working in Ghana, pleaded guilty to passing classified information to a Ghanaian official. What, of course, was not known at this time, and would not be for several more years, was that the greatest damage to U.S. intelligence assets in Moscow was being caused by a Soviet informant at the very center of the CIA— Aldrich Ames.

As this crisis in human intelligence played itself out during 1985, an even more serious crisis began to unfold in the area of imagery intelligence. It all began some years earlier with the decision to phase out the

KH-8 and KH-9 programs because of the success and the cost of the KH-11 electro-optical system. Thus by 1985 there were no more KH-8s or KH-9s in orbit and only a single KH-9 remaining as backup. As for the KH-11 system, it too was about to be phased out and replaced by the Advanced KH-11. The plan was to launch the final KH-11 (5507) in August to join the one remaining KH-11 (5506) that had been launched the previous December. On 28 August, however, the seventh and final KH-11 was lost on launch, leaving only a single KH-11 in orbit (Burrows 1986, 303). Imagery, which had been so abundant a few months before, was now available for only the highest priority targets. The situation would improve only with the launch some months later of the first Advanced KH-11 (referred to by the media as the KH-12).

The Advanced KH-11 was by definition an improved version of the KH-11. Weighing nearly twice as much as a KH-11, the Advanced KH-11 possessed two significant advantages over its predecessor: higher resolution and a longer operational life. In terms of resolution, the best way to think of the Advanced KH-11 was as a Hubble Space Telescope pointed back toward Earth. This system, with its advanced electronics, was capable of providing "sharper images than the KH-11, comparable in quality to the best of the film return satellites, with a resolution approaching ten centimeters" (Pike 1997c). As for its longer operational life, the Advanced KH-11 was designed to be launched, refueled, and repaired by Shuttle astronauts, although as it turned out the Titan 4 became its primary launch vehicle. The additional weight of the Advanced KH-11 was accounted for by its expanded fuel-carrying capacity. The seven tons of fuel carried by an Advanced KH-11 vastly increase its operational life while allowing system operators to freely change the satellite's orbit in order to acquire imagery of high-priority targets (Pike 1997c). One Advanced KH-11 is already in its ninth year of successful operation (Covault 1997, 25).

In spite of the successful launch of the Advanced KH-11, tragedy continued to plague America's space activities. On 28 January, during a nationally televised launch, the *Challenger* space shuttle blew up, killing all aboard. The *Challenger* was carrying a relay satellite, which for the first time would have enabled the U.S. Landsat system to acquire multispectral imagery of eastern Siberia. And, then, on 18 April 1986, the final

KH-9 was lost when the Titan 34D carrying it into space erupted into a massive fireball on launch. The intelligence community would be dependent for the next couple of years on an aging KH-11 and a single new Advanced KH-11. For many analysts, whose targets were neither high priority nor located in northern latitudes, coverage might be acquired only two or three times a year.

If Ronald Reagan's approach to the Soviet Union during his first term was a combination of military strength and belligerent rhetoric, during his second term the rhetoric would give way to dialogue. The U.S. military buildup would continue, and by 1986 U.S. defense spending would approach $300 billion. The centerpiece of Reagan's military remained SDI, but his language began to soften. While he continued to insist that SDI was not to be viewed as simply a "bargaining chip," Reagan was beginning to suspect he could get an agreement from the Soviets without it. The fact also remained that if he desired to do so, Gorbachev could counter SDI fairly inexpensively by adding more warheads to his MIRVs.

During Reagan's first term he had not met with Brezhnev, Andropov, or Chernenko, yet within eight months of Gorbachev's becoming general secretary the two would participate in their first summit meeting. Gorbachev quickly and publicly made clear his eagerness for an early summit meeting with President Reagan, and to increase the chances for one "he announced a unilateral moratorium on deployment of SS-20 intermediate-range missiles in Europe" (Kaiser 1991, 95). He had probably already concluded that "the long-term benefits of reaching arms control agreements with Reagan, justified any short term sacrifices" (Blumenthal and Edsall 1988, 194), a view consistent with Reagan's that Gorbachev would have to come to him because the Soviet economy was failing and the country could not continue to spend the $250 billion annually it was presently spending on defense (LaFeber 1991, 315).

The first summit in Geneva produced no strategic breakthroughs; none had been anticipated. Nevertheless, both Reagan and Gorbachev considered the summit a success. There was no fixed agenda, so the two had ample time to talk and take the full measure of one another. They came away convinced they could work together to slow the arms race, and they agreed to meet on an annual basis. Gorbachev realized early on that improved relations with the United States would be a long-term process and would require incredible restraint in Soviet foreign policy. To make his point Gorbachev literally reversed decades of Soviet expansionism. In a five-year period "he withdrew Soviet forces from Afghanistan, cut adrift the Sandinistas in Nicaragua, withdrew from Indochina, and pulled back in Africa. Most important, he did nothing to prevent the former Soviet satellites in Eastern Europe from asserting their independence and ending Communist Party domination" (Kaiser 1991, 121).

Though Gorbachev appeared sincere in his push for arms control negotiations, imagery analysts continued to find evidence that the USSR's program to modernize and diversify its strategic forces was steadily moving ahead. New systems were being deployed while even newer ones were being tested. All this activity suggested that the Soviets had every intention of replacing existing strategic forces—ICBMs, SLBMs, and strategic bombers—with even more advanced systems. Imagery analysts now counted 1,400 silo and mobile ICBM launchers, over 800 of which had been replaced since 1972. These included 150 SS-17s, 308 SS-18s, and 360 SS-19s; the deployment of these fourth-generation systems was now essentially complete. Yet already analysts had identified 70 deployed launchers for the fifth-generation SS-25. They likewise found evidence that the Soviets were dismantling older SS-11 and SS-13 sites to compensate for the SS-25s as required by SALT I (Department of Defense 1986, 25–26).

In terms of ballistic missile submarines, the USSR now possessed the world's largest force, with 62 modern SSBNs carrying 944 SALT-accountable nuclear missiles. Of these 62, 4 were *Typhoon*-class, the world's largest submarine and capable of carrying 20 SS-N-20 MIRV missiles with a range of four thousand nautical miles (five thousand miles). Not included among the 62 were another 13 older *Golf*-class submarines with a total of 39 missiles.

Finally, Soviet Long Range Aviation possessed 180 Bear and Bison heavy bombers as well as another 125 Backfire bombers, which the U.S. Air Force continued to claim "could be equipped with a probe to permit inflight refueling to increase its range . . . [and] improve its capabilities against the contiguous United States" (Department of Defense 1986, 32). A new strategic bomber, the Blackjack, was in the process of being flight-tested. It was alleged to be faster than the American B-1B and to have a similar combat radius. Once again, the preciseness of these figures underscored the importance of overhead surveillance. Only the more experienced analysts could remember how difficult it was to generate such figures during the 1950s and early 1960s.

In April an incident took place that provided a severe test of Gorbachev's new policy of *glasnost*, or "openness," while at the same time demonstrating the impact satellite reconnaissance could have on U.S.-Soviet relations. At 1:00 A.M. on 26 April 1986, one of the four operating reactors at the Chernobyl nuclear power plant near Kiev exploded, spewing vast amounts of radioactive debris into the atmosphere. The Soviet government said nothing about the accident, but as the debris began settling over Poland, Finland, and Sweden, these nations demanded to know what was happening. In the absence of any word from the Soviet government, highly exaggerated rumors began to spread quickly both within the Soviet Union and in the West. One American newspaper, for example, reported that over one thousand people had died as a result of the accident. The Soviets would ultimately wait ten days before finally calling a press conference, but government spokesmen provided little specific information.

As it turned out the fire resulting from the explosion would take nearly nine days to contain; only the heroic efforts of those fighting the blaze prevented a much greater loss of life. Intercepted telephone and two-way radio messages in combination with KH-11 imagery enabled intelligence analysts to make "detailed assessments of the catastrophe as it was unfolding" (Richelson 1991, 41). Analysts monitoring Soviet efforts to keep the fire from spreading to the neighboring reactor were nevertheless taken aback at the sight of helicopter pilots exposing themselves to the escaping radiation as they dumped sand and other fire retardants directly into the damaged reactor. This information permitted the U.S. government to formulate a reasoned and sympathetic response to the situation, though the Soviets themselves had to this point said nothing.

The intelligence community was aided immeasurably in its analysis through the use of data provided by civilian satellites. Landsat, the U.S. government–owned satellite system, was able to publish images of the Chernobyl site within three days of the accident; higher resolution images acquired by France's SPOT satellite were published three days after that. The Landsat Thematic Mapper image of 29 April displayed a "hot spot" on two infrared bands in the vicinity of the number four reactor. By 8 May, when another TM image was acquired, the hot spots were no longer in evidence, indicating that the heat emanating from the burning reactor had been reduced (EOSAT 1986). The information provided by the civilian satellite systems played a significant role in dampening the rumors being spread by the more sensational media.

In an earlier time Gorbachev could have gotten away without making any public statement because news of the accident would have been suppressed, but with satellite images of the burning reactor appearing on the front pages of Western newspapers he was forced to respond. On 14 May, eighteen days after the accident, Gorbachev finally went on Soviet television to discuss Chernobyl, but his frustration with having to do so became quickly evident. Rather than taking the opportunity to reassure Soviet citizens that the government was doing everything possible to minimize the consequences of the accident, Gorbachev attacked the West for the manner in which it had reported the accident, conveniently ignoring the fact that the Soviet government had made no effort to provide any information of its own. He claimed that opponents of arms control in the West were using the Chernobyl accident to discredit Soviet proposals for eliminating nuclear weapons. Chernobyl "was one of Gorbachev's worst moments," and it dealt "a devastating blow to Gorbachev's hopes for building popular trust and enthusiasm" (Kaiser 1991, 127).

But it was easy in those days to underestimate Gorbachev, and those who believed he had now shown himself to be just another *apparatchik* would be in for a surprise. As with so many instances of this kind, Gorbachev would turn it to his own advantage. He now used the accident as an excuse to speed up the pace of reform and began speaking openly for the first time about opponents within the party who were trying to undermine his reform efforts. In the aftermath of Chernobyl his policy of openness also began to change: "*Glasnost*, until then merely a slogan, began to take on a life of its own" (Kaiser 1991, 129).

The impact that Landsat and SPOT imagery had on forcing Gorbachev to be more forthcoming on the Chernobyl accident quickly led to additional exposés. In August 1986 a Swedish company, Space Media Network, released a set of SPOT photos of the Semipalatinsk nuclear test site that purported to show that the Soviets were making preparations for a new series of tests. These photos provided the public with its first indication that the Soviets were about to end their moratorium on underground nuclear testing (Broad 1986). Over the next several months Space Media Network would prepare several more such stories for release to the media—on the Soviet Union's strategic defense laser weapons facilities at Sary Shagan and Nurek, on the accident that reportedly took place at the Kyshtym nuclear research complex in 1957, and on the SS-20 IRBM complex at Yur'ya.

As it turned out, Space Media Network's piece on the Soviet Union's laser weapons facilities would draw a significant response from Soviet leaders. Until the release of the SPOT photos of facilities at Sary Shagan and Nurek, few people inside or outside the Soviet Union knew of that country's laser research activities; on the other hand, literally everyone in the world was familiar with America's SDI, or "Star Wars," program. Thus, when the press printed photos of the Soviet laser facilities, along with a discussion of their role in countering SDI spacecraft and "blinding" intelligence satellites, the Soviets immediately denied the facilities were meant for such activities. They claimed, in fact, the alleged laser facility, located high on an isolated mountaintop near Nurek and secured by double fences, was nothing more than a gigantic radio telescope for tracking space vehicles (Larsson 1987, 1). Soviet authorities even had a special correspondent from *Pravda* visit the "mystery complex" and report back on the construction activities taking place there (Pokrovskiy 1988, 1, 3). The denials would continue until Gorbachev himself, in an interview on American television, would finally admit that the Soviets were conducting research on laser weaponry.

The Gorbachev admission would not be the only indication of the extent of the Soviet Union's new openness. During the fall of 1987 the Soviet Union announced the creation of two new agencies—Soyuzkarta and Glavkosmos. The former, Soyuzkarta, was established to begin marketing Soviet satellite photos of the earth in competition with Landsat and SPOT. Specifically, Soyuzkarta planned to sell five-meter resolution photos acquired by the Soviets' KFA-1000 camera; until now the highest resolution photos available to the public were SPOT's ten-meter photos. There would be one restriction, however; Soyuzkarta would not sell photos of the Soviet Union or any other Socialist country. The other new agency, Glavkosmos, would offer the international community a wide range of space-related services, including satellite launching. As a part of its marketing campaign, Glavkosmos invited potential customers to inspect its heretofore top secret launch complex at Baikonur in Kazakhstan (Sawyer 1987, A29).

During all of this Gorbachev was trying desperately to keep his dialogue with Reagan going. He wanted another summit, though initially his price was Reagan's withdrawal from SDI. When it became obvious that Reagan was not about to abandon SDI as a condition for a summit, Gorbachev dropped it, hoping "Reagan would ultimately yield on SDI in exchange for the huge reductions in nuclear weapons he professed to want" (Dobrynin 1995, 621). The two would meet in Reykjavik, Iceland, on 11–12 October 1986, in what may have been the cold war's "most bizarre meeting" (Kaiser 1991, 139). Before it ended the two were talking about eliminating all nuclear weapons. Later, when European leaders complained to Reagan that he was negotiating away their nuclear umbrella without even consulting them, Reagan denied the discussion had taken place. Much to his embarrassment, however, Soviet leaders proceeded to release a transcript of the discussion "with the exact words of the President already quoted" (Prados 1991, 528).

One of the proposals made by Reagan at Reykjavik involved eliminating all intermediate-range ballistic missiles in Europe, the so-called Euromissiles. While Gorbachev was not yet prepared to accept their total elimination, he agreed to "equal global ceilings of one hundred warheads, none in Europe" (U.S. Senate 1988, 22). This proposal, as attractive as it was to the United States, had subsequently to be rejected when Gorbachev attempted to once again link it to SDI. In February, however, Gorbachev unilaterally announced that he was prepared to separate the issue of intermediate-range missiles from long-range missiles in order to move forward with an agreement. Until this point it had largely been the United States that had shaped arms control negotiations, but now "it was the Soviets who initiated the arms control dialogue and offered concession after concession" (Blumenthal and Edsall 1988, 195). SDI was paying dividends. Gorbachev had become persuaded "that an SDI system would give the United States a first-strike advantage in nuclear conflicts" (Dobrynin 1995, 621).

The INF Treaty signed by Gorbachev and Reagan in Washington on 8 December 1987 was another historic arms control document in that the two sides agreed to destroy twenty-six hundred missiles. No previous agreements, including SALT I and SALT II, had involved the actual elimination of strategic nuclear weapons. While this number admittedly represented only a fraction of the missiles possessed by the two powers, these particular missiles "had unnerved Western Europe for a decade and had forced the North Atlantic Treaty Organization to install offsetting missiles" (*USN&WR* 1987a, 24).

Specifically, the INF Treaty required the elimination of all ballistic missiles in the 500-to-5,500-kilometer (270-to-3,000-nautical-mile) range; intermediate-range missiles would have to be destroyed within three years, shorter-range missiles within eighteen months. The United States was required to destroy all single-warhead Pershing II missiles, a total of 859 warheads, while the Soviets had to eliminate all SS-4, SS-12, SS-20, and SS-23 missiles and launchers for a total of 1,836 warheads. Weapons would be transported to "elimination facilities," where they would be either launched without warheads or cut up and burned. The United States was the clear winner in this agreement, especially in terms of the SS-23s, which the Soviet military had not wanted Gorbachev to give up. The one-sidedness of it "was a belated and reluctant admission of the fact that the initial deployment of SS-20s had been a gross miscalculation" (Dobrynin 1995, 430).

The INF Treaty was unprecedented in that for the first time on-site inspection would play a critical role in the verification process of a strategic arms control agreement. Gorbachev, unlike his predecessors, supported them enthusiastically as long as the obligations involved were shared equally. Under the terms of the treaty inspectors would be employed to verify the numbers of missiles declared by each side, to verify that these missiles and launchers had, in fact, been destroyed. In addition, inspectors would continuously monitor missile plants at Magna, Utah, and Votkinsk, USSR, for a term of thirteen years to ascertain that no prohibited missiles were being produced. At another seventy sites in the Soviet Union and Eastern Europe as well as twenty-three sites in the United States and Western Europe inspectors would be authorized to make short-notice visits (*USN&WR* 1987b, 28).

Imagery analysts, however, would bear the burden of monitoring compliance. They would not only help provide the questions for which on-site inspectors were to find the answers but also keep watch over the many facilities inspectors would not be visiting and where, accordingly, violations were most likely to occur. To make it at least a little easier for imagery analysts, the INF negotiators had agreed that the ban on the types of missiles covered by the treaty would be a total one. Therefore, it would not be necessary to count, say, SS-20s; any SS-20 detected would represent a violation of the treaty. As an additional concession to U.S. imagery analysts, the Soviets were required for up to six times a years to open the roofs of their SS-25 garages on short notice to demonstrate that no SS-20 missiles were hidden there; SS-25 launchers were to be moved into the open where they were clearly visible to orbiting satellites. The verification regime created under this treaty was without question "the most stringent and comprehensive" in arms control history (U.S. Senate 1988, 24).

As it turned out, the greatest obstacle facing analysts was the availability of satellite imagery. Analysts monitoring arms control agreements had to share the two operating systems with those whose responsibility it was to monitor military activities around the globe; there were no satellite-imaging systems dedicated exclusively to arms control monitoring. But, in fact, the Soviets complied with all INF deadlines. The destruction of weapons systems began in August 1988 and was completed ahead of schedule in June 1991. They even removed much of the debris away from the demolished missile sites, something not mandated by the agreement. Imagery analysts were surprised to find them removing prefabricated concrete roads until it was later discovered that they were simply moving them to other facilities. The work of imagery analysts was aided immensely by representatives of the United States On-Site Inspection Agency (OSIA), whose responsibility it was to personally visit sites in the Soviet Union and witness the destruction of weapons systems.

In December 1988 the imaging capabilities of the intelligence community were dramatically expanded when the space shuttle *Atlantis* deployed the first synthetic aperture radar satellite (Kokoski 1990, 26). Referred to as Lacrosse by the media, the system provides its own energy rather than depending upon reflected sunlight for illuminating targets. It, therefore, has the capability to penetrate darkness, clouds, and some natural camouflage. The Lacrosse satellite is distinguished by a very large radar antenna and a series of solar panels for providing electrical power to the radar transmitter (Pike 1997d). It operates by emitting bursts of microwave radiation toward the earth's surface. Landscape features reflect this radiation back to the satellite, where it is captured by the system's antenna, converted to a digital format, and relayed to a ground receiving station, all in a matter of seconds. Like any digital data, radar data may be analyzed either in "soft-copy" format or in the form of black-and-white images that resemble satellite photographs. The resolution of the so-called Lacrosse system is estimated to be between two and five feet, which would allow for the identification of weapons systems as small as an individual tank or armored personnel carrier (Kokoski 1990, 26–27). High resolution inevitably comes at the expense of broad-area coverage, so the system tends to employ a variety of scanning modes including a low-resolution mode capable of scanning a several-hundred-kilometer square (Pike 1997d).

The major advantage of radar systems like the Lacrosse is their day-night, all-weather capability. The need for such a capability has been there for years; I&W is impossible without it. For I&W to be effective, Warsaw Pact and other Soviet forward bases had to be monitored on a continuous basis, but this could not be done with conventional imaging systems incapable of penetrating the cloud cover and long hours of darkness so common to northern latitudes during much of the year. Radar gave experienced analysts the opportunity to count aircraft, tanks, and APCs at forward bases on a daily basis, something that had proven impossible with conventional systems. As one example, Richelson reported that satellite photography taken of Czechoslovakia several days before the invasion in 1968 revealed no indication of an attack, but a second bucket of film "returned after the invasion that carried images taken just before the attack showed unmistakable signs of Soviet troops massing along the border" (Richelson 1991, 38). It is exactly this type of intelligence failure that radar satellites were designed to avoid.

Like all systems, though, there is a downside to radar: it is difficult to exploit, and a great deal more training is required if it is to be used effectively. While radar imagery, for example, may appear similar to an aerial or satellite photograph, it is not. Radar returns are influenced by the physical properties of landscape features such as surface roughness, orientation, moisture content and composition, as well as by the specific wavelength of the radar signal itself. What this can mean is that a particular object may not appear the same on consecutive images; it may vary according to the orientation of the radar, the wavelength employed, or whether it has rained. Many analysts gave up trying to use it. Fortunately, perhaps, by the time the system had truly become operational, the Warsaw Pact had disappeared, along with much of the Soviet threat to invade Europe, and analysts could get back to employing imagery from the Advanced KH-11s.

In retrospect, the INF treaty represented a turning point in the relations between the United States and the Soviet Union. In signing it, Gorbachev essentially took the Soviet Union out of the cold war on the West's terms; he obtained literally no concessions from the United States and certainly none on SDI. Malia has concluded that "Gorbachev at last drew the realistic conclusion that nuclear war was neither thinkable nor winnable, a position that was the essence of his *new thinking* in international affairs" (Malia 1994, 416). Others have been less charitable. Dobrynin described Gorbachev as becoming so carried away by his international acclaim that "he moved forward without seriously contemplating the consequences" (Dobrynin 1995, 626).

Reagan and Gorbachev had become a team. Even as they were signing the INF Treaty in Washington, they were expressing the hope that a START Treaty could be concluded before Reagan left office. This agreement would dwarf the INF Treaty in significance. Whereas the INF Treaty led to the destruction of twenty-six hundred warheads, START would eliminate twelve thousand; and unlike the INF Treaty, which eliminated the Euromissiles, START would require the destruction of missiles capable of striking the United States. Unfortunately, the issues raised by the proposed treaty were too great to be resolved before Reagan's term ended. Critics pointed out that if the agreement were signed as it presently existed, the three-to-one advantage in warheads held by the Soviets would increase to five-to-one if certain sublimits were not introduced.

This did not discourage Gorbachev from pursuing his own arms control agenda. In December of 1988 before the UN General Assembly he declared his intention to unilaterally "cut Soviet armed forces by half a million troops and a thousand tanks" (Beschloss and Talbott 1993, 39). Though this speech won Gorbachev high praise in the West, it was in Eastern Europe that Gorbachev's words had their greatest impact. Within a year of his UN speech the Communist governments of this region had all been swept away in a series of largely bloodless coups. Though Gorbachev appears never to have anticipated such a reaction, to his credit he refused to employ Soviet military forces to maintain the Communists in power. On 19 November 1990, he signed the Conventional Forces in Europe (CFE) Treaty, which reduced even further the level of conventional forces on both sides. After nearly half a century the threat of a Soviet attack on Western Europe had been completely eliminated.

From this point on, however, Gorbachev would steadily lose whatever degree of control he exercised over the forces of change he had set in motion. Having destroyed the Communist Party, the backbone of Soviet society, he failed to create a new political structure to take its place. He did much the same with the economic system. Thus, as the economy slipped into free-fall and the various ethnic minorities began declaring their independence of the Union, Gorbachev became relegated to the role of witness to his own country's disintegration.

During this period George Bush, who had replaced Ronald Reagan in the White House, did his best not to make Gorbachev's position more untenable. Boris Yeltsin was largely ignored, with the exception of one disastrous visit to Washington; Gorbachev, on the other hand, would meet with Bush in four separate "summits." The White House would even warn Gorbachev that it had evidence indicating that a coup was being prepared against him, though the warning "made little impression on him" (Andrew 1995, 528). When the Baltic republics of Lithuania, Latvia, and Estonia declared their independence of the Soviet Union, the Bush administration hesitated recognizing them for fear such recognition would only hasten the Soviet Union's disintegration. Ironically, these republics had been the only ones whose annexation by the Soviet Union was never formally recognized by the United States.

For all the drama of the events taking place in the Soviet Union, Washington found its attention increasingly focused on the Middle East, where in August of 1990 Iraqi troops overran the neighboring country of Kuwait. In the months that followed, President Bush would pull together a remarkable coalition of nations to confront Saddam Hussein and demand his troops' withdrawal from Kuwait. When Saddam refused to do so, Operation Desert Storm was initiated on 16 January to drive his forces from the country. After several weeks of air and cruise missile attacks, a massive ground assault began on 23 February. It ended less than one hundred hours later in total victory for the coalition forces. The Soviet Union was little more than a bystander to the conflict.

By the summer of 1991 the Soviet Union had become once again the center of Washington's attention. On 31 July at a summit in Moscow, George Bush and Mikhail Gorbachev put their signatures to the START I Treaty, which mandated the destruction of nearly 30 percent of the two countries' strategic arsenals. Specifically, the treaty required the two sides to reduce the aggregate number of ICBMs, SLBMs, and strategic bombers to 1,600; warheads for those systems could not exceed 6,000. Of the latter figure, a maximum of 1,100 could be accounted for by mobile missiles. To attain these levels the Soviet Union would be forced to eliminate 900 missiles, or 36 percent of its nuclear arsenal, while the United States would have to rid itself of 622 missiles, 28 percent of its arsenal (Sur 1992, 50). The United States would, however, have to eliminate a slightly larger number of warheads than the Soviets. While critics of START claimed that the permitted levels were still too high, the reductions in missiles and warheads demanded by the treaty all but guaranteed that neither side would now possess a first-strike capability.

To assure compliance, a verification process was established that was as historic as the number of missiles and warheads to be destroyed under the terms of the treaty. The verification measures would be far more comprehensive and intrusive than those of any previous treaty, reflecting the complexity of START's requirements. For unlike the SALT treaties, which involved the monitoring of large, and in most cases, immovable launchers (i.e., missile silos and nuclear submarines), and the INF Treaty, which required the elimination of all missiles of a certain class, START I authorized specific missile and aircraft systems "to be quantitatively reduced and constrained within some qualitative parameters" (Sur 1992, 50). These qualitative parameters involved such things as missile throw-weight, numbers of warheads on missiles, and types of deployment arrangements.

The bulk of the monitoring required by START I would be carried out by each side's national technical means of verification; those tasks that could not be met in this way would be handled by a combination of on-site inspections and continuous monitoring of designated missile production facilities. As in previous treaties, a number of procedures were built in to make the job of imagery analysts somewhat easier. A case in point is provided by mobile missiles such as the MX and the SS-25. Under the terms of START I mobile missiles may only be placed within certain "restricted deployment areas" whose number and size are fixed. Furthermore, upon appropriate notification, one side may request the other to openly display these missiles in order that they may be imaged by satellites passing overhead. Even with these provisions, however, effectively monitoring missiles that were specifically designed to elude detection by satellites would not be an easy task.

Within three weeks of the Treaty's signing, Gorbachev was temporarily removed from office in a coup. Though the coup itself turned out to be a dismal failure, it had the result of propelling Boris Yeltsin onto Moscow's center stage while further reducing Gorbachev's already waning authority. When in August Parliament banned the Communist Party, Gorbachev became a leader without followers, and when in December Yeltsin took the Russian Federation out of the Soviet Union to form the Commonwealth of Independent States (CIS), Gorbachev became a leader without a country. On 25 December, with little fanfare and even less sympathy, Gorbachev resigned. The Soviet Union officially ceased to exist on 1 January 1992, at which time by definition the cold war ended as well.

For imagery analysts the last two or three years of the cold war were anticlimactic; there was no longer a sense of urgency or impending threat. There was not even a need for as many analysts, since the number of collection targets had been reduced. The Warsaw Pact was gone and with it the necessity to monitor Soviet forces in Eastern Europe. Within the Soviet Union itself there had been major cutbacks in both conventional and nuclear forces. Many imagery analysts who had formerly monitored events in the Soviet Union were temporarily shifted to handle responsibilities associated with the Gulf War, since the imagery demands created by this conflict were unprecedented. For the first time since the cold war had begun, the Soviet Union was not the primary collection target for the intelligence community (Andrew 1995, 522), and when the Gulf War ended, most imagery analysts were given new assignments, few of which had anything to do with the former Soviet Union. For imagery analysts it was clearly the end of an era.

The field of imagery analysis had truly come of age during the years of the cold war. By the late 1980s imagery analysts in the intelligence community numbered in the thousands compared to perhaps several hundred in the early 1950s. Even more impressive was the technological evolution in imaging systems. Those several hundred photointerpreters who worked with the first U-2 photography could scarcely have imagined that within a few years comparable quality imagery would be routinely acquired by orbiting satellites. These technological changes were a direct result of the enormous demands for information placed upon the intelligence community by the development of strategic nuclear weapons. However, as imaging technology evolved to meet these demands, it also began to impact the progress of the cold war. For example, with each new imaging system, the shroud of secrecy that blanketed much of Soviet society was drawn back further until finally the United States and its allies were able to compose a fairly complete and accurate appraisal of the Soviet Union's strategic capabilities. Initially, it was these systems that provided the crucial intelligence exposing the myths of both the bomber and the missile gaps. Later, these same systems would provide an effective and nonintrusive means of verifying compliance with arms control agreements, without which the early SALT treaties might never have been signed.

It was, in fact, the success of the SALT treaties that played a significant role in stabilizing political relations between the two governments and creating an atmosphere of trust and confidence that, until that point, had been largely nonexistent. Though this trust would be severely strained in the early 1980s with the Soviet Union's invasion of Afghanistan and Reagan's election as president, it was never eroded entirely. President Reagan and Mikhail Gorbachev would later not only reestablish this sense of trust but extend it to the point where the United States and Soviet Union would ultimately agree to unprecedented cuts in their nuclear arsenals. "Trust but verify" became Reagan's favorite expression during this period, though Gorbachev apparently found it insulting. Nevertheless, the expression probably reflected accurately the views of both governments. Each side was prepared to make significant reductions in its nuclear arsenal, but only if it could be certain the other side could not cheat and get away with it. While a variety of on-site inspections were built into these treaties, by themselves they were insufficient to ensure compliance; only imaging satellites with their ability to monitor the numerous facilities and areas not covered by inspections could effectively do this.

The treaties, requiring the destruction of huge numbers of missiles and warheads, were signed and ratified; both sides complied with the treaties' provisions. With the threat of nuclear war significantly diminished Soviet leaders could no longer ignore their country's growing economic crisis. What would begin as Gorbachev's attempt to solve this crisis would ultimately end in 1991 with the collapse of the entire Soviet system.

# 7

## An Uncertain Future

It should have come as no surprise to anyone familiar with our nation's history that the cold war's end would bring with it significant changes for the imagery community. After all, in the years following both World Wars I and II the military literally dismantled the photographic interpretation institutions that had been built up during the course of those conflicts. While nothing quite so drastic has occurred to the imagery community in the cold war's immediate aftermath, it has not escaped unscathed. Budget cuts, along with a series of organizational reforms, have weakened both morale and capabilities. How much these in turn have weakened our nation's security remains a question yet to be answered.

It did not help the imagery community that the post–cold war era began in scandal. The National Reconnaissance Office, the Defense Department agency responsible for purchasing and operating the nation's intelligence satellites, and which heretofore had been largely unknown to the American public, was accused of having secretly spent $350 million to build itself lavish new headquarters in the Virginia suburbs. But this, as it turned out, was not all. Two years later, in 1996, the NRO was forced to acknowledge that it had accumulated nearly $4 billion in unspent appropriations for new satellites. Though no one would ever be charged with any wrongdoing, the scandal obliged Congress to more closely scrutinize the entire intelligence community's budget. Congressmen were already searching for a "peace dividend," and with a budget of $28 billion, 70 percent of which was directed at the former Soviet Union, the intelligence community was an obvious place to start. The country, or so it seemed, could well afford to reduce the number of analysts tracking Soviet weaponry.

But the NRO scandals had another unintended consequence; they reinforced the notion that it was time to reorganize the imagery community. The Pentagon, through its supporters in Congress, had been pressing for such a reorganization for years. Military leaders had never forgiven President Eisenhower for placing control of imaging satellites in the hands of the CIA and had waged an unremitting struggle "to right this wrong." Their determination was finally rewarded on 1 October 1996 with the formal establishment of the National Imagery and Mapping Agency under Department of Defense authority. Needless to say, such a major reorganization was bound to create significant problems under any circumstances, but the manner in which this one was conducted served only to exacerbate them.

The reorganization process began with the establishment by Congress of the Commission on the Roles and Capabilities of the United States Intelligence Community. Unfortunately, the Commission was not up to the task, and its recommendations were criticized as far too modest. This enabled John Deutch, the new DCI, to undertake a reorganization of his own, quite independent of the commission's activities. The focus of his reorganization would be almost exclusively the imagery community.

In fact, Deutch's predecessor, Robert Gates, had already begun the process of reorganizing the imagery community. Although he too proposed consolidating many of the intelligence community's imagery operations into a single institution, his suggestions were rejected by the Pentagon, which controlled over 80 percent of the intelligence community's budget. Gates had to settle for a more modest organization, the Central Imagery Office (CIO), created in 1992 with a budget of approximately $1 billion. As a part of this reorganization COMIREX was merged into the CIO and the agency's Office of Imagery Analysis was transferred back to NPIC. It was planned that NPIC would then become part of the CIO, but Deutch replaced Gates as DCI before the latter could complete his reorganization.

Upon becoming DCI in 1993, Deutch immediately began putting his plans for reorganizing the imagery community into motion. His proposal was very similar to Gate's plan with one major exception—any new imagery agency would be controlled by the Defense Department, not by the CIA. The National Imagery Office, as the proposed agency was originally to be called, would be formed by consolidating the Defense Mapping Agency, the CIA's NPIC and CIO, as well as the imagery support resources of the DIA, the Defense Airborne Reconnaissance Office, and the various military services into a single organization of about nine thousand employees. The NPIC and DMA would cease to exist, as OIA had previously. By this reorganization the Pentagon had further increased its control over the intelligence process, especially within the field of imagery analysis.

Deutch's proposed reorganization of the imagery community was approved by Congress, and on 1 October 1996, the new National Imagery and Mapping Agency became official, though without a budget of its own. In having NIMA report directly to the Pentagon, the reorganization ran clearly counter to Eisenhower's admonition against placing the nation's imagery analysis capabilities in the hands of the military. Eisenhower had specifically given the DCI considerable control of imagery operations over the objections of the military. He was extremely concerned about the conflict of interest involved in having the Defense Department conduct military assessments of potential adversaries. He had never entirely forgotten that the air force had gone "over his head" at the time of the so-called bomber gap to convince Congress to authorize the purchase of more B-52s than he had proposed. Eisenhower, therefore, demanded that assessments be done independent of the military, and the CIA became his choice to undertake them.

In the view of many analysts, Deutch came over to the CIA with the specific intention of reversing Eisenhower's decision by returning control of the intelligence community's imagery capabilities to the military. Testimony by various Pentagon officials at the time the reorganization was being debated in Congress did little to undermine this notion. First and foremost, these officials made clear they would support no reorganization unless NIMA was a part of it, but they also demanded that any changes in the intelligence community must support those directly engaged in fighting wars. Sounding more like the secretary of defense than the DCI, Deutch claimed that the purpose of the reorganization was to enable military commanders in the field to have so much information that they would have a distinct advantage over their adversaries in any future conflict (Pincus 1995).

Uncertain Future

During the months of debate over the reorganization much was made of the failure of imaging satellites to meet the needs of battlefield commanders during the Gulf War. That there were problems no one in the imagery community would dispute. For one thing, military commanders had to compete for coverage with a host of other users; COMIREX determined collection priorities on a national level, which meant ultimately that less than half the targets attacked on any given day were covered by imaging satellites. Then, too, many battlefield units found they lacked the ability to task or receive satellite imagery, and even those who did often found their imagery dated. The vast number of images required by the military strained the intelligence community's processing capabilities and led to delays of as much as eighteen hours in imagery reaching the field (Pike 1997a).

Still, much of the criticism directed at the imaging community was unfair, some might even go so far as to say vindictive. Among the latter were those who believed the Pentagon was infuriated by an OIA assessment during the Gulf War that the bombing campaign directed at Iraq was not as effective as the military was claiming, something later even the military admitted to. Then there was the generally recognized fact that the overwhelming victory won by the United States and its coalition allies was accomplished through a combination of superior weaponry and superior intelligence. The bulk of that superior intelligence was acquired in turn by a vast array of imaging satellites, reconnaissance aircraft, and unmanned air vehicles hosting an equally impressive array of imaging sensors. These included not only conventional sensors using the visible portions of the electromagnetic spectrum but forward-looking infrared (FLIR) systems, useful for detecting the heat emitted by camouflaged or half-buried tanks, and advanced synthetic aperture radar (ASAR), an especially effective device for finding military vehicles moving across the flat expanses of the Persian Gulf region under cover of darkness, clouds, and smoke. The military was even able to call on civilian imagery companies like EOSAT and France's SPOT for large-area coverage. In fact, military commanders frequently had so much imagery available, they had difficulty exploiting it to best advantage.

When the Gulf War began the United States had four imaging satellites in orbit—three Advanced KH-11 and one Lacrosse. Using imagery from these systems, analysts detected Iraqi troops massing on the Kuwait border several days before the invasion took place. The White House, however, refused to believe that Saddam Hussein would actually invade; it was totally in the dark as to his intentions and the intelligence community could provide little help. It was clearly an intelligence failure, but the imaging satellites had done their part; the failure was one of human intelligence, not technical intelligence.

And what about during the course of the war? What role did imaging satellites play? Satellite imagery provided the first evidence of SCUD missiles; it showed the Iraqis laying mines in the Persian Gulf and constructing oil-filled trenches in the desert sands to impede attacking troops. The imagery was employed to create detailed maps of the entire battlefield, displaying the location of mine fields and wire entanglements. While these systems were never designed to detect the location of fighting vehicles in real time or provide bomb damage assessments in a matter of hours, the NRO nevertheless demonstrated that it could reprogram satellite orbits in a relatively short period of time to respond to changes in battlefield conditions.

In fact, whether imagery satellites performed poorly or well during the Gulf War is probably irrelevant to the central question: Who should control the nation's imagery assets, the military or some civilian agency? In the long term it is simply not in our best interests to have the Defense Department exercise total control over our imaging systems. There are numerous reasons for this, but the simplest is that the primary users of intelligence from imaging satellites are civilian policymakers, not the military. Though the cold war may be over, there are no shortage of threats to our national security or other tasks for which policymakers need the kind of intelligence that only imaging systems can provide.

Even in the short term the reorganization of the imaging community has created problems. For one thing it has drastically reduced morale among imagery analysts. To be fair, some of this would have happened anyway, since the cold war's end brought with it an inevitable loss in a sense of mission. There is no longer a readily identifiable enemy, now that the Soviet Union has collapsed. Nonetheless, the morale problem has unquestionably been exacerbated by the reorganization. For one thing, imagery analysts now find themselves a minority within their new agency, since over 70 percent of NIMA's employees came from DMA. For another, most imagery analysts are career CIA employees who now find themselves reporting to a very different boss—the Defense Department. This has created an awkward situation in which they continue to be paid by the CIA, but for most other things, including promotions, they are dependent on the military. Unfortunately, only their retirement will probably change the situation. Not surprisingly, then, many of them, including the bulk of the more experienced analysts, have chosen to do just that or else move to nonimagery positions elsewhere in the intelligence community, with the result that the number of imagery analysts in NIMA has declined by nearly half (Schmitt 1999, 6).

The degree to which the imagery community's analytic capabilities has been weakened by the loss of such personnel may be illustrated in the case of the nuclear tests undertaken by India in May 1998. The tests took the intelligence community totally by surprise. Analysts, who had reviewed imagery of the sites just prior to the tests, failed to detect the telltale indications that a detonation was imminent—burial of the actual nuclear devices, capping the holes with concrete "stems," attaching the cables for recording the test data. This failure was compounded when analysts once again failed to detect preparations for another set of tests that took place two days later. It was another classic case of mirror-imaging. In spite of well-publicized comments by government leaders that they intended to conduct such tests, imagery analysts had convinced themselves the Indians would not dare to do it. Accordingly, they did not give the sites the intense scrutiny they deserved. Critics of the intelligence community, including former DCI James Woolsey, placed the blame for this squarely on the loss of experienced imagery analysts (Pincus 1998). The failure proved to be more than just an embarrassment for the imagery community, for America's failure to prevent the tests led directly to Pakistan conducting nuclear tests of its own.

An equally costly error that has been laid at NIMA's doorstep was the bombing by American aircraft of the Chinese Embassy in Belgrade, Yugoslavia, resulting in the death of three embassy employees (Graham and Pearlstein 1999). The pilots responsible for the bombing were operating under the mistaken assumption they were attacking the Yugoslav Procurement and Supply warehouse; they had been given faulty intelligence. The target had been selected from maps prepared by NIMA several years earlier and were not up-to-date; analysts working with imagery of Belgrade failed to notice that the warehouse had been replaced by the Chinese Embassy. The mistake has served only to worsen relations already badly strained by charges of Chinese spying at U.S. nuclear weapons laboratories.

The loss of so many experienced imagery analysts is compounded further by the inability of NIMA to find young people eager to enter the field. In the past there was always a reservoir of potential analysts provided by the military services, but today that career path has largely dried up; without compulsory military training, few people opt for it on their own. To this must be added the fact that a career as a government imagery analyst is not as attractive as it once was. Imagery analysts in NIMA will increasingly fill technical slots with definite limitations as to how high they may rise in grade. Many of those recently retiring were slotted as "all-source" analysts with grades as high as GS-15s. Such grades will be impossible to attain in the future. Already NIMA is experiencing such a shortage of technical personnel that it recently awarded a $600 million contract to a group of commercial cartographic and imagery companies to help it keep up with its workload (Schmitt 1999).

But it is in the long term that the military's control over our nation's imagery assets may prove most costly. Take, as just one example, the issue of arms control, which remains a critical element in the U.S.-Russian relationship. The ABM Treaty signed with the Soviet Union in 1972 is still in force, and its various provisions are continuously monitored for possible violations, though there are indications that the United States may choose to abrogate or revise the treaty in order to begin construction of a new strategic missile defense system. The START I Treaty requires similar inspection, as will START II recently ratified by the Russian Duma; the U.S. Congress ratified it back in January 1996. START II would require each side (since all former republics have agreed to give up their nuclear arsenals, only the United States and Russia are signatories of START II) to reduce its total number of warheads to thirty-five hundred. In the meantime, unfortunately, both sides have felt compelled to maintain nearly half their deployed missiles at high levels of readiness—Russia to compensate for the gaping holes in its early warning network caused by the breakup of the former Soviet Union, the United States because it worries about the effectiveness of Russia's central command and control system. So while in theory one might expect the shrinking of nuclear stockpiles to enhance international security, this is not what has been happening. Instead, Michael Krepon has suggested, there are now so many ballistic missiles on hair-trigger alert, it has become "a recipe for disaster" (Krepon 1999).

Adding to the threat is the belief that NIMA may not be monitoring Russia's aging missile systems with the care they deserve. For one thing the bulk of NIMA's imagery analysts have been pulled away from such activities to produce "target packages" to support bombing campaigns in Kosovo and Iraq. As for those analysts who are still involved in monitoring arms control compliance, they may not be receiving sufficient imagery to do their job effectively. Since there are no systems dedicated solely to arms control activities, analysts who monitor treaty compliance must compete for target coverage with a host of other users. Prior to the reorganization, the CIA, which was deeply involved in the arms control process, made certain that analysts had sufficient imagery for monitoring purposes. The Pentagon, however, has a very different mission for NIMA that has changed targeting priorities. Now these analysts may go for weeks without receiving the imagery they need.

So great are these concerns they almost dwarf the once crucial issue of how potential treaty violations should be handled. Within the CIA arms control was traditionally given a high priority, in part because the CIA was a major player. Agency analysts were generally supportive of the arms control process and often found themselves in disagreement over arms-related issues with their DIA counterparts, who typically adopted a harder line. NIMA analysts, including even the CIA careerists among them, may find themselves pressured to read a more sinister intent into potential violations detected on imagery, especially if the military feels it can bully Russia because of its weakened economic condition, but also if the Pentagon decides it does not want to further reduce the size of its nuclear arsenal.

Arms control, however, represents only one of numerous responsibilities confronting civilian policymakers for which intelligence supplied by imaging satellites is required. For all the military resources invested in Iraq and the Balkans, we are involved primarily for what we claim to be "humanitarian" reasons, which is another way of saying that our national security is not directly threatened by what goes on in these places. So while an enormous amount of our imagery assets are devoted to these conflicts, there is danger that longer term strategic concerns are not being sufficiently addressed. For example, which countries will present the gravest threats to our national security a decade from now? What are their foreign policy objectives? And what capabilities are they developing to meet these objectives? These are critical questions, and our imaging satellites should be directed toward providing intelligence to help shape the answers.

Again, Russia represents a good example. For all its present political and economic problems, it is no postwar Japan or Germany, primed to be rebuilt in America's image. And though for the moment Russia's weakness allows Washington to pursue its foreign policy objectives with near total disregard for its concerns (e.g., NATO expansion, the bombing of Yugoslavia), it would be a grave error to underestimate the country. Its vast size, including its enormous reserves of petroleum and natural gas; its aging though still powerful force of nuclear weapons; and its long history of aggression against smaller neighbors all combine to make Russia a nation we must take seriously.

Much the same may be said of China. Although no immediate threat to the United States, it is in the process of developing both a market economy and a modern nuclear arsenal, which in time will combine to alter the balance of power in Asia. Inevitably this will mean rubbing against longstanding American interests in places like Taiwan and the South China Sea. If China were for any reason to attempt to take Taiwan by force or to assert control over the critical sea lanes of the South China Sea, the United States would find itself under great pressure to intervene. It is in America's best interests, therefore, that policymakers develop the kind of long-term, stable relationship with China that would, if not prevent, at least reduce the chances of such a confrontation taking place.

Beyond the long-term strategic threats posed by Russia and China are the proliferation concerns. The list of nations now capable of building and delivering missiles with nuclear, biological, or chemical warheads is rapidly expanding, India, Pakistan, North Korea, Iran, Iraq, and Libya being only the most worrisome. Such is the concern that the concept of an American missile defense system is gaining congressional support, even at the cost of scrapping the ABM Treaty signed with the former Soviet Union in 1972. Underlying this concern is the fact that many of these same nations are the chief sponsors of international terrorism, of which the United States is a frequent target.

190

The demand for imagery by Washington policymakers is expanding rapidly. Beyond the traditional users—the intelligence community itself, the Departments of State, Interior, Treasury—a host of new users have been added. These include the FBI, the Drug Enforcement Agency (DEA), the Environmental Protection Agency (EPA), and the Federal Emergency Management Agency (FEMA). It goes without saying that the flow of imagery to these agencies should not be impeded by the military's requirement for battlefield intelligence or mapping activities that only indirectly serve the nation's security. To prevent this the NRO must develop new satellite systems that can satisfy the needs of military commanders without endangering this large and growing customer base.

Designing systems for the new millennium must begin now for the lead time is five to ten years, but it's not going to be an easy task. For example, one thing the NRO must determine is what exactly the various constituencies need, yet they are not always certain themselves. Take the case of the Pentagon. It has often expressed frustration with the present generation of imaging satellites because of their difficulty in providing broad-area coverage of battlefields or vast areas of ocean, and since the Gulf War considerable attention has been paid to the issue. Yet, ironically, the military's newest operational doctrine stresses the use of smaller, more agile forces along with precision, long-range ordnance, which "presumes access to precise, dynamic, real-time, target quality data" (Behling and McGruther 1998–99, 116). Clearly, a great deal more thought must be given to the design of future systems. Then there is the cost factor to consider. Present systems, such as the Advanced KH-11, which were designed to provide high-resolution imagery of the type best suited for examining individual ABM radars or SS-25 launcher garages, are extremely large and cost nearly $1 billion each (Pear 1995), all of which suggests that future satellites will tend to be smaller and less expensive than today's systems; there will also probably be far more of them.

It will not, however, only be intelligence satellites that will increase in number, but imaging satellites of all kinds. The world will become so open, so transparent, it will be easy to forget that there was a time not long ago when only the United States and the Soviet Union possessed a satellite imaging capability. In the years since then, China, France, India, the European Space Agency, Japan, Canada, and Israel have joined the club.

By the year 2010 it is estimated that there may be as many as ten nations that have satellite imaging systems with resolutions of one meter or better (Behling and McGruther 1998–99, 113).

Even the United Nations is considering acquiring its own satellite imaging system from the European Space Agency. The purpose of the system is to monitor the cultivation of illegal drugs, but, of course, if it proves effective there is certainly no shortage of other tasks to which it could be applied. As just one example, the UN would seem to be the perfect organization to compile evidence on the mass killings in the Balkans first revealed on imagery acquired by American satellites and reconnaissance aircraft (Rohde 1999). The primary reason the United Nations is getting into the monitoring business is because of concern over the crop figures produced by the CIA. Several drug-producing countries have complained that the CIA's figures are politically biased; the UN, they argue, would be more impartial (Wren 1999).

Of course, the idea of developing an international monitoring organization is not entirely new. As early as 1978 French president Giscard D'Estaing proposed the creation of an International Monitoring Agency (ISMA) before the UN General Assembly. The proposal, however, received little support from either the Soviets or the Americans, who at the time had no desire to share their "monopoly of necessary technologies" (Jasani and Sakata 1987, 39), and was shelved. The idea did not die, however, and in 1985 several nations, including Switzerland and Sweden, came forward with a proposal of their own for a smaller Regional Satellite Monitoring Agency (RSMA) for Europe as a politically more palatable alternative. This time it was the Soviet Union's collapse that undermined the proposal by making such an agency appear unnecessary.

But the largest number of imaging satellites in the future may be launched by private companies. Already a number of American companies have plans to place one-meter systems in orbit over the next several months. These systems are the result of a bill President Clinton had signed back in March 1994, which permitted for the first time American companies to market satellite imagery with one-meter resolution. Following the signing a number of companies launched lower-resolution systems, but they now seem ready for the high-resolution business. Their market will be governments and corporations that do not possess their own imaging capability.

In addition to this bill, President Clinton also signed an Executive Order in February 1995 that authorized the declassification of imagery acquired by the first generation of photoreconnaissance systems, that is up to and including the KH-4 system (Corona). The imagery would be made available to the public through the U.S. Geological Survey's Earth Resources Observation Systems (EROS) Data Center in Sioux Falls, South Dakota. Analysts, who for so many years were forbidden to even mention the code name Talent-Keyhole, may now take home KH-4 photography to show their families. The next step will be the release of KH-8 and KH-9 photography. In fact, the process of declassifying this photography and preparing it for transfer to the public domain is already under way.

President Clinton's decision to declassify KH-4 photography may have been influenced in part by Russia's decision in 1992 to begin marketing high-resolution imagery as a way of earning foreign exchange. The Russian Space Agency and the Ministry of Defense have recently established the Converted Technologies Center to prepare the imagery for sale. The center will have access to imagery from a variety of Russian satellites—military, environmental, and meteorological. High-resolution imagery from Russian military satellites will be degraded "at the site to resolutions no better than 2 meters" (*Aviation Week and Space Technology* 1996). Recently, the Russians have gone one step further than the Americans by announcing they will use their satellites to acquire new imagery for clients who have the dollars to pay.

Potentially the greatest contributor to global transparency is the proposed Open Skies Treaty, which has been signed, though not ratified, by some two dozen nations, including Russia and the United States. The significance of the treaty is not only a function of the number of nations involved but the vastness of the territory it will cover. Depending upon which nations choose to ratify the treaty, it could cover Canada and the United States, Europe, and all of the former Soviet Union, although not every former republic had indicated an interest in signing. Open Skies will permit participants to conduct aerial overflights of the territory of all other participants on a regular basis. The treaty is not meant to be just another means of verifying arms control agreements, though it may in fact be used for this purpose. Rather, the treaty is a cooperative measure that seeks to "enhance the feeling of security of participating states by allowing each of them a means of satisfying themselves of the peaceful intentions of the other participants (Sur 1992, 157–58).

If the Open Skies Treaty is ratified, and this is not at all certain, it will permit each participant to conduct a specified number of overflights over the national territory of other participants on an annual basis. These overflights are to be conducted by aircraft and have nothing to do with "unilateral and national satellite capabilities" (U.S. Senate 1992b, 19). The number of overflights is a function of a nation's geographic size, though all participants must accept a minimum of our overflights. Ironically, Russia was the first nation to conduct a training mission under the terms of the treaty, though it has yet to ratify it. In July 1997 an Antonov An-30 aircraft with a Russian crew and an American observation team spent several days photographing military installations located throughout the eastern half of the United States. Until all signatories ratify the treaty, only training flights will be permitted ("Russian Jet Flies" 1997).

It is thus ironic that as other nations and international organizations come to recognize the importance of imagery analysis and begin developing their own imaging satellite capabilities, our own has been allowed to slip. It is not irreversible, however, for the problem is more organizational than technological. For example, the NRO has made certain that several systems are operating at all times with sufficient redundancy that if anything were to happen to one of the systems, it would not generate a crisis similar to 1985, when for a critical period only a single KH-11 system was providing imagery. Furthermore, the resources of the civilian community can be tapped more easily if it became necessary. Both Landsat and SPOT are now used routinely by the military. To all this may be added the fact that the NRO has new, more sophisticated systems prepared to go in the immediate future.

Much of the problem, then, lies with NIMA itself. The decision to reduce the status of imagery analysts to technicians with accompanying low grades and salaries is not the way to bring intelligent, well-educated people into the field. This approach may have worked reasonably well for the military over the years, since in large part the tasks required of military analysts are relatively narrow, but it will not be sufficient for the broad range of intelligence required by civilian policymakers. Imagery analysts should enjoy a comparable status to all intelligence analysts. It simply doesn't make sense to spend billions of dollars designing and operating sophisticated imaging satellites only to have the analysis conducted by inadequately paid and trained technicians. In the intelligence community, as elsewhere in society, "you get what you pay for." Therefore, if you want experienced, well-trained imagery analysts you must be prepared to pay for them.

This, of course, gets to the heart of the main issue—the military's control over our nation's imagery assets. While it is a perfectly good idea to have a national organization like NIMA where cartographic, imagery, and information systems are brought together for intelligence purposes, such an organization need not, and probably should not, be controlled by the military. The Clinton administration was pushed by the Pentagon into authorizing a reorganization of the intelligence community's imagery assets that does not serve the nation's best interests. President Eisenhower recognized nearly half a century ago that there is a basic conflict of interest with the military controlling the flow of intelligence to civilian policymakers. The numerous disagreements between the military and the CIA over the interpretation of imagery-derived data were in large part a reflection of this conflict. The military has all too often read the worst-case scenario into its interpretations, except, of course, when it was evaluating its own performance. Though the CIA's interpretations may have been too optimistic on many occasions, they added an important balance that now appears to have been lost. Tension between civilian policymakers and the military is an inevitable component of democratic societies; it is one of the things that distinguishes democracies from military dictatorships. Whatever the reason for reorganizing the imagery community into its present structure, whether it was budgetary or to eliminate interagency disputes or to provide battlefield commanders with better operational information, the bottom line remains the same: the decision was a shortsighted one that potentially could harm the intelligence process. Planning should begin immediately, therefore, to either bring NIMA under civilian control or establish an independent imagery analysis capability within the CIA as a means of restoring some balance between the civilian and military communities. It was this balance, after all, that proved so effective in providing a series of American presidents with the strategic intelligence they required to successfully prosecute the cold war and bring it to an end without the use of nuclear weapons.

# Literature Cited

Adam, John A. 1986. "Peacekeeping by Technical Means." *IEEE Spectrum*, July, 42–80.

———. 1988. "Ways to Verify the U.S.-Soviet Arms Pact." *IEEE Spectrum*, February, 30–34.

Adamsky, Viktor, and Yuri Smirnov. 1994. "Moscow's Biggest Bomb: The 50-Megaton Test of October 1961." *Bulletin, Cold War International History Project* 4 (Fall): 3, 19–21.

Allison, Graham T. 1971. *Essence of Decision: Explaining the Cuban Missile Crisis.* Boston: Little, Brown.

Ambrose, Stephen E. 1981. *Ike's Spies: Eisenhower and the Espionage Establishment.* Garden City, N.Y.: Doubleday.

———. 1989. *Nixon: The Triumph of a Politician, 1962–1972.* New York: Simon & Schuster.

American Society for Photogrammetry and Remote Sensing. 1997. *Manual of Photographic Interpretation,* 2d ed. Washington, D.C.: American Society for Photogrammetry and Remote Sensing.

Andrew, Christopher. 1995. *For the President's Eyes Only: Secret Intelligence and the American Presidency from Washington to Bush.* New York: Harper Collins Publishers.

Anselmo, Joseph C. 1994. "Remote Sensing to Alter TV News." *Aviation Week,* 5 December, 61.

Arms Control Association. 1989. *Arms Control and National Security: An Introduction.* Washington, D.C.: Arms Control Association.

Aspin, Les. 1979. "The Verification of the SALT II Agreement." *Scientific American,* February, 38–45.

Associated Press. 1988. "Soviets Offer to Scrap Radar If ABM Pact Is Extended." *Boston Globe*, 20 July, p. 6.

Avery, Thomas Eugene, and Graydon Lennis Berlin. 1985. *Interpretation of Aerial Photographs*, 4th ed. Minneapolis: Burgess Publishing.

*Aviation Week and Space Technology*. 1996. "Russian Military, Civil Imaging Center Formed." 14 October, 33.

Bates, Col. E. Asa. 1978. "National Technical Means of Verification." *Journal of the Royal United Services Institute for Defence Studies*, March, 64–72.

Behling, Thomas, and Kenneth McGruther. 1998–99. "Planning Satellite Reconnaissance to Support Military Operations." *Studies in Intelligence* (Winter): 113–21.

Beschloss, Michael R. 1986. *May Day: Eisenhower, Khrushchev and the U-2 Affair.* New York: Harper & Row.

Beschloss, Michael R., and Strobe Talbott. 1993. *At the Highest Levels: The Inside Story of the End of the Cold War.* Boston: Little, Brown.

Bingham, Roger. 1985. "The Politics of Mistrust." *Science*, December, 34–40.

Bissell, Richard M., Jr., with Jonathan E. Lewis and Frances T. Pudlo. 1996. *Reflections of a Cold Warrior: From Yalta to the Bay of Pigs.* New Haven, Conn.: Yale University Press.

Blumenthal, Sidney, and Thomas Byre Edsall, eds. 1988. *The Reagan Legacy.* New York: Pantheon Books.

Bohlen, Charles E. 1973. *Witness to History.* New York: W. W. Norton.

Boyne, Walter J. 1997. *Beyond the Wild Blue: A History of the U.S. Air Force, 1947–1997.* New York: St. Martin's Press.

Brands, H. W. 1993. *The Devil We Knew: Americans and the Cold War.* New York: Oxford University Press.

Broad, William J. 1986. "Photos Said to Show New Activity at Main Soviet Nuclear Test Site." *New York Times*, 4 August, p. A3.

———. 1987. "U.S. Designs Spy Satellites to Be More Secret than Ever." *New York Times*, 3 November, pp. C1, C3.

———. 1992. "Russia Is Now Selling Spy Photos from Space." *New York Times*, 4 October, p. 10.

Brugioni, Dino. 1991. *Eyeball to Eyeball: The Inside Story of the Cuban Missile Crisis.* New York: Random House.

Burr, William. 1994. "Soviet Cold War Military Strategy: Using Declassified History." *Bulletin, Cold War International History Project* 4 (Fall): 1, 9–13.

Burrows, William E. 1986. *Deep Black: Space Espionage and National Security.* New York: Random House.

Bush, George P. 1989. "Remarks by the President at Texas A&M University." 12 May, 1–5.

Calvo-Goller, Notburga K., and Michel A. Calvo. 1987. *The SALT Agreements: Content-Application-Verification.* Dordrecht: Martinus Nijhoff Publishers.

Central Intelligence Agency. Center for the Study of Intelligence. 1996a. *Newsletter* 5 (Spring).

———. 1996b. *Newsletter* 6 (Summer).

Chang, Laurence, and Peter Kornbluh, eds. 1992. *The Cuban Missile Crisis, 1962: A National Security Archive Documents Reader.* New York: New Press.

Covault, Craig. 1991. "Recon Satellites Lead Allied Intelligence Effort." *Aviation Week and Space Technology*, 4 February, 25–26.

———. 1997. "Advanced KH-11 Broadens U.S. Recon Capability." *Aviation Week and Space Technology*, 1 January, 24–25.

Day, Dwayne A., John M. Logsdon, and Brian Latell. 1998. *Eye in the Sky: The Story of the Corona Spy Satellites.* Washington, D.C.: Smithsonian Institution Press.

Department of Defense. 1986. *Soviet Military Power.* Washington, D.C.: Department of Defense.

———. 1989. *Soviet Military Power: Prospects for Change.* Washington, D.C.: Department of Defense.

Department of State and Department of Defense. 1985. *The Soviet-Cuban Connection in Central America and the Caribbean.* Washington, D.C.: Department of State and Department of Defense.

Diamond, John. 1996. "Accounting Woes Put Spotlight on Spy Agency." *Washington Post*, 16 May 1996, p. A21.

Dobrynin, Anatoly. 1995. *In Confidence: Moscow's Ambassador to America's Six Cold War Presidents.* New York: Times Books.

Donovan, Robert J. 1982. *Tumultuous Years: The Presidency of Harry S. Truman, 1949–1953.* New York: W. W. Norton.

Dutton, Lyn, David de Garis, Richard Winterton, and Richard Harding. 1990. *Military Space.* London: Brassey's.

Earley, Pete. 1997. *Confessions of a Spy: The Real Story of Aldrich Ames.* New York: G. P. Putnam's Sons.

Eckholm, Erik. 1999. "It's Not the Cold War, but There's a Nip in the Air." *New York Times*, Week in Review, 16 May, pp. 1, 6.

EOSAT News Release. 1986. "May 8, 1986 Chernobyl Data." Lanham, Md., 12 May.

Finn, Peter. 1997. "At CIA, a Vocation of Imitation." *Washington Post*, 8 September, pp. A1, A6.

Freedman, Lawrence. 1977. *U.S. Intelligence and the Soviet Strategic Threat.* London: Macmillan.

Gaddis, John Lewis. 1997. *We Now Know: Rethinking Cold War History.* Oxford: Clarendon Press.

Goodman, Melvin A. 1997. "Ending the CIA's Cold War Legacy." *Foreign Policy* (Spring): 128–43.

Gorbachev, Mikhail. 1987. *Perestroika: New Thinking for Our Country and the World.* New York: Harper & Row.

Gordon, Michael R. 1996. "Despite Cold War's End, Russia Keeps Building a Secret Complex." *New York Times*, 16 April, pp. 1, A6.

Graham, Bradley, and Steven Pearlstein. 1999. "Outdated Map Faulted." *Washington Post*, 10 May, pp. 1, A19.

Graybeal, Sidney N., and Michael Krepon. 1987. "The Limitations of On-Site Inspection." *Bulletin of the Atomic Scientists*, December, 22–26.

Greenwood, Ted. 1973. "Reconnaissance and Arms Control." *Scientific American*, February, 14–25.

Gribkov, Gen. Anatoli I., and Gen. William Y. Smith. 1994. *Operation Anadyr: U.S. and Soviet Generals Recount the Cuban Missile Crisis*. Chicago: edition q.

Halloran, Richard. 1979. "U.S. Spy Plane Takes Pictures Over Cuba." *New York Times*, 7 October, p. 18.

Henderson, Nell. 1986. "Civilian Satellites Penetrate Soviet Secrecy, Photograph Plant." *Washington Post*, 2 May, p. A1.

Hoffman, David. 1996. "Liftoff, $35; Landing, Free." *Washington Post*, 16 July, p. A11.

Infield, Glenn B. 1970. *Unarmed and Unafraid*. New York: Macmillan.

Isaacson, Walter, and Evan Thomas. 1986. *The Wise Men: Six Friends and the World They Made*. New York: Simon & Schuster.

Jasani, Bhupendra. 1987. "Military Use of Outer Space." *World Armaments and Disarmament: SIPRI* Yearbook 1987. Oxford: Oxford University Press.

———. 1989. "Soviet Photo-reconnaissance Satellite Programme." *Jane's Soviet Intelligence Review*, May, 223–26.

Jasani, Bhupendra, and Toshibomi Sakata, eds. 1987. *Satellites for Arms Control and Crisis Monitoring*. New York: Oxford University Press.

Jensen, John R. 1986. *Introduction to Digital Imaging Processing: A Remote Sensing Perspective*. Englewood Cliffs, N.J.: Prentice-Hall.

Jervis, Robert. 1989. "Strategic Intelligence and Effective Policy." *Studies in Intelligence* (Winter).

Kaiser, Robert G. 1991. *Why Gorbachev Happened: His Triumphs and His Failure*. New York: Simon & Schuster.

Kennan, George F. 1986. "The Origins of Containment." *Containment: Concept and Policy*. Vol. 1. Edited by Terry Deibel and John Lewis Gaddis. Washington, D.C.: National Defense University Press.

Kennedy, Robert F. 1969. *Thirteen Days: A Memoir of the Cuban Missile Crisis*. New York: W. W. Norton.

Kent, Sherman. 1972. "The Cuban Missile Crisis of 1962: Presenting the Photographic Evidence Abroad." *Studies in Intelligence* (Spring): 19–42.

Kissinger, Henry A. 1982. *Years of Upheaval*. Boston: Little, Brown.

Klass, Philip J. 1971. *Secret Sentries in Space*. New York: Random House.

Koch, Scott A., ed. 1993. *Selected Estimates on the Soviet Union, 1950–1959*. Washington, D.C.: Central Intelligence Agency.

Kokoski, Richard. 1990. "National Technical Means." *Verification of Conventional Arms Control in Europe.* Edited by Richard Kokoski and Sergey Koulik, 17–31. Boulder, Colo.: Westview Press.

Krass, Allan. 1985. *Verification: How Much Is Enough?* London: Taylor & Francis.

Krepon, Michael. 1986. "Arms-Treaty Verification: A Political Problem." *Technology Review* (May/June): 34–47.

———. 1987. "CIA, DIA at Odds over Soviet Threat." *Bulletin of the Atomic Scientists*, May, 6–7.

———. 1999. "Invitation to Nuclear Disaster." *Washington Post*, 25 May, p. A15.

Khrushchev, Nikita S. 1971. *Khrushchev Remembers.* Translated and edited by Strobe Talbott. New York: Bantam Books.

LaFeber, Walter. 1991. *America, Russia, and the Cold War 1945–1990.* New York: McGraw-Hill.

Lardner, George. 1990. "Satellite Eyes and Ears Check Moves on Mideast Chessboard." *Washington Post*, 10 August, p. A29.

Larsson, Christer. 1987. *Discovered: The Secret of Soviet Star Wars.* Stockholm: Space Media Network.

Leary, William M., ed. 1984. *The Central Intelligence Agency: History and Documents.* Tuscaloosa: University of Alabama Press.

Lebow, Richard N., and Janice G. Stein. 1994. *We All Lost the Cold War.* Princeton, N.J.: Princeton University Press.

Leffler, Melvyn P. 1994. *The Specter of Communism: The United States and the Origins of the Cold War, 1917–1953.* New York: Hill and Wang.

Malia, Martin. 1994. *The Soviet Tragedy: A History of Socialism in Russia, 1917–1991.* New York: Free Press.

Marchetti, Victor, and John D. Marks. 1974. *The CIA and the Cult of Intelligence.* New York: Alfred A. Knopf.

May, Ernest R., and Philip D. Zelikow, eds. 1997. *The Kennedy Tapes: Inside the White House During the Cuban Missile Crisis.* Cambridge: Harvard University Press, Belknap Press.

McAuliffe, Mary S. 1992. *CIA Documents on the Cuban Missile Crisis 1962.* Washington, D.C.: Central Intelligence Agency.

McCullough, David. 1992. *Truman.* New York: Simon & Schuster.

McDonald, Robert A. 1995. "Corona: Success for Space Reconnaissance, a Look into the Cold War, and a Revolution for Intelligence." *Photogrammetric Engineering and Remote Sensing* 61 (June): 689–718.

McDougall, Walter A. 1985. *The Heavens and the Earth: A Political History of the Space Age.* New York: Basic Books.

McFarland, Stephen L. 1997. *A Concise History of the U.S. Air Force.* Washington, D.C.: Air Force History and Museums Program.

Meese III, Edwin. 1992. *With Reagan: The Inside Story.* Washington, D.C.: Regnery Gateway.

Mintz, John. 1995. "Lockheed Martin Works to Save Its Older Spies in the Sky." *Washington Post*, 28 November, p. D1.

National Photographic Interpretation Center (NPIC). 1991. *Thirty . . . and Thriving*. December. Washington, D.C.: NPIC.

Newton, Verne W. 1991. *The Cambridge Spies: The Untold Story of McLean, Philby, and Burgess in America*. Lanham, Md.: Madison Books.

Norris, Robert S., and William A. Arkin. 1994. "Nuclear Notebook: Estimated U.S. and Soviet/Russian Nuclear Stockpiles, 1945–1994." *Bulletin of the Atomic Scientists*, November–December, 58–59.

Orlov, Alexander. 1998–99. "The U-2 Program: A Russian Officer Remembers." *Studies in Intelligence* (Winter): 5–14.

Payne, Samuel B., Jr. 1980. *The Soviet Union and SALT*. Cambridge, Mass.: MIT Press.

Pear, Robert. 1995. "Shake-Up Over Agency's Secret Money." *New York Times*, 25 September, p. A11.

Peebles, Curtis. 1997. *High Frontier: The United States Air Force and the Military Space Program*. Washington, D.C.: Air Force History and Museums Program.

Peterson, Neal H. 1984. "Intelligence and U.S. Foreign Policy, 1945–1954." *Studies in Intelligence* (Winter).

Pike, John. 1997a. "Desert Star." *FAS Space Policy Project*. 10 July. Page on the Federation of American Scientists (FAS) web site. Http://www.fas.org.spp/military/program/ds/images.htm.

———. 1997b. "KH-11 Kennan/Crystal." *FAS Space Policy Project*. 10 July. Page on the FAS web site. Http://www.fas.org/spp/military/program/imint/kh-11.htm.

———. 1997c. "KH-12 Improved Crystal." *FAS Space Policy Project*. 10 July. Page on the FAS web site. Http://www.fas.org/spp/military/program/imint/kh-12.htm.

———. 1997d. "Lacrosse/Vega." *FAS Space Policy Project*. 10 July. Page on the FAS web site. Http://www.fas.org/spp/military/program/imint/lacrosse.htm.

———. 1997e. "NRO History." *FAS Space Policy Project*. 10 July. Page on the FAS web site. Http://www.fas.org/irp/nro/nrohist.htm.

Pincus, Walter. 1987. "U.S. Insists Moscow Alter Radar." *Washington Post*, 14 December, p. A17.

———. 1995. "Another Intelligence Image Faces Change." *Washington Post*, 15 October, p. A3.

———. 1997. "Intelligence Community Faulted by House Panel." *Washington Post*, 19 June, p. A19.

———. 1998. "2 New Tests Again Catch U.S. Intelligence Off Guard." *Washington Post*, 14 May, p. A28.

Pokrovskiy, A. 1988. "Reportazh s 'zagadochnovo kompleksa': Tuman pri yasnoy pogode." *Pravda*, 2 January, pp. 1, 3.

Pope, Ronald R., ed. 1982. *Soviet Views on the Cuban Missile Crisis: Myth and Reality in Foreign Policy Analysis*. Washington, D.C. University Press of America.

Prados, John. 1982. *The Soviet Estimate: U.S. Intelligence Analysis and Russian Military Strength*. New York: Dial Press.

———. 1991. *Keepers of the Keys: A History of the National Security Council from Truman to Bush*. New York: William Morrow.

Ranelagh, John. 1986. *The Agency: The Rise and Decline of the CIA*. New York: Simon & Schuster.

"Return of the Titans." 1987. *Space World*, December, 8.

Rich, Ben R., and Leo Janos. 1994. *Skunk Works*. Boston: Little, Brown.

Richelson, Jeffrey T. 1984. "Keyhole Satellite Program." *Journal of Strategic Studies* (June): 121–53.

———. 1985. *The U.S. Intelligence Community*. Cambridge, Mass.: Ballinger Publishing.

———. 1991. "The Future of Space Reconnaissance." *Scientific American*, January, 38–44.

———. 1997. *A Century of Spies: Intelligence in the Twentieth Century*. New York: Oxford University Press.

Rohde, David. 1999. "A High-Tech Threat with a Low-Tech Track Record." *New York Times*, 4 April, p. 6.

Rositzke, Harry. 1977. *The CIA's Secret Operations*. New York: Readers Digest Press.

Rostow, W. W. 1982. "Eisenhower's Open Skies Proposal, July 21, 1955." Draft. Austin, Texas.

Ruffner, Kevin C., ed. 1995. *Corona: America's First Satellite Program*. Washington, D.C.: Central Intelligence Agency, Center for the Study of Intelligence.

Rusk, Dean. 1990. *As I Saw It*. Edited by Daniel S. Papp. New York: Norton.

"Russian Jet Flies Across U.S., Taking Photos of Military Bases." 1997. *New York Times*, 5 August, p. A13.

"Russia's Arms for Oblivion." 1996. *Economist*, 30 November, 47.

Sawyer, Kathy. 1987. "Soviet Invite U.S. Customers, Others to Baikonur Launch Site." *Washington Post*, 9 October, pp. A29, A33.

Schecter, Jerrold L., and Peter S. Deriabin. 1992. *The Spy Who Saved the World*. New York: Charles Scribner's Sons.

Schmitt, Eric. 1999. "Smart Bombs, Dumb Map." *New York Times*, Week in Review, 16 May, p. 6.

Scott, Robert T. 1984. "Now a 'Warhead Gap.'" *Bulletin of the Atomic Scientists*, November, 43–44.

Shulsky, Abram N. 1993. *Silent Warfare: Understanding the World of Intelligence*. 2d ed., rev. New York: Brassey's (U.S.).

Smirnov, Yuri, and Vladislav Zubok. 1994. "Nuclear Weapons after Stalin's Death: Moscow Enters the H-Bomb Age." *Bulletin, Cold War International History Project* 4 (Fall): 1, 14–18.

202

Smith, R. Jeffrey. 1985. "High-Tech Vigilance." *Science*, December, 26–33.

Sorensen, Theodore C. 1965. *Kennedy*. New York: Harper & Row.

"Spy Satellite Is Launched." 1996. *New York Times*, 21 December, p. 8.

Stares, Paul B. 1987. *Space and National Security*. Washington, D.C.: Brookings Institution.

Steury, Donald P., ed. 1996. *Intentions and Capabilities: Estimates on Soviet Strategic Forces, 1950–1983*. Washington, D.C.: Central Intelligence Agency.

Sur, Serge, ed. 1992. *Verification of Disarmament or Limitation of Armaments: Instruments, Negotiations, Proposals*. New York: United Nations.

Swahn, Johan. 1989. *Open Skies for All: The Prospects for International Satellite Surveillance*. Goteborg, Sweden: Chalmers University of Technology.

Swedish Space Corporation. 1988. *Technical Study of a Satellite System for Arms Control Verification*. Executive Summary. Solna, Sweden, 12 September, 1–5.

Talbott, Strobe. 1984. *Deadly Gambits*. New York: Alfred A. Knopf.

Thompson, Robert Smith. 1992. *The Missiles of October: The Declassified Story of John F. Kennedy and the Cuban Missile Crisis*. New York: Simon & Schuster.

Trachtenberg, David J. 1988. "Inside View: Looking through a Shrinking Keyhole." *Defense News*, 29 August, 24.

Trachtenberg, Marc. 1994. "American Policy and the Shifting Nuclear Balance." In *Origins of the Cold War*, edited by Melvyn P. Leffler and David S. Painter, 107–22. New York: Routledge.

Tsipis, Kosta, David Hafemeister, and Penny Janeway, eds. 1986. *Arms Control Verification: The Technologies that Made It Possible*. Elmsford, N.Y.: Pergamon Press.

Turner, Stansfield. 1985. *Secrecy and Democracy: The CIA in Transition*. Boston: Houghton Mifflin.

"The Uses of Space." 1991. *Economist*, 15 June, 3–22.

*U.S. News & World Report* (*USN&WR*). 1987a. "Arms Control: Is It Good for Us?" 14 December, 24–28.

———. 1987b. "The Big Problems Restarting START." 21 December, 26–28.

———. 1993. "Special Report." 15 March, 30–52.

U.S. Senate. 1988. Committee on Foreign Relations. *The INF Treaty: Hearings before the United States Senate Committee on Foreign Relations*. 100th Cong., 2d sess. 25–28 January, 1–37.

———. 1992a. Committee on Foreign Relations. *The START Treaty: Hearings before the United States Senate Committee on Foreign Relations*. 102d Cong., 2d sess. 6, 19, 25, 27, 28 February, 3, 5, 10, 11, 17 March, 213–33.

———. 1992b. Committee on Foreign Relations. *Treaty on Open Skies: Hearing before the United States Senate Committee on Foreign Relations*. 102d Cong., 2d sess. 22 September, 16–36.

Usowski, Peter S. 1990. "Photo Intelligence and Public Persuasion." *Studies in Intelligence* (Spring).

Verrier, Anthony. 1983. *Through the Looking Glass: British Foreign Policy in an Age of Illusions*. New York: W. W. Norton.

Volkman, Ernest. 1985. *Warriors of the Night: Spies, Soldiers and American Intelligence*. New York: William Morrow.

Volkogonov, Dimitri. 1988. *Stalin: Triumph and Tragedy*. New York: Grove Weidenfeld.

Warner, Michael. 1998–99. "The CIA's Internal Probe of the Bay of Pigs Affair." *Studies in Intelligence* (Winter): 93–101.

Williams, Robert Chadwell. 1987. *Klaus Fuchs, Atom Spy*. Cambridge: Harvard University Press.

Wren, Christopher S. 1999. "U.N. to Create Own Satellite Program to Find Illegal Drug Crops." *New York Times*, 28 March, p. 10.

# Index

A-12 (Project Oxcart), 50, 60–61. *See also* SR-71

ABMs. *See* antiballistic missiles

ABM Treaty, 100, 124, 129–30, 187; Soviet violations, 161–63

ACDA. *See* Arms Control and Disarmament Agency

Acheson, Dean, 19–20

Adenauer, Konrad, 78

Advanced KH-11 (KH-12) satellite, 165, 175, 184–85, 190

Advanced Reconnaissance System (Weapon System 117L, WS-117L), 95–96

advanced synthetic aperture radar (ASAR), 184

aerial photography: Cuban missile crisis and, 10–11; World War II and, 23

aerial photointerpretation, 11–12

aerial reconnaissance, 6; ferret flights, 27–28, 50. *See also* photoreconnaissance

Afghanistan, 8, 151, 157, 167

Africa, 167

Agena booster rockets, 96

aircraft: bomber gap myth, 2, 29, 37, 44, 100–101; bombers modified for reconnaissance missions, 24; ferret, 27; reconnaissance, 3, 24–25, 57; strategic bombers, 59. *See also specific aircraft*

*Air Force One*, 57

Alaska, 43

*Alexandrovsk*, 90

all-source analysis, 9, 155, 187

Ames, Aldrich, 164

analysis. *See* imagery analysis

Anderson, George, Jr., 139

Anderson, Rudolf, 84

Andropov, Yuri, 164

Angola, 157

antiballistic missiles (ABMs), 2, 115–17, 122; ABM Treaty, 100, 124, 129–30, 161–63, 187; Safeguard system, 120

antisatellite (ASAT) capability, 99–100

Antonov An-30 aircraft, 192

Argon system, 103–4

arms control, 7–8, 11, 38, 189; ABM Treaty, 100, 124, 129–30, 161–63,

intelligence gathering *(continued)*
administration, 61; interim cold
war, 29–62; Project Corona, 10, 61,
95–122; second cold war, 153–80;
on Soviet Union, 23–26. *See also*
reconnaissance
intercontinental ballistic missiles
(ICBMs), 7, 48, 59; and Caribbean
crisis, 80; complexes, 106–7, 127;
deployment of, 124; reduction of,
177; SALT I ceiling on, 146; SALT
II ceiling on, 149; silos, 107; Soviet,
51, 112, 122, 154. *See also* surface-
to-surface missiles (SSMs)
"Interdiction of the Delivery of
Offensive Weapons to Cuba" order,
80–81
Interim Agreement on Offensive
Weapons, 124, 127–29, 132; Unilateral Statement, 133–34
intermediate-range ballistic missiles
(IRBMs), 45, 47; on Cuba, 76–78,
80, 86; elimination of, 172;
Euromissiles, 171; Operation
Anadyr, 67; Soviet, 76–78, 80, 86,
107–8; Yur'ya complex, 170. *See
also* surface-to-surface missiles
(SSMs)
Intermediate-Range Nuclear Forces
(INF) Treaty, 2, 143, 171–72, 175;
compliance monitoring, 172–73;
verification, 172–73
International Geophysical Year
(IGY), 98
International Satellite Monitoring
Agency (ISMA), 191
Iran, 43, 148, 189; U.S. Embassy
seizure by, 151–52
Iraq, 189; invasion of Kuwait by,
176–77, 184–85
IRBMs. *See* intermediate-range ballis-
tic missiles
Island of Yuri, 26
Isle of Pines, 72
ISMA. *See* International Satellite
Monitoring Agency

Israel, 190
Italy, 47
Itek Corporation, 97
I&W. *See* indication and warning

Japan, 26, 190; operation Tu Go, 39
Johnson, Clarence "Kelly," 32, 34, 50
Johnson, Lyndon, 109, 114, 116–17
Johnston Island, 100
Joint Chiefs of Staff, 72, 116–17
Joint Study Group, 101
Jupiter missiles, 47, 65, 83–85

KAL 007, 58, 160
Kampuchea, 157
Kapustin Yar Missile Test Range
(KYMTR), 102
Kapustin Yar–Vladimirovka missile
test facility, 45
*Kasimov*, 72, 77
Keegan, George, 141–42
Kemerovo, 23
Kennedy, John: antisatellite installa-
tions, 100; blackout directive,
103–4; Caribbean crisis, 11, 63–64,
74, 78–91, 108–9; and CIA, 114;
Executive Committee (EXCOM),
74–76, 78; importance of photoreconnaissance to, 41, 91; military
buildup, 108; and missile gap myth,
61, 105; and Operation Mongoose,
66–67; summit with Khrushchev,
64–65; test-ban treaty, 109; U-2
program, 58, 63–64
Kennedy, Robert, 67, 85, 90–91
Keyhole camera systems: Advanced
KH-11 (KH-12), 165, 175, 184–85,
190; KH-1, 105; KH-4, 104, 109–10;
KH-4A (J-1), 104–5, 112; KH-4B (J-
3), 104–5, 111, 121; KH-6, 104; KH-
7 (Gambit), 109–10, 112, 121, 127;
KH-8, 111–13, 117, 121–22, 127,
142–43, 165; KH-9 (Hexagon) (Big
Bird), 121–22, 124–25, 142–43, 165;
KH-11 (Kennan/Crystal), 12,
143–45, 152; KH-11/6, 144

Overflights," 88; A-Team/B-Team Experiment, 139–40; and Caribbean crisis, 79–80; Executive Committee (EXCOM), 74–76, 78, 80–81, 83–85; NSC-68, 21; NSSM-28 Panel, 126; Verification Panel, 126, 130

national technical means of verification (NTM), 128, 149–50

NATO. *See* North Atlantic Treaty Organization

Naval Photographic Intelligence Center. *See* National Photographic Interpretation Center (NPIC)

*Newport News*, 79

Nicaragua, 157, 167

NID. *See* national intelligence daily

NIEs. *See* national intelligence estimates

Nike-Zeus, 115

Nikolayevsk shipyard, 127–28

NIMA. *See* National Imagery and Mapping Agency

9th Strategic Reconnaissance Wing, 111

NIOs. *See* National Intelligence Officers

Nitze, Paul, 21

Nixon, Richard, 55, 61–62, 93, 123; and CIA, 121; Moscow Summit with Brezhnev, 135; Safeguard ABM system, 120; SALT I, 124; SALT II, 135; SS-9 dispute, 119–20

Nizhny Tagil, 23

North Atlantic Treaty Organization (NATO), 1, 19, 28, 156; designations, 117

North Island Naval Air Station, San Diego, Calif., 57

North Korea, 16, 20, 189

Norway, 39, 43

Novaya Zemlya test site, 65

NPIC. *See* National Photographic Interpretation Center

NRO. *See* National Reconnaissance Office

NSC. *See* National Security Council

NSSM-28 Panel, 126

NTM. *See* national technical means of verification (NTM)

nuclear submarines: *Delta*-class, 138; Soviet fleet, 93, 127, 134–35; Trident, 129, 153. *See also* submarines

nuclear weapons, 1, 30–31; warheads, 89–90, 172. *See also specific weapons*

nuclear weapons testing, 59, 65–66, 109; in India, 186; Limited Test Ban Treaty (LTBT), 92; monitoring, 92; Operation Bravo, 31; Semipalatinsk nuclear test site, 169–70; Soviet, 20

Nurek facility, 170

Office of Imagery Analysis (OIA), 35, 155, 182, 184

Office of Missile and Satellite Systems, 4

Office of National Estimates (ONE), 9. *See also* national intelligence estimates

Office of Naval Research, 39–40

Office of Strategic Research (OSR), 130

Office of the Secretary of the Air Force, 4

OIA. *See* Office of Imagery Analysis

oil, 158–59

*Omsk*, 70

ONE. *See* Office of National Estimates

On-Site Inspection Agency (OSIA), 173

Open Skies Treaty, 37–38, 192–93

Operation Anadyr, 67–68, 70–71

Operation Bravo, 31

Operation Desert Storm, 176–77

Operation Genetrix (119L), 39–40

Operation Grand Slam, 52–53

Operation Mongoose, 66–67, 70

Operation Zapata, 64

OSIA. *See* On-Site Inspection Agency

# About the Author

David T. Lindgren was born in Ipswich, Massachusetts, and educated at Boston University. For the past thirty or so years he has been a member of the faculty at Dartmouth College in Hanover, N.H., where his teaching and research have focused largely upon the two areas of remote sensing and the former Soviet Union. In addition to these activities, he served for several years as chairman of the Department of Geography and more recently served a term as the college's associate dean of the faculty for the social sciences.

The author of numerous articles, monographs, and a book on remote sensing, Professor Lindgren has served as a consultant to several government agencies including the Central Intelligence Agency, National Aeronautics and Space Administration, the Department of Interior, and the Census Bureau. He has also taught remote sensing in Greece and the Netherlands. In 1987 Lindgren was awarded a grant from the MacArthur Foundation to explore the national security implications of civil imaging satellites such as the American Landsat and the French SPOT systems.

At present Professor Lindgren is dividing his time between Hanover, N.H., Washington, D.C., and Quito, Ecuador, where his wife is serving as representative for the Interamerican Development Bank.

**The Naval Institute Press** is the book-publishing arm of the U.S. Naval Institute, a private, nonprofit, membership society for sea service professionals and others who share an interest in naval and maritime affairs. Established in 1873 at the U.S. Naval Academy in Annapolis, Maryland, where its offices remain today, the Naval Institute has members worldwide.

Members of the Naval Institute support the education programs of the society and receive the influential monthly magazine *Proceedings* and discounts on fine nautical prints and on ship and aircraft photos. They also have access to the transcripts of the Institute's Oral History Program and get discounted admission to any of the Institute-sponsored seminars offered around the country.

The Naval Institute also publishes *Naval History* magazine. This colorful bimonthly is filled with entertaining and thought-provoking articles, first-person reminiscences, and dramatic art and photography. Members receive a discount on *Naval History* subscriptions.

The Naval Institute's book-publishing program, begun in 1898 with basic guides to naval practices, has broadened its scope in recent years to include books of more general interest. Now the Naval Institute Press publishes about one hundred titles each year, ranging from how-to books on boating and navigation to battle histories, biographies, ship and aircraft guides, and novels. Institute members receive discounts of 20 to 50 percent on the Press's more than eight hundred books in print.

Full-time students are eligible for special half-price membership rates. Life memberships are also available.

For a free catalog describing Naval Institute Press books currently available, and for further information about subscribing to *Naval History* magazine or about joining the U.S. Naval Institute, please write to:

Membership Department

**U.S. Naval Institute**

291 Wood Road

Annapolis, MD 21402-5034

Telephone: (800) 233-8764

Fax: (410) 269-7940

Web address: www.usni.org